Restoring the Law of Restitution of Cultural Property

This groundbreaking book covers the restoration of the law of restitution of cultural property, matching the time, space, and depth dimensions of the law with the time, space, and ontology of events that violated persons and desecrated their heritage in the colonial era.

Using the contested ownership of the Parthenon Sculptures and the Zhanggong Zushi mummy encased in a Buddha statue as the main points of orientation, the book shows how the law of restitution could be 'defragmented' and 'restored' in respect of claims for the return of colonial-era and Indigenous cultural property disputes. The study argues that the secondary legal norms and common arguments of Private International Law can unlock governance functions and strategies that counter the effects of the narrow definition of the 'sacred' and the consistent refusal to consider an alternative chronosophy in restitution claims. When called upon to resist the detrimental effects of the mimetic dynamic in complex colonial contexts, the law stands to benefit from a legal-theoretical perspective that views law in relation to ethics and considers Private International Law, a model of ethics.

The book will be of interest to researchers in the field of cultural property law, heritage studies, Indigenous law, provenance, and applied ethics.

Christa Roodt is Senior Lecturer in the School of Culture and Creative Arts, University of Glasgow, UK. She specialises in the provenance and restitution of cultural heritage and acts as consultant on projects designed to achieve a more appropriate international regime for the protection and return of cultural objects removed from colonial, archaeological, and Nazi-era contexts. She is a serving member of the British Committee for the Reunification of the Parthenon Marbles.

Cultural Heritage and International Law

Regulating Transnational Cultural Heritage
Diversity, Memory and Identity
Merima Bruncevic

Transboundary Heritage and Intellectual Property Law
Safeguarding Intangible Cultural Heritage
Patricia Covarrubia

Cultural Heritage, Sustainable Development and Human Rights
Towards an Integrated Approach
Edited by *Laura Pineschi*

Legal Protection of Intangible Cultural Heritage
Perspectives from Indonesia and Malaysia
Diyana Sulaiman

Intentional Destruction of Cultural Heritage and the Law
A Research Companion
Alberta Fabbricotti

Restitution of Cultural Property and the Law
Complex Colonial Histories
Christa Roodt

Restoring the Law of Restitution of Cultural Property
Complex Colonial Histories
Christa Roodt

Restoring the Law of Restitution of Cultural Property

Complex Colonial Histories

Christa Roodt

Routledge
Taylor & Francis Group
LONDON AND NEW YORK

First published 2025
by Routledge
4 Park Square, Milton Park, Abingdon, Oxon OX14 4RN

and by Routledge
605 Third Avenue, New York, NY 10158

Routledge is an imprint of the Taylor & Francis Group, an informa business

British Library Cataloguing-in-Publication Data
A catalogue record for this book is available from the British Library

ISBN: 978-1-032-95249-9 (hbk)
ISBN: 978-1-032-95260-4 (pbk)
ISBN: 978-1-003-58396-7 (ebk)

DOI: 10.4324/9781003583967

Typeset in Times New Roman
by Deanta Global Publishing Services, Chennai, India

Contents

Acknowledgements

If crisis descends, move further away from the phenomena than what the 'spirit of technical competence' would usually require. This was Theodore Adorno's suggestion in a lecture he delivered at a meeting of the German Werkbund in Berlin called 'Functionalism Today', on 23 October 1965. His advice was prescient. As I stepped away from teaching Private International Law (PrIL) to focus on provenance studies more than a decade ago, the emancipatory potential of the 'sacred' in art and cultural heritage absorbed my attention but the predominant modes of thought that underpin the core business of PrIL also captivated me more and more.

The same people who gave so freely their time and attention during the writing of the preceding study, *Restitution of Cultural Property and the Law: Complex Colonial Histories*, supported the work that went into this study. I am grateful for the efficient and energetic support provided by Nicola Sharpe and Diksha Bhugra, the editorial team at Routledge. You made it all happen with seeming ease! I am indebted to colleagues who provided more support at crucial junctures than I could have asked for—Professor Clare Willsdon, Professor Debra Strickland, Steph Scholten, Giovanna Vitelli, Andy Mills, Marta Iljadica, and Elena Cooper, to name a few. This book would not have seen the light of day without Andreas Giorgallis' tireless research assistance, rendered with astonishing skill, accuracy, and speed. He also provided support with the indexation process, for which I am hugely grateful. Haoyang Zhao helped to unlock the content of the Chinese rulings on the Zhanggong Zushi mummy exactly when I needed it. Maggie Cacot's first-class editorial work and professionalism made a lasting impression on me. I am deeply grateful for your editorial inputs, much more than words can say.

Koos, your boundless generosity of spirit made light of every challenge. What a difference your steady companionship has made over all these years.

Scotland, August 2024

Abbreviations

ADR	Alternative Dispute Resolution
AFFORD	African Foundation for Development
AMNH	American Museum of Natural History
APABE	Advisory Panel on the Archaeology of Burials in England
ARPA	Archaeological Resources Protection Act of 1979
BABAO	British Association for Biological Anthropology and Osteoarchaeology
CLT	Classical Legal Thought (1850–1914)
CT	Contemporary Thought (1945-early 2000s)
DCMS	United Kingdom Department for Digital, Culture, Media and Sport
DMB	Deutscher Museumsbund (German Museums Association)
EU	European Union
EurCtHR	European Court of Human Rights
FNSCORA	First Nations Sacred Ceremonial Objects Repatriation Act
ICJ	International Court of Justice
ICOM	International Council of Museums
ICPRCP	Intergovernmental Committee for Promoting the Return of Cultural Property to its Countries of Origin or Its Restitution in Case of Illicit Appropriation
IDA	Institute of Digital Archaeology
ILA	International Law Association
NAGPRA	Native American Graves Protection and Repatriation Act
NMAI	United States National Museum of the American Indian
NSPA	National Stolen Property Act
OAS	Organization of American States
OJ L	Official Journal of the European Union, Legislation
PrIL	Private International Law
PublIL	Public International Law
SLT	Socially Oriented Legal Thought (1900–1968)
SOGO	Sale of Goods Ordinance (Cap 26) Hong Kong
UK	United Kingdom of Great Britain and Northern Ireland
UMAC	University Museums and Collections
UNCITRAL	United Nations Commission on International Trade Law

UNDRIP	United Nations Declaration on the Rights of Indigenous Peoples
UNESCO	United Nations Educational, Scientific and Cultural Organisation
UNIDROIT	International Institute for the Unification of Private Law
UNTS	United Nations Treaty Series
US	United States of America

Table of cases

Regional

African Commission on Human and Peoples' Rights

European Court of Human Rights (EurCtHR)

National

Australia

Brazil

Canada

India v Bumper Development Corporation (1995) 171 AR 166 (QB) 74–76, 80

China

Yunchun Village and Dongpu Village Committees v Oscar van Overeem, Design & Consultancy B.V. and Design Consultancy Oscar van Overeem B.V., Fujian Province Sanming Intermediate People's Court, 2015 San Min Chu Zi No. 626, 4 December 2020 81–82 87 141 143 151

Oscar van Overeem, Design & Consultancy Oscar van Overeem B.V. v Yangchun Village and Dongpu Village Committees, Fujian Province Higher People's Court, 2021 Min Min Final No. 302, 19 July 2022 3 82 87 88 141 144 146 147 151

Colombia

Quimbaya Treasure, Judgment SU-649/17, Republic of Colombia, Constitutional Court, Plenary Chamber, 19 October 2017 44–45

France

Tribunal civil de la Seine, Duc de Frias v Baron Pichon, 17 April 1885, Clunet 1886, 593 132

Court de Cassation, Fondation Abegg v Ville de Genève D.1988.325

Cour d'Appel de Montpellier, Ville de Genève et Fondation Abegg v Consorts Margail D.1985.208 137

Italy

Associazione nazionale Italia Nostra Onlus c. Ministero per i beni e le attività culturali et al., Tribunale Amministrativo Regionale del Lazio (Sez. II-Quarter) Case No. 3518, 28 February 2007; Consiglio di Stato, Case No. 3154, 23 June 2008 44–45

Namibia

Swartbooi and Others v Speaker of the National Assembly and Others High Court of Namibia Case No. HC-MD-CIV-MOT-REV-2023/00023 20 January 2023
Swartbooi and Others v Speaker of the National Assembly and Others High Court of Namibia Case No. HC-MD-CIV-MOT-REV-2023/00023 [2024] NAHCMD 602 7 October 2024 43

Netherlands

Amsterdam District Court, Village Committee of Yangchun and Dongpu v Oscar van Overeem et al, No. ECLI:NL:RBAMS:2018:8919, 12 December 2018 80–81, 129–130, 132, 146–147

South Africa

United Kingdom

United States

National Courts

Regional and International Courts

Table of legal instruments

Constitutions

Civil Codes

National laws

Conventions

EU Law

Inter-governmental agreements

Declarations

Joint Declarations on Return of Benin Bronzes

Model Legislative Provisions

EU Reports and Resolutions

Table of museum guidelines and policies

Federal Ministry for Arts, Culture, the Civil Service and Sport *Recommendations of the Advisory Committee for Guidelines for Collections in Austrian Federal Museums from Colonial Contexts* 20 June 2023 152
Glasgow Life Museums Policy on Repatriation and Spoliation 2022 32
ICOM Code of Ethics for Museums 2017 31–32
ICOM Code of Ethics for Natural History Museums 2013 28
National Museum of the American Indian (NMAI) *A Step-by-Step Guide through the Repatriation Process* 2020 27
Natural History Museum Human Remains Policy 2019 25
Quebec Basic Principles of a New Museology 1984 32
Sarr and Savoy *The Restitution of African Cultural Heritage: Toward a New Relational Ethics* 2018 19 28 31 69 102 152 161
University Museums and Collections (UMAC) 2022 *Guidance for Restitution and Return of Items from University Museums and Collections* 26 33

1 Questions of 'normativity' and the 'sacred' in restitution claims

1.1 Recapitulation

This study traces a new role for Private International Law (PrIL is known as 'conflict of laws' in much of the Anglosphere). It follows on from *Restitution of Cultural Property and the Law: Complex Colonial Histories* (Roodt 2024b), which focuses on claims for the return of colonial-era and Indigenous cultural property and heritage. It argued for better integration of law, ethics, history, anthropology, and provenance research, and it proposed a method to bridge the material and the sacred world in adjudication and policy formulation. A purely legal analysis of civil claims to restitution of tangible cultural objects does not ordinarily encompass social systems and intangible knowledge systems that give expression to the relational dimension of objects in the material world. Narrowly conceived approaches do not lead to a satisfactory treatment of the subject. The adjudicatory responsibility to settle a case authoritatively, bringing an end to conflicting claims, necessitates moving beyond both the confines of 'law,' and the content of the legal norm, to achieve an evaluation that would make it possible to reach a decision. When equally ranked legal principles at the same hierarchical level of argument and counterargument compete for application, non-legal factors and extra-judicial principles provide a way out (Soirila 2022: 12, 20). Factors external to the system of law must be considered (Zeidler 2016: 52, 210; Childress III 2011: 4; Chechi 2008: 180).

Of the relationship between discursive practices and material phenomena, it has been said that neither is 'ontologically or epistemologically prior' since matter and meaning are mutually articulated (Barad 2003: 822). Epistemology focuses on 'what to think' and ontology focuses on how we determine that things exist and are 'real.'

Restitution of Cultural Property and the Law: Complex Colonial Histories highlights the encompassing, challenging, and far-reaching theory conceived and formulated in the humanities in the last century by René Noël Théophile Girard (1923–2015). He was an eminent theorist, historian, literary critic, and philosopher of social science. Born and raised in France, he made his career as a professor at Stanford University. Girard's theory offers a way to trace the effects of pervasive racism in colonial empires and their politics of annihilation and war; it can also be

DOI: 10.4324/9781003583967-1

applied in studies of the contests over legal ownership and protection of cultural heritage removed unethically during the colonial era.

The anthropology of mimesis explains human desire as collective and driven by an imitative and competitive urge. The blind conviction that we can acquire another's admired essence if we have what they possess, is tempered and contained by the sacred. Girard's theory explains the societal role and function of human sacrifice and self-sacrifice as society's way to rein in the relentless mimetic rivalry that starts with the idealisation of the other and soon gives way to competition and ultimately aggression. The propensity to resort to violence imparts a limiting identity to humans that the sacred transcends. Sacrifice enables communities to control aggression and to survive, become better integrated, and live in harmony alongside others.

Girard never applied his theory to cultural property and heritage, but the common definition of the 'sacred' and the notion of 'sacrifice' he outlined offer a theoretical framework in which the question of restitution of sacred cultural heritage can progress across the multi-layered structure of cultural property law and ethics frameworks. The theory simplifies and enhances national, trans-national, and international alignment in the commitment to restitution. The same object that 'in the hands of a collector or museum is of aesthetic, monetary, or art-historical value, may be held sacred by the former owner' (Campfens 2021: 40). If held sacred, its removal to museums and private collections in other nations touches the construction and nurturing of self and the flourishing of community. A common definition and argument about the threat which removal poses to security at the deepest level is necessary to achieve change across the humanities and social sciences.

Among the obstructions in the path to repatriation are the dynamics that hamper conversations about and attempts at returns. Each side sees what is right from its vantage point but fails to appreciate the position of the other side, and their conceptions of time and material shape their priorities. Their competitive stances may intensify and garner normative effect if left unchallenged. If the mechanisms that produce mimetic competition remain unidentified, normative effects can more easily be attributed to brutality.

The doctrinal characterisation of cultural assets underwent frequent shifts in the 19th century—from monarchic goods or national monuments to universal assets, and from 'public' to 'private' property (Spitra 2021: 128–129). Alteration of one's perspective on the significance of how an object's component material features are described also results in differing descriptions, definitions, and categorisations, particularly for complex objects. The Parthenon Sculptures and the encased mummy of Zhanggong Zushi confirm this.

The fate of the Parthenon Marbles is among the most highly charged and longest-running cultural property and heritage disputes. From 1983 onwards, the British Foreign Office and the UK government have formally and systematically rejected claims for the Parthenon Sculptures. UNESCO offered to mediate in the dispute between Greece and the UK in 2013, but the UK government declined in 2015. Only one court case has considered a claim, but the European Court of Human Rights (EurCtHR) declined jurisdiction (*Syllogos ton Athinaion v United*

Kingdom, Application No. 48259/15, First Section, 31 May 2016, ECHR 23 June 2016). The EurCtHR is a body with compulsory treaty-based jurisdiction under the 1950 European Convention for the Protection of Human Rights and Fundamental Freedoms, to which Greece is a signatory. The UK is also bound by the jurisdictional rules of the EurCtHR (section 2 Human Rights Act of 1998). The approach that was followed by the EurCtHR depletes substantive normativity and maintains the status quo of western museums. It is in need of refinement.

The international civil cases brought by the Chinese village committees of Yangchun and Dongpu concern the return of the Zhanggong Zushi mummy, artefactual human remains of a self-mummified monk from the Song Dynasty encased in a Buddha statue, which was smuggled into the West via Hong Kong in 1994–1995. The Buddha statue containing the remains of their ancestor has been worshipped by local villagers in south-eastern China since the 12th century. The name Zhanggong Zushi was conferred on Zhang Qisan by the Ch'an Buddhist community he belonged to. A human subject, through self-mummification, merged into a physical object which the monastery considered to be a master of Ch'an. In Ch'an the subject would be part of a sacred lineage of enlightened patriarchs who trace their ancestry back to the Buddha (Sharf 1992: 6). Patriarchs are considered the 'collective (communal) property' of the monastery. Such mummies held high importance for monastery economies in local forms of Buddhism and attracted the devotion of believers (Faure 1994: 161, 167–168). Their spiritual communities adhered to the 'cult of relics' to defend themselves against spiritual and physical aggression. Their desirability explains the prevalence of theft in China and Japan (Robson 2003: 155; Faure 1994: 161; Sharf 1992: 10). The Zhangong Zushi mummy was sold to a Dutch buyer after it was smuggled via Hong Kong into the Netherlands in the final years of Britain's 99-year lease, when Hong Kong was a British colony and had semi-autonomous status in China. The litigated cases present comparatists and PrIL lawyers with a wide array of issues to think through related to material, matter, method, status, definition, normativity, and time (*Oscar van Overeem, Design & Consultancy Oscar van Overeem B.V. v Yangchun Village and Dongpu Village Committees*, Fujian Province Higher People's Court, 2021 Min Min Final No. 302, 19 July 2022).

The material frame of reference and methodology of materiality refer to the sacred in discussions about restitution, but in legal debates over ownership, such references are less frequent and far more random. When the sacred does feature in the discussion, no systematic approach is followed or sought. The term 'sacred' is routinely used to depict what is religious, transcendent, or set apart from the mundane. However, the scope of its meaning is broader than is commonly drawn in western cultural and educational institutions. Efforts to introduce a typology and nomenclature that would provide conceptual refinement have yielded frustrating results (Evans 2003: 32ff). Existing North American legislation systematises issues in a way that refutes the idea of animism. The spiritual and personal significance of cultural heritage are mostly disregarded in definitions of sacred material (para 3001(3)(C) of the Native American Graves Protection and Repatriation Act (NAGPRA) US Code Title 25 (Indians) Chapter 32; Alberta's provincial First

Nations Sacred Ceremonial Objects Repatriation Act (FNSCORA) Article 1 (e); Coody Cooper 2008: 65; Conaty 2015: 55, 63). The FNSCORA protects sacred objects vital to a First Nation to practice sacred ceremonial traditions while the NAGPRA defines sacred objects as 'specific ceremonial objects which are needed by traditional Native American religious leaders for the practice of traditional Native American religions by their present day adherents.' These definitions do not integrate the tangible and intangible dimensions and nor do they defragment the dichotomies that contribute to an unstinting belief in a single, unified chronology for complex colonial histories. The lawsuit which anthropologist and author Elizabeth Weiss filed against her employer, San Jose University, exemplifies the issue. Weiss claimed that NAGPRA's prioritisation of religion over science in repatriation of Native American skeletal remains and burial objects undermines scientific research (*Elizabeth Weiss v Stephen Perez, et al.*, Case No. 22-cv-00641-BLF (N.D. Cal. 19 October 2022)). For a fuller understanding of the resonance between different cultural conceptions of the sacred as a non-legal factor in restitution claims, systematic treatment across the social sciences and humanities is required.

Drawing attention to the material-discursive forces that may be important to processes of materialisation, Barad observes that 'the knowing subject is enmeshed in a thick web of representations …[and] all that is visible [to the mind] is the sticky problem of humanity's own captivity within language' (Barad 2003: 811–812). One of the difficulties of inter-disciplinarity is that phrases that belong to different genres of discourse can be 'linked one onto the other,' but they cannot be 'translated from one into the other' (Lyotard tr. Van Den Abbeele 1988: xii). In the field of law, concepts that characteristically admit of substantive disagreements which cannot be settled to everyone's satisfaction could result in a 'hard case.' The interpretation, creation, application, applicability, and/or observation of the law may make it difficult to identify a single appropriate and just solution in a transnational dispute. The component features of essentially contested concepts characteristically compete with one another to influence the applications of the concept. They could lead to mutually incomprehensible cultural positions since different conceptions may be incommensurable and impossible to measure by a common unit or a single scale (Flanagan 2016: 143). The disagreements arising in legal circles over the issue of ownership of material removed unethically during the colonial era are not confined to legal norms; they are also semantic, semiotic, and conceptual. Semantic ploys aim to secure semiotic advantage. They protect 'blind spots.' For instance, dichotomising classifications between 'commercial' and 'non-commercial' in the colonial era shaped both the determination of adjudicatory competence and the outcome of legal argument. They were power circuits for the imprints of the 'frivolous Distinctions' on legal thought in the Hobbesian state of the *Leviathan*.

Claims for the return of colonial-era and Indigenous cultural property and heritage may focus on tangible material but they also evoke intangible qualities that are found in relationships, knowledge, and community. If the systems of knowledge associated with the tangible and the intangible are fragmented, it is easier to ignore the loss of the intangible inritual practice or forms of sacrifice underpinned by an ecumenical contemplative aspect. Rituals typically need to be performed when sacred relics are received and the denial of an opportunity to do so may invite objections that an ancestor is objectified and treated disrespectfully. This was the case when the National Museum of Denmark returned a sacred cloak made of ibis feathers that was removed from Brazil in the 1640s and inventoried in Denmark in 1689 to the National Museum of Rio de Janeiro. The leaders of the Tupinambá de Olivença Indigenous people complained about having been sidelined and denied the opportunity to meet the cloak whereas the feathers were given a period to adjust to the different climatic conditions of Brazil before being shown (Rogero 2024). The denial of the intangible is particularly severe in the case of the Parthenon Sculptures. Their original intangible role as embodiments of the sacred has been long neglected, prioritised only by the inimitable Melina Mercouri in a famous speech at the Oxford Union on 12 June 1986 in her capacity as Greek Minister of Culture and Science. She declared that the Sculptures are the sacrifices, aspiration and essence of 'Greekness' (melinamercourifoundation.com/en/oxford-union-june-12-1986). This woeful history relates the most damaging consequences of their dispersal. Greece's restitution claims are regularly met with automated responses that focus on the surface-level cultural iconography of the Parthenon Sculptures and their survival. The Parthenon Sculptures are synonymous with restitution in a symbolic and emblematic sense but as material objects they also stand for themselves. Objectifying symbolic practices obviates the boundary between the metaphor (the representation) and the material (the corporeal). The same symbolic obviation occurs in legal disciplines (Riles 2005: 1022). It is replicated in the structure, method, approaches to normative conflicts, and in the failure to identify cultural heritage and the sacred. It is fair to say that the Parthenon Sculptures dispute is paradigmatic of the fragmentation in legal and ethical frameworks that affect cultural sectors including higher education, and in the splits and conflations that occur in and across subject specialisms. A prominent example is the public-private divide in international law. Emperor Justinian defined public law as pertaining to the state, whereas private law concerned the well-being of the individual as determined by natural precepts that are observed generally by nations and those of a given state (*Institutiones* 1.1.4–text reproduced in Thomas 1975: 1ff, 3). The Roman Empire was governed by the distinction between public law and private law. Notwithstanding the futility of drawing a rigid dividing line between PrIL's 'private' dimension in opposition to its 'public' face, the public-private legal divide again became foundational to legal epistemology in the 19th century. Contemporary European legal systems have each put their stamp on the public-private divide but PrIL's dogmatic link to the civilian understanding of private law became irrevocable, and the compartmentalisation of specialisms in international law followed.

Patterns of exclusion and resistance to the legitimisation of natural law's transcendental principles gradually supplanted natural law ideology. Thomas Aquinas professed in the 13th century that all peoples and nations had legal principles in common (Neidhardt 2018: 101). The aspiration to foster the equality of nations and the universality of law was anchored in natural law doctrine (Alexandrowicz

1967: 2). The principles of natural law were strongly identified with principles of justice and equality, so that 'natural international law' applied to Europeans and non-Europeans alike. For instance, Samuel von Pufendorf (1632–1694) upheld the application of international law to all nations as a common bond and not just to the 'Christendom' that European states had in common (Miles 2011: 29, 33). Major parts of the Law Between the Peoples or *jus inter gentes*, were incorporated into the Law of Nations (the *jus gentium*), which regulated private and public affairs. Throughout the 18th century, the *jus gentium* continued to be applied to the intercourse between European and Asian powers, but not always on equal terms (Alexandrowicz 1967: 224). Jurist, diplomat, and author Henry Wheaton (1785–1848) wrote that every nation's Law of Nations differed according to place and time. Public International Law (PublIL) was limited to the 'civilized and Christian people of Europe or those of European origin,' but agreement was possible among nations because international law directed intercourse with all nations regardless of their faith and without reciprocity (Wheaton 1866: paras 11, 13). German scholars insisted that reciprocity was intrinsically part of international law, with some going as far as to say that reciprocity was its foundation (e.g. Heffter 1844: para 2). However, the expansionist interests of European nations caused them to observe reciprocity to some but not to others (Labadie 2021: para 10).

Pufendorf conceived of international law as a branch of ethics (Wheaton 1866: para 7). Its principles derived from the basic understanding that all human activity was bound by an overarching morality (Anghie 1999: 11). While earthly power lodged in the state, this power was subject to natural and divine law—a law prior to, above, and beyond the state (Glenn 2011: 249). State practice confirmed the universality of the natural law ideology. However, in the late 19th century, aspirations of the equality of states were frustrated by a constant reproduction of the distinction between those considered the 'norm' and those labelled the 'exception.' The emergence of the name 'private international law' had common roots and coincided with the creation of 'PublIL' as a discipline (Hatzimihail 2021: 5, 15, 40, 51). An international discussion constituted both the fields of PrIL and PublIL. Both claimed to operate in international or transnational conflicts. Notwithstanding their common ground, the split into public and private spheres became a permanent feature (Paul 1988: 153–154). The doctrinal ideals of PrIL were rooted in local contexts and its discourse was merged with strong domestic discourse; PublIL de-emphasised the local origins of its intellectual roots (Hatzimihail 2021: 52, 91). *Lex mercatoria* and transnational business law aimed to include a wider set of materials concerning the global operation of the economic system, but the understanding of PrIL rules and procedures was seen to be limited to national legal systems and their relation to one another. PrIL's 'international' reach mirrored PublIL's representation of a world of multiple territorial states (Muir Watt 2014: 1–2).

Conceptions of PrIL and those of PublIL urgently require 'defragmentation.' They are not strictly separate nor do they share the same space. They work together to achieve stability and legitimacy (van den Berge 2018: 119). Their interaction also has a darker side which deserves closer scrutiny.

This study has no pretense of a standalone work on PrIL in restitution and repatriation claims to cultural heritage removed unethically during the colonial era. It proceeds from a more broad-based, inter-disciplinary understanding about law, ethics, and cultural material such as human remains, 'object-beings,' ceremonial and ritualistic practices, and knowledge about these as manifestations of the sacred. Humans transmit skills, knowledge, consciousness, and culture. What gives them strength, nurtures community, and is essential to the security of society constitute sacred cultural material. Chapter 1 starts with the challenges to restitution in legal thought. It then considers 'normativity' and the normative in relation to ethics and legal thought.

1.2 Challenges to restitution in legal thought

The law is an important ideology for survival, but it does not offer a paradigm for restitution that can forecast all the twists and turns brought by new claims for return. There is no consistency in the modes of reasoning that characterise legal thought, but a helpful linguistic analytical model of the modes of reasoning was devised by Duncan Kennedy, American legal philosopher, deconstructionist, and founding member of the Critical Legal Studies movement (Kennedy 1991: 811ff). His model differentiated Classical Legal Thought ('CLT' 1850–1914) from Socially Oriented Legal Thought ('SLT' 1900–1968), and Contemporary Thought ('CT' 1945–early 2000s). The (fictional) authority of CLT took Christianity to be the purpose underlying law, whether by 'tacit premise' or open declaration. The 'civilised/uncivilised dichotomy' that formed part of this mode of reasoning promoted the view that the 'civilised states' referred to the 'Christian states of Europe,' and that the Law of Nations was exclusive to the Christian Empire (Alexandrowicz 1967: v).

PublIL cannot be presented simply as a unifying force that supports interdependence and integration among states. Traditional PublIL smoothed the way for the expansionist drive of European empires in overseas territories while the 'civilising mission' of imperialism proclaimed rights that promoted inequality between nations. Epistemologies implicit in modern PublIL derive from rules developed by the conquerors for application among themselves. Different moral standards were applied abroad. PublIL rules originated in a world where justice and human civilisation prevailed, but outside it, people had free rein to pillage. Colonisers whose cultural policies and practices promoted Darwinist conceptions of cultural evolution could apply or suspend these concepts and rules when it suited them (Vrdoljak 2008: 171). Some social Darwinist thinkers argued that racial extermination would result in moral progress for humanity. By their twisted logic, since the civilised Europeans were morally superior to primitive races, the extermination of the latter would rid the world of immorality (Weikart 2003: 274).

Ideas concerning modernity, progress, development, and emancipation abound within western legal disciplines, but the 'civilised/uncivilised dichotomy' at times still pervades mainstream discourse about 'decolonisation.' In cultural heritage law, 'decolonisation' is considered achievable by returning heritage taken as colonial loot to its original locations (Bruncevic 2021: 46, 53–54, 92). The rejection of the racist distinctions between so-called 'civilised' and 'uncivilised' nations is used as a measure of the decolonisation of law, yet it is seldom acknowledged that decolonisation implies radical divestment from mummified colonial thinking—culturally, linguistically, and psychologically. Coloniality emits a temporality. The impacts of colonialism and imperialism differ depending on 'when' the coloniser undertook certain actions. Our understanding of these impacts can be reworked by drawing upon authentic ideas that circulated before Europe made 'discoveries' prior to colonisation, when Indigenous peoples had authority over their lives. Account would need to be taken of pre-colonised time. However, the focus on pre-colonised time dims when the analysis centres only on how Indigenous peoples were colonised, what that meant in their immediate past, and how it impacts their present and future (Tuhiwai Smith 2021: 25–27). How much of the narrative of the 19th and 20th centuries has been co-opted remains unclear.

It is no wonder that the law grapples with the challenges of the interplay between historical events and the legal mechanisms premised on time as a gatekeeper. Time bars and the passing of time are advanced as reasons why the merits of a transnational case cannot be heard and an order for restitution cannot be issued.

The consistency of restitution among international, domestic, and regional legislative frameworks poses challenges (Frigo 2023: 182). 'Legal colonialism' survives in the vestiges of racial inequality built into the structure of the law, so that legal strategies for restitution are best evaluated from within the structure and system of international and domestic law (Koskenniemi 2017: 14). Wood (2016: 220) has a sense that the inherent complexity of the law stems from:

> uncertainty about cause and effect, disagreements about what the law should say and who it should protect, national cultural differences and histories, and disputes about how much law there should be and how intrusive it should be.

Wood's explanation does not mention howthe law is subject to rapid changes as well as increased 'internal tiering' across legal systems. Blind spots may be operating in transnational litigation, both at the level of legal norms and the structure and method of international law. Rules and principles rooted in the property and privilege of the former colonialist-imperialist world order foster legal uncertainty that undermines the success of restitution claims. Normative conflicts may arise between the space and time dimensions of different spheres and units of domestic law, and between different norms deriving from general international law or *jus cogens*. In the absence of applicable international standards, requests for restitution will be governed by domestic or national laws. Under ordinary commercial or property law rules, the person making a restitution claim must prove that they used to be the owner, and most legal actions fail at the early stage of having to prove ownership (Thielecke & Geißdorf 2021: 158). States generally do not have specific legal regimes in place for cultural objects and many states treat them as ordinary commodities, subject to the provisions governing private property or contract law. Ordinary commercial or property law rules are unlikely to support a claim for restitution without adjustments being made. When requests for restitution go beyond national borders, PrIL rules and techniques claim application, but the commercial orientation of these rules can promote commercial competition and dichotomised classifications that highlight technical grounds on which adjudicators may decline to hear the merits.

Conceptual disagreements may also occur over the decoupling of 'law' and 'ethics' which promote polarised narratives and stale, circular arguments. Non-compliance with moral standards puts pressure on 'justice' yet it is a by-product of formalist legal argument based on positivist notions of what 'law' is and what 'law' does. A positivist conception of what law is adheres to a narrow view of sources, confining them to international conventions and laws promulgated by a state's legislative authority. The decoupling of 'private' and 'public' in law's subject specialisms add to the complications. The discourse about what colonial powers considered worth protecting was interrelated with the administration of culture as part of the international, discriminatory legal system. For example, the 1797 Peace Treaty of Tolentino between the Holy See and the French Republic was an unequal wartime treaty that imposed peace on the papacy. The harsh terms forced the Papal States to surrender the diplomatic functionaries of Bologna, Ferrara, and Ravenna. One year later the strident terms were extended to all of Italy. The treaty's attempt to paper over plunder did not constitute a legitimate basis for possession (Miles 2011: 32, 40). Adjudicators and policymakers are expected to formulate novel responses when faced with the special social question raised by claims to cultural heritage looted and trafficked during the colonial era. The 'depth' dimension of law and ethics approaches accentuates the hollow ring of replicated mummified thinking. For instance, monument ordinances and other excavation and exportation regulations passed by colonial powers would expose the insidious underlying thinking that only the culturally 'advanced' state could properly care for the material heritage of their colonies (Spitra 2021: 138).

The preceding study on restitution of cultural property and the law argued that the intangible heritage value of sacred material is the non-legal factor that drives successful restitutionary claims to sacred heritage but that the courts on the demand-side of the trade do not identify this factor and lack the legal tools to accommodate it. A dispute about sacred cultural heritage may be characterised as a violation of PublIL or of human rights, a moral claim, or a property dispute. Characterisations other than 'proprietary' are possible but they do not fill the glaring gaps in the protective regime for the intangible cultural heritage associated with the sacred displays. The sacred underpinning of claims is seldom part of the way in which claims concerning humanitarian misdoing, human rights infringements, property, or moral grounds, are framed. The elements that mark the mummified monk as sacred would be 'oral tradition,' 'ritual,' and 'knowledge and practices about nature and the universe' in the taxonomy of the 2003 The United Nations Educational, Scientific and Cultural Organisation (UNESCO) Convention for the Safeguarding of Intangible Cultural Heritage (Article 2.2; UNESCO Guidance Note for Inventorying Intangible Cultural Heritage under the 2003 Convention for the Safeguarding of the Intangible Cultural Heritage; Intangible Cultural Heritage Inventory; Roodt 2024a: 165). Ritual shapes the relationship of human beings to reality. It inculcates a slowness that nurtures community and non-duality between human and nonhuman, subject and object, mind and matter (in general, Barad 2003: 829). The father of western philosophy insisted on the separation of human subject and physical object. Descartes (1596–1650) drew a problematic distinction between mind and matter that turned humans into spectators of life's process, supposedly occurring independently of them (Descartes 1937: 60–62, 73). Mechanistic science in the West claims superiority in the 'science'/'sacred' dichotomy and amplifies the gaps in monochronic provenance practices, but in processes of contemporary science, the distinction between the human and material realms blurs.

In *Ancient Law* (1861), Sir Henry Maine gained an important insight that the rules of the Law of Persons and the Law of Things were 'inextricably mingled together.' He condemned the distinction between the *jus personarum* and the *jus rerum* in Roman law as 'entirely artificial' and based on nothing but convenience. He believed that the artificial separation between the Law of Persons and the Law of Things could not be meaningful in the context of the law in its infancy and has 'evidently done much to divert inquiry on the subject before us from the true direction' (Maine 1861: 152). While later jurisprudence drew this distinction, he was convinced that historians who confined their attention to 'the proprietary rights of individuals' alone would learn nothing of value about the history of property. The erroneous notion of human subjects' priority over physical objects has since been rejected by others as well. Mr Justice Markby agreed that the only use of a division of law into the Law of Persons and the Law of Things is 'as a convenient arrangement of topics in a treatise or a code' (Markby 1905: sec. 163).

Cultural property law and heritage studies bear imprints of conceptual and material fragmentation. The labyrinthine jurisprudence that has emerged around community-centric resource governance of human remains encased in cultural property highlights the differences between the language of the sacred and of legal and scientific language. The fragmentation occurring at the level of language, disciplinary division, and legal categorisation is also visible in the lack of acknowledgment of the process elements that the Polish Jewish lawyer Raphael Lemkin identified in the undifferentiated violence of genocide (Lemkin & Schabas 2008: 84–85, 95). Hobbes targeted the '*frivolous Distinctions, barbarous Terms, and obscure Language*' which the 'Schoolmen' taught at Universities in *The Leviathan* (chapter XLVII: 636). The reconstruction of legal domains must take account of 'deep differences' in core beliefs and assumptions arising at the level of language, steering clear of rhetoric.

Fragmentation embeds the mummified assumptions about normativity and normative conflicts that erode the already inadequate and tenuous dispute resolution process in restitution disputes. During the colonial era, the law concerning the protection of embodiments of tribal authority as found in oral traditions, customs, and e.g., stones, statues, and temples, either remained uncodified or the codifications were distorted understandings of the underpinning norms. The erosion of the authority embedded in material culture and tribal infrastructure hinders identification of cultural objects as sacred cultural heritage in transnational litigation. Language contributes to the challenge of ascertaining the applicable 'law.' Moreover, a purely legal approach frequently leaves 'a residue of discontent, with at least one of the parties feeling that the important questions were not asked or not fully answered' (Shapiro 1998: 95). Thinking about the role that law should play in repatriation raises questions about the risk of reinforcing neocolonial dynamics between museums and Indigenous communities and the unintended consequences of doing so. The different understandings that attach to diverse cultural conceptions of the sacred also get in the way, for they affect how cases are dealt with, and they explain why courts may have recourse to the same evidence and legal instruments yet reach clashing outcomes.

Both heritage and legal debates will benefit from firming up their grasp of the interplay between law and ethics as normative phenomena. Normativity and the spectrum of the normative emerge as core questions at the meeting point of law, history, and applied philosophy. This spectrum is at once wider and more clearly defined than many would suspect. Ethics comprise a normative order premised on theory and philosophy. Most ethics frameworks consider theoretical and practical elements of the philosophy of conduct in relation to critical contemporary issues, values, and unregulated spheres of social life. Every ethical concept or category involves some kind of norm, be it practical or epistemic. Anyone may cultivate practical action-oriented skill sets to inform these norms.

Legal and ethical rules are also embodied in material. Barad suggests that the blinkers of disciplinary-defined causes and their corresponding effects prevent us from realising the intra-actions among material-discursive forces at work in 'knowing in being' (Barad 2003: 810, 829). This implies interactive practices as opposed to dogmatic or taught knowledge. Since these intra-actions create humans and objects, they matter a great deal. Barad submits that practices of knowing in being are best conceived 'onto-epistemologically.'

The unity of history, the ontological status of present and past, and historical time are long-neglected big questions about the historical condition (Bevernage 2012: ix, 109, 169). This neglect stands in the way of law reform. Working out the implications for restitutionary claims on an elongated temporal horizon can resist short-term thinking and quick fixes at a policy level when historical wrongs and deceit prompt economic reparations and redress ormaterial restitution of human remains and sacred cultural material stolen or looted outside the territory of the coloniser state.

A superficial and short-term human perception could yield but a blurred impression of historical fact. Academic historians are increasingly brought into the core of the legal inquiry by being put on the stand in court. While the perspectives of historians do not necessarily diminish the distance between history and justice, their perceptions of changes in cause-and-effect relationships may yield more clarity. Likewise, perceptions based on an anthropologist's systemic explanations of possible synchronicities may clarify matters (Libera 2011: 597).

1.3 Erosion and overlap of normative phenomena: law, morals, ethics

The normative overlap between moral and legal rules is indisputable. The law assumes normativity in supplying reasons to behave in particular ways when it is required, while the standard that someone sets for their own conduct would be—for them—a moral norm. It is a destabilising fact that the dominant PrIL view remains firmly predicated on, and attuned to, legal positivism, despite the indefensible differentiation between law and morals in PrIL.

Emmanuel Lévinas (1909–1995), a Talmudic scholar who survived the Holocaust, studied the philosophical distance between ethics and ontology. He encouraged a deeper understanding of singularity and promoted respect for the singularity of the other through recognition of the other as a self. If the self were to become identified with the other or the other's separate existence struck out, respect for the other would become impossible. They would be reduced to an object that cannot affect my self ('me') (Shepherd 2003: 484). The ethical dimension of Lévinas's philosophy is antithetical to objectification. The individual face of the other resists possession. The distance that separates the self from the other is impossible to erase. Even if I have the stranger 'at my disposal' 'I' have no power over them (Lévinas 1969: 39). The primordial second-person relatedness is wholly constituted by the responsibility of the self—to and for every other person—in a face-to-face encounter with the other's irreducible individual entity. As 'I' welcome the stranger who is different because of not being from 'my' place (being 'foreign'), 'I' may find an increased capacity to welcome the fundamentally alien and radically other and may discover the capacity for hospitality (Saldukaityte 2019: 78).

To acknowledge the universal need for recognition of the other as another self, while respecting their singularity, the normativity of moral theory and ethical precepts must work in tandem with the law. The non-factual ethical dimension of claims for return cannot be overlooked. A significant complicating factor is that the idea of a normative order, that speaks with one voice and contains a single truth, is illusory (Bollée 2019: 349). There are no universal truths in restitution, no single overarching law or body to assert jurisdiction, and no comprehensive rulebook of procedure containing generally applicable procedures for effecting restitution of cultural material removed from colonial contexts. Conventional frameworks present uniform sets of rules, but no set of universal laws governs all spheres of reality pertinent to the primordial debate. Social life is not based on universal principles that hold true for everyone (Zeidler 2016: 213). Nonetheless, a wide range of sources beyond law and ethics—anthropological and philosophical writings and oral history, for instance—can reconnect practice with theory and put technique in the service of not just formal law but also its substance.

Rules with normative qualities in political-moral terms that do not constitute legally binding norms are growing and spreading. Vague and imprecise provisions may be confused with specific instructions, but 'soft law' may also possess strong power to persuade and be considered to have 'relative normativity' (Chechi 2014: 247–248). Customary international law demonstrates how the ethical dimension helps to explain the origin of normativity (Glenn 2011: 258, 261). Ethics provide guidance regarding what one ought to do considering the realm of moral obligation or duty. In the example of handling human remains, ethics theoretically examines the right thing to do as part of a moral evaluation preceding the issuing of practical guidance (DMB *Recommendations for the Care of Human Remains in Museums and Collections* 2013: 62). Practice guidelines may exhort museums to treat all human remains in a respectful and reverent manner but the imperatives and prohibitions deriving from principles of good social co-existence or an inner sense of duty do not always inform ethical stances. Placing western interests in knowledge and scientific data above the religious sentiments of relatives who make claims concerning human remains is a form of utilitarian ethics that does not value good social co-existence. The norms that concern agency are not the same as those concerning inquiry, and practical and epistemic norms pull in different directions. It is hard to weigh practical reasons against epistemic grounds for a course of action or belief (McHugh et al. 2018: 1, 8).

The precise kind of normativity implicit in different ethical concepts, such as moral wrongness, virtue, and well-being, is energetically debated. Objectivists maintain that what a person ought to do is determined by the facts, without restriction. Perspectivists maintain that perspective determines a person's deliberation on a decision and what that person ought to do. Different versions of perspectivism produce different answers to the question of what constitutes a person's perspective (McHugh et al. 2018: 5). Ethical pronouncements—whether by objectivists or by perspectivists—tend to precede the development of legal rules (Chechi 2014: 301–302). Whereas legal duties or obligations can be so conclusive as to rule out any uncertainty (a court may hold a person liable to do x), a duty based on a set of moral values or norms will always leave scope to make a choice. Moral and ethical responsibilities spur active engagement and reflective responses to claims for restitution. They may render a claim tenable. The line of argument that brings the normative into human rights arguments concerning the right to possess, access, and control holds much appeal. Arguably, denying the villagers of Yangchun and Dongpu access to the mummified monk is to deprive them of an opportunity to participate in their cultural life. The villagers regard the re-emergence of their Buddha statue as a spiritual manifestation and a sign of Zhanggong's desire to come home (Liu 2017: 223, 226–227). While intangible cultural heritage law interacts with human rights, the two remain separate when it comes to implementation (Hance 2020: 96). This reality underlines the importance of identifying the ways to approach moral reasoning and the most complicated ethical issues associated with righting the wrongs of colonialism.

1.4 Ethical reasoning in a context of normative uncertainty

International claims for restitution and repatriation of cultural material are increasingly based on normative phenomena such as reputational pressure or ethical standards. For example, the 2021 DMB *Recommendations for the Care of Human Remains in Museums and Collections* state that the circumstances under which museums and collections acquired their holdings should be evaluated in light of today's ethical standards (at 21). Ethical considerations or moral conviction may guide a museum towards compliance with the United Nations Declaration on the Rights of Indigenous Peoples (UNDRIP) and other guidelines for the museum sector. Policy guidelines that incorporate references and guidance on legal aspects clarify the scope of the operation of the law. Policy frameworks that align with legal rules or principles on substantive and institutional aspects are likely to garner more traction than those that do not find resonance with primary legal norms. Not all legal theorists contend that law necessarily makes moral claims, but those who do are likely to recognise that ethics are often hidden in rules. Concealment does not negate the ethical dimension (Bix 2015: 143). An unwaveringly solid, globally supported ethical grounding of a legal rule may still meet with great evidential and interpretive uncertainty (Sugarman 2015: 15).

'Legal normativity' invites recurring questions in the philosophy of law (Bix 2015: 143). What is the relationship between law and rules? What is the relationship between law and morality? Both questions have a bearing on the normative uncertainty that plagues restitution discourses. An ill-defined framework for restitution fosters normative uncertainty and invites political polarisation, especially as more people stop complying with a religious moral regime and turn towards the ethic of the legal system. Societies may decide to do without religions, but they cannot do without law (Wood 2016: 179). Arguments about the scope of the law can be employed to effectively put holding institutions 'beyond the reach of the law,' but communities cannot be denied the freedom to conduct their own cultural practices in accordance with their own world views.

Neither the 1970 UNESCO Convention on the Means of Prohibiting and Preventing the Illicit Import, Export and Transfer of Ownership of Cultural Property, nor the 1995 UNIDROIT Convention on Stolen or Illegally Exported Cultural Objects calls specifically for the return of culturally significant remains and artefacts taken during colonial times, nor do they specifically exclude collections of ethnological interest from their scope and purview. These conventions have partly cemented existing inequalities through codification. While it is understood that the state itself may be responsible for depriving groups in the territory of their traditional culture, the public-private law dichotomy prevents the development of any legal protection of property against the state. These conventions refer to the protection of states against takings and illegal trade by individuals and groups, but not to the protection of individuals and groups against takings by the state (e.g. 1970 UNESCO Convention and the 1976 Inter-American Convention on The Protection of the Archaeological, Historical and Artistic Heritage of the American Nations). Instead of creating rights in international law that limit sovereignty, these instruments establish mechanisms for cooperation that reinforce sovereign prerogatives, often at the expense, directly or indirectly, of communities. Being protective of state sovereignty, they are widely ratified (Lixinski 2019: 50).

Attempts by political theorists and legal scholars to clarify the moral responsibility of present-day generations for the actions of their ancestors highlight the complicated relationship between rectificatory justice and distributive justice. Butt, focusing on rectificatory duties, argues that the wrongdoer's injustice gives rise to (moral) duties of rectification. These are duties to repair harm, reverse acts in cases of stolen property, pay compensation to counterbalance losses, and offer apologies. If these duties remain unfulfilled, the injustice of the actions continues and is not remitted. The ongoing injustice is only remitted by giving a stolen thing back, and failure to do so is another injustice (Butt 2009: 177). Society would be at risk of committing new injustices if cultural institutions were to give up on making amends for the colonial past. Modern society must endeavour to right historical wrongs even if past injustice cannot be undone (Provenance Research Manual of the German Lost Art Foundation 2019: 9).

The fact that moral theories cannot supply a universal moral framework for restitution claims does not mean that no normative obligation ever exists to restore certain cultural material and the intangible knowledge associated with that material. The philosophical question about the relationship between law and morality concerns the question of justice. A universal moral framework for restitution is lacking, but it is conceivable that legal norms may resonate across space. Legal diversity makes it more likely that competing regimes from different locations in the world will be in opposition. The 'chronotype' of colonialism and its discourse of exclusion lodge within configurations of time, but coloniality also calls up a locality. 'Local knowledge' can be permitted to contribute to globalised dispute-resolution. Implicit in the notion of 'Indigenous identities' is the factual dichotomy between comparable global experiences and the profound local specificity of the signs and symbols to which communities relate. The original location of cultural material is an important part of its provenance and its cultural origin provides insight into the culture embodied in the heritage. The colonial territories that were claimed and the cultural property and heritage appropriated from them are equally specific. Both one's point of view and one's vantage point could affect conceptions of the original location of the object or the object-being in question, as well as one's conception of the priority between a human subject and a physical object. Ontological materialism foregrounds physical objects, substances, things, and matter with properties or qualities, but this is not the only way of seeing. There are ways of worldmaking that notice only processes, events, and their impermanence.

The legal dimension of ethics and the ethics that underpin legal standards become more visible when museums acknowledge and implement cultural rights. An awareness of the gaps in object documentation can be expressed to shape and refine musem practice. However, incorporating ethical and religious considerations into deliberations is difficult when the domestic legal framework in question lacks clear procedures and criteria for restitution. Ethical considerations are tied to what museums consider to be their central role in preserving the source culture (cultural preservation) and preserving intangible cultural heritage (Byrne 2015: 19–20, 33–34). In the British legal order, however, a case must be made to allow for the return of cultural materials from national UK museums and galleries without primary legislation that outlines circumstances in which collection items may be de-accessioned (7th Report of the House of Commons Select Committee on Culture, Media and Sport *Museums: Acquisition and Return* para 166). Repatriation policies and ethical codes of practice do not refer to cultural rights. UK museums are not required to formally recognise cultural rights, and yet their responsibility to respect cultural rights is central to the rule of law. Since repatriation policies and ethical codes of practice do not reference cultural rights, national museums do not always conceive of the retention of human remains as ongoing violations of cultural rights in repatriation decisions, and some museums simply cannot conceive of culture as a right that Indigenous or other communities may exercise. The concept of 'inalienable cultural heritage' is unknown. Cohesion is lacking in respect of principles, criteria, and procedures for all aspects of collections of human remains (Woodhead 2002: 317, 346–347). The absence of resident Indigenous populations pressuring governments to address historic injustices delays the start of interrogations of certain colonial histories (Howes 2020: 84). This lacuna creates ethical dilemmas for many museums which were not alleviated by the pressure which the conservative government piled on the museum sector to adopt an unattainable value-neutral stance. The Arts Council of England (ACE) policy guidelines replicate this oversight in respect of cultural rights (*Restitution and Repatriation: A Practical Guide for Museums in England* 2022). No mention is made of structures of injustice, object itineraries, or histories. The terminology reveals nothing of the violence that accompanied colonial takings (Stahn 2023: 474).

The Museums Association situates the guidelines issued by ACE in the context of the wider movement to decolonise museums and the Supporting Decolonisation in Museums guidance (*Restitution and Repatriation: A Practical Guide for Museums in England* 2022). However, ACE's guidance oversimplifies the understanding of cultural restitution in the 2020s (Stahn 2023: 46). The distinction between conditional and unconditional loans is glossed over and no attempt is made to explain how to resolve conflicting claims or why it is important to identify a legal basis for categorising and claiming objects. A three-year time limit applies to export permits issued for loans of the Parthenon Sculptures (Hansard HL Deb. vol 834, col. 2006, 14 December 2023). Persisting with its patchy restitution track record, the former Conservative UK government required export licences for artefacts that are being restituted (announcement by Arts Minister Stephen Parkinson, 17 February 2023). While it is hoped that ACE's *Practical Guide* could reduce the level of confrontation between cultural institutions and government in Britain, its notification that the advice does not change any law or policy is misleading. Policy guidance that cannot affect policy must necessarily block meaningful development of the policy framework.

Whether a moral obligation exists to undertake restitution can be ascertained by a framework that foregrounds normative phenomena regarding the sacred and removes ambiguity in respect of colonial contexts. It cannot be predicated on any one morality, nor can it pretend that western institutional values are 'universal' (Smith 2022 unpublished, based on refinements of the framework advanced by Thompson 2003: 251). Affirmative responses to the following discrete questions will indicate that a moral obligation exists:

a) is there a valid group claim to sacred cultural material?
b) is the group claim morally justifiable? and
c) are there moral values that may displace valid and justifiable claims to restitution?

Validity in a) is assessed with reference to whether the object was created by or can be proven to have been acquired other than by force, forced sale, or under duress through power imbalances or the racist laws and discriminatory practices that marked the colonial era; and whether the object is essential to the dispossessed group's self-identity or their sacrifice (and not simply of historical or cultural importance in a more general sense). If a claim can be supported by morally justifiable arguments under b), the material does not qualify to be sold or circulated, e.g., that the human remains or other sacred material in question were acquired by a different collectivity under circumstances considered immoral or illegal by modern standards, under structures of oppression, without consent. To determine whether any moral values of western academic institutions identified by societal discourse outweigh a valid and justifiable claim, museums are required by c) to demonstrate how other values—such as compliance with the law or protecting and conserving sacred cultural heritage—outweigh their moral responsibility to restitute sacred material.is.

Robertson (2019: 124–125) poses a question about the ethical implications of the retention of collections items 'unfit to be retained.' 'Legality' means something different in the US where many museums are independent, and in France, where laws and regulations that control museum collections have come under review. The 1963 British Museum Act permits the Trustees of the British Museum to sell, exchange, give away, or otherwise dispose of collection items that are duplicates of another such object in the collection under s 5(1)(a). Since 1945, more than 30 Benin Bronzes in the museum's collection have been sold. The Benin Bronzes were seized during the British 'punitive expedition' against the Benin ruler in 1897 from the royal palace of the Kingdom of Benin. In 1972, plaques of a mudfish and a crocodile were de-accessioned despite not fitting the 'duplicate' exception (Forbes, 6 June 2013). The British Museum acknowledges that the wood and stone altar tablets knows as the Ethiopian Tabots were looted by British soldiers after the Battle of Maqdala in 1868. They represent the Ark of the Covenant and the Ten Commandments. Kept in the 'Holy of Holies,' only a small circle of Ethiopian Orthodox priests is entitled to access and see them (Binns 2017: 80). Hidden from view, they have never been on public display. In 2003 the British Museum announced that museum staff are prohibited from entering the room where the Ethiopian Tabots are kept (House of Commons, Culture, Media and Sport Committee, First Report of Session 2003–04. H.C. 59: paras 58, 59). Arguably, 'legality' would be upheld if sacred cultural objects were designated as 'unfit to be retained' and repatriated to their source community (Smith 2022 unpublished).

Scholars who recognise that the gap between law and ethics needs bridging in claims for the return of Nazi-spoliated art have turned the focus on the practice of advisory committees and panels mandated to hear such claims. Nonetheless, attempts to keep questions of ownership and restitution separate from victim-focused, policy-based, morality-driven paradigms continue in post-war restitution studies (Veraart & Winkel eds. 2011: 7; Oost 2018: 139). The disrupted relationship between law and ethics contributes to the isolation of certain legal disciplines.

1.5 On the 'sacred' and the 'normative'

Since it is imperative that the reasoning that underpins a unifying method for restitution claims is understood more widely, the resonance between different cultural conceptions of the sacred and the ethics that govern it deserves systematic treatment. This section aims to clarify the role and ethics of sacred property and heritage in society. It investigates conflicting claims by different stakeholders for 'colonial objects' in museums and whether claims are connected to cultural obligations to care for the dead and for sacred objects. A unifying conceptual framework of the sacred and the obligations and duties engendered by it is necessary to restore the ability of the material to challenge hierarchical thinking not just in regard to the colonial past but also in the present. Such a framework can be expected to dissolve disciplinary boundaries that befuddle restitutions, repatriations, and returns of unethically collected heritage.

What are the priorities in restitution? Scholarly arguments about what ought to be prioritised for unconditional repatriations adhere to the definition of religious heritage as the sites, buildings, artefacts, and practices that form part of living religions (Lixinski 2024: 473). Priority is usually assigned to religious objects linked with active cults alongside war objects. It has been suggested that the best way to properly qualify sacred objects is to 'contextualize them within the current living practices and traditions of the claimants' (Hai 2013: 208). Hai reasons that sacred objects should not become separated from any meaning they continue to hold or the part they play in contemporary culture. 'Dead' religions and 'dead' culture are not necessarily given any consideration (for more detailed discussion see section 1.5.1).

The category of 'religious objects,' 'cult,' or 'practiced ritual' does not capture the essence of the sacred material in western ethnographic collections. All religions utilise holy places and relics. None of these definitions take account of mimetic human desire, which plays out, for example, on sacred sites that are used as military strongholds and in attacks on sanctuaries and places of worship, bringing destitution to the tangible and intangible heritage located within them. Religious intolerance threatens sacred cultural heritage directly. Even if a person's faith tradition cannot be outwardly perceived, their practices may render them identifiable to the intolerant. The phenomenon is not new. The pogroms that commenced in Roman and medieval times continued in the wake of the First World War. The scope of the sacred is much broader than is commonly thought in western cultural and educational circles. It extends to the ritualised destruction of sanctuaries and sacred sites throughout history; venerated objects used in ritual, ceremony, or contemplation; temple idols believed to embody deities or the souls of ancestors or gods and kings; and objects that reflect and support the structure of the self. The profound lack of knowledge about ethnographic collections is akin to a form of epistemic violence (Weber-Sinn & Ivanov 2020: 73).

The ritual value of 'culturally- sensitive' material is often relegated to 'myth' and fantasy under a western, mechanical world view, but secret or restricted culturally-sensitive material must be included. Their viewing or handling is reserved for certain members of Indigenous communities, but displayed as emblems of power in western cultural structures and researched in western institutions their true nature remains veiled. The desire to conquer, control, and eradicate certain beliefs left deep imprints on this material. It is submitted that the mimetic propensity and the sacred, which controls this propensity, will highlight priorities for restitution.

The full range of sacred material of culture(s) forms part of a programme of behaviours that determines the sequence of events, the history, and the results of events in practical life, much like a 'semiotic system' (Libera 2011: 597–599). Although actions are programmed by culture, 'culture(s)' is not the best term to use because of varying understandings of what 'culture' is. In western conceptions it refers to all non-biological aspects of humanity and human development that form and shape spiritual values; however, the diversity of Indigenous cultures and histories cannot be captured by any single accepted definition (*Centre for Minority Rights Development (Kenya) and Minority Rights Group International on behalf of Endorois Welfare Council v Kenya*, African commission on Human and People's Rights Communication 276/2003, 2010).

The category of 'cultural heritage' is hard to read when premised on unjustifiable distinctions. Not only is the terminology overgeneralised, but unjustifiable distinctions have been drawn between material looted during armed conflict and material taken by way of economic conquest (e.g., Mastalir 1993: 1033, 1049). Such a distinction is spurious for trade can be tantamount to war, just as liberty can be extolled by those who perpetuate oppression. Calls for peace rarely mean aggression is relinquished as the tool to achieve it. Initiatives such as the 2018 Sarr and Savoy Report foregrounds 'war booty' and 'punitive missions; collection by ethnological missions and scientific "raids" funded by public institutions; objects originating from such operations, passing through private hands, and gifted to museums by the heirs of officers or colonial civil servants'. The 2021 Dutch Council for Culture's *Policy Vision on Collections from a Colonial Context* recommends that circumstances surrounding an object's removal, including the social, political, and market conditions of the country of origin at the time, should factor into restitution decisions. However, the common denominator category can be made much more specific. Policy frameworks will be more effective if they pay closer attention to dishonourable conduct towards the sacred resulting from mimetic rivalry with family members, neighbouring and other empires, and colonisers. This approach displays greater potential than 'culture' to achieve policy aims and objectives because it supports the dismantling of the frivolous, artificial distinctions drawn in the humanities and social sciences.

Sacred material is not 'religious' in the sense of having a universal quality that belongs to all. What is truly unversal is the craving for a sanctuary or sacred space. Ritual and ceremony are somatically adhered to, and as the experience engages the body and the senses in the present, it concretises the sacred. Behaviours that honour the sacred—ceremonies, pilgrimages, rituals—introduce a 'slowness' that nurtures community and peaceful co-existence because they interrupt the mimetic drive to get even. Without such behaviours, humans enter a violent, undifferentiated simultaneity (Girard 2010: 56–57). Importantly, without a broader agreement of what the sacred entails, the contentious classification will continue to obstruct lasting change through a more unified regulatory and ethics framework for adjudication and policymaking.

Girard's reading of the sacred challenges researchers, policymakers, and adjudicators to identify how the sacred shapes systems of knowledge and develops the normative. Sacralised objects and object-beings provide the best argument for their belonging and return, because they demonstrate the normative implication of the sacred. The communal obligations they engender give them authority. Essential to the survival, continuity, and integration of culture, these obligations steer towards a unifying model that resists personal and sectarian interests undermining claims for return. Claims to cultural heritage may be lodged to recover identity and ancestral memory, but sacred cultural objects stand for more than just their identity value for the people involved. Integral to political sensibilities, relationships and subjectivities, they are what communities require to survive and thrive. How those obligations fit within the argument for re-unification within the juridical framework of exception is a fascinating yet challenging research objective that this Chapter will address.

Material philosophies are embedded in everyday practice rather than in abstract thought. Contrastingly, however, western legal frameworks are grounded in abstract systems of thought that emerge from the reflection and study of individuals who are permitted to separate themselves from everyday life by a specialised institutional structure. The legal frameworks and rules that are front and centre in the West make it much harder to identify or quantify the ethical and spiritual dimensions of cultural material (Kreps 2003: 3). Adhering to Girard's theoretical framework, this section singles out material phenomena that evoke the sacred and sacrifice, along with the systems of knowledge associated with the sacred and the traces of *res extra commercium* in western European legal systems. Knowledge about norms and their effects is implicit in the materiality of the sacred and so is the 'normative.' Does sacred cultural property and heritage qualify as a special, separate category of property? In gift economies and begging traditions in Buddhist communities the obligations engendered by the sacred are manifest. The question is whether they can counter the normative thrust of mimetism and reframe perceptions that collections will be lost.

1.5.1 The ethics of 'sacred' property and heritage

In the 1980s, Oleg Grabar (1929–2011), distinguished Aga Khan Professor of Islamic Art and Architecture at Harvard, noted how underdeveloped the ethics of spiritual property were in discourses about religious monuments and holy places. Religious politics easily become all bound up with power displays that undermine the ethics of this type of property and heritage. The political skirmishes between Hindu and Muslim constituents over the new Ayodhya Hindu Temple in India, which was built on the site of the ancient Hindu Temple of Ram, indicate that power continues to rule. Ever since litigation commenced in 1857, a range of state organs has failed to effectively implement and enforce legal rights and guarantees granted to the minority Muslim community. Unwilling to use their power to implement guarantees , the political conflict has deepened over time. The lack of confidence in the federalist, secular principles enshrined in the Constitution has put the secular basis of India's constitutional order at risk (Edge & Rajan 2020: 228–230). In France, the principle of secularism which forms part of the bedrock of the identity of the French state isinterpreted as prohibiting public entities from granting subsidies to religious events. It is designed to foster stability (Hance 2020: 174–175).

Cultural monuments and traditions represent heterogeneous mixtures of inventions and influences that have accumulated over long periods of time. Aesthetic qualities of sites and monuments across cultures may overlap and find agreement; however, spiritual values are not interchangeable in the same way. Grabar argued that holy sites and monuments are bound by common integrity and spiritual, aesthetic, and cultural values which are peculiar to them. Religious monuments represent national heirlooms and can be considered as belonging to all, but as expressions of piety, they are for specific groups or individuals only (Grabar 1988: 31). A Muslim shrine cannot be interpreted in terms of the Jesuit faith or with reference to Buddhist tradition. The Parthenon temples are readily acknowledged as a 'religious architectural form' and feature among examples of the appropriation of this form (e.g., Connelly 2014: xx; 141–142). Yet interpreting sacred art and monuments such as the Parthenon through the lens of another religion will result in contradictions and theological dilemmas.

In the Christian West, sacrality vests in relics through their ceremonial use by the clergy. Some objects are more sacred than others (Mairesse 2019: 16). For example, Christian relics and reliquaries are person-objects that are paraded in birthday processions for saints to celebrate the connection they foster between the material and spiritual world. The skull of Sainte Foy (Saint Faith), a girl martyred for refusing to make pagan sacrifices, is enshrined in a gold and gem-encrusted reliquary in the museum of Conques, France. The reliquary has been listed as a historical monument since 1895. Every October, the reliquary is taken out for the procession of Sainte Foy despite its protected status, re-inforcing participants' sense of belonging. The ceremonies and rituals depicted on the Parthenon Frieze may invite comparisons to those associated with Passover and Holy Week, but the likeness is superficial. Crude comparative studies between religions, like those of the early 20th century, cannot add much to our understanding of the intangible cultural heritage without taking extraneous factors into account (in general, Faure 1994: 157). Restitution ethics cannot be resolved by means of a research imperative that seeks to compare and differentiate. For instance, undertaking a comparison of sacred bodies in rival traditions—Confucianism versus Daoism; or the ideology of Ch'an versus general Buddhist eschatology—is useful only to understand the element of mimetic competition; yet the sacralisation of the body lies central in Buddhism and beyond (Faure 1994: 157). Overlooking commonality when differentiating between traditions of sacralisation may diminish the interdisciplinary validity of research results across the social sciences and humanities. Focused on the peace and stability that every culture needs for its cohesion and survival, Girard's understanding of the sacred directs attention to the core characteristic that the sacred shares across cultures and religions. Pointing to what lies beyond the religious ideas, values, or feelings they give expression to, it is unconcerned with the tenets of individual belief systems, religious communities, or individual religious works referenced in historical art writings. It does not end with a supernatural event or a religious consensus on God or prophets or sites and phenomena. The sacred is found where cultural and natural elements resonate. Temples built as sanctuaries are the artificial mountains that communities ascend to help them transcend a profane world (Eliade 1959: 41, 58–59, 75).

Misclassifications cannot change the inherent character of the sacred, but the discourse is complicated if the ethics of sacred property and heritage are omitted from restitution debates. The Vatican's return of the heads of a horse and a boy, which used to be part of the frieze, and the head of a bearded male from one of the metopes in 2022, was not based on any formal bilateral agreement between the Holy See and Greece, yet did not highlight the sacred either. As a religiously inspired donation, it reiterated the ecumenical truth that, if you steal something, you must give it back instead of grasping at the financial gains to be had from serial theft. The omission makes it easier to trivialise the sacred. Colonial affinities and hostilities denatured the Parthenon Sculptures into artworks that Lord Elgin could flog in England. Despite their close association with the Parthenon Temple and the Acropolis as a place of worship for the dominant religion through the ages, the law and ethics discourses about their repatriation have allowed their sacrality to fade into the background. Traditional Greek polytheism competed with Christianity until Roman emperor Theodosius I decreed Nicene Christianity the official religion of the Roman Empire in 380 (Connelly 2014: xvi). Pagan Hellenic rituals and practices were banned, and other Christian sects were deprived of their legal status. Between the 5th and 6th centuries, the construction of a Christian church within the Parthenon damaged its eastern pediment and friezes. In the 13th century AD, it was used as a Roman Catholic cathedral; when Athens fell to the Ottoman Turks in 1458, it was rebuilt as a mosque. In 1687 the Ottomans were using the Erechtheion as a gunpowder magazine. A Venetian mortar struck the temple and caused significant damage to the temple frieze (St Clair 1998: 47). The small mosque that arose from the rubble of what had been the Parthenon's inner room or cella that housed the statue of Athena physically survived until 1843 (Connelly 2014: xvii). The contribution of this history to law and ethics frameworks for spiritual property seems rather obscure, but Girard's theory on mimetic competition and the sacred ascribes meaning to the intense competition for control of religious centers and sacred spaces.

Repatriation wins support more readily when religious rituals are still practiced by a living culture (e.g., Campfens 2021: 169). Time seems less distant. The widespread assumption that the Parthenon Sculptures symbolise a 'dead culture' and a 'dead religion' and that no living culture supports the system of knowledge they hold, renders the urgency of their return 'arguable' in ethical frameworks that require Athens to prove the sustained importance of the Parthenon Sculptures over time (e.g. Thompson 2003: 256–257).

A more coherent reading of the ethics of sacred property and heritage is that the rituals that create order and inspire trust within a community live on, whether actively practiced or not. Girard's conception of the sacred carries no implication that sacred material must be used as living heritage or in present-day rituals to have spiritual significance. Rather, his theory challenges assertions that material objects cannot be sacred unless they can be re-introduced to their original religious contexts within traditions that continue to be practiced by source communities. The unique sacred connection of the Parthenon Sculptures with the spirit of the Athenian people is not a function of the survival of ancient Greek religion—although remnants of Greek mythology continue to influence Athenian society—but is based on knowledge that remains essential to the well-being of Athenians.

John Henry Merryman (1920-2015) set two requirements for a hypothesised legal obligation to return an ethnographic object to the culture of origin, which scholars have yet to interrogate: First, that the culture claiming return must be alive, and second, that the object must be used for the ceremonial purposes it was made for (Merryman 1988: 497). He argued that together, the two requirements make for 'essential propinquity,' or an inextricable link between some objects and their culture of origin, which establish a binding obligation to return them, and declared this the only instance where an obligation exists to effect return. Since the ethics of sacred heritage does not begin and end with living religions, Merryman's requirements for a hypothesised legal obligation to return an ethnographic object to the culture of origin ring hollow. His ill-conceived pre-set criteria may promote the restitution argument for human remains, encased human remains, and sacred bundles, for example, but they do not align with the ethics of sacred heritage.

The spiritual values of abandoned religions cannot be trivialised just because their sites of origin no longer have clear roles in society. To discard the knowledge of the ceremonies, liturgies, and beliefs of the abandoned religions that made monuments possible undermines their spiritual integrity, which is as important as their physical integrity. Both are expressed through the information provided about them. A society's cultural values influence its interpretation of other religions in ways that may interfere with a community's relationship to their past, but one does not need to believe in the holiness of a religious monument or value its aesthetics to appreciate the power, creativity, and diversity instilled in it. A monument's embodiment may be tied to a specific location, but its qualities are universal. Even in a secular dispensation, the meaning of religious monuments and holy places can be conveyed to people of all beliefs and none (Grabar 1988: 27, 31). If the religion which the material is associated with is transcended, transcendental meaning is achievable (Evans 2003: 33, 38). In this sense, the material 'forms community' and issues a call for spiritual practice.

The interpretation of the mummified monk as a Chinese religious folk relic, subject to the laws protecting cultural relics created before 1795 from export or sale to foreign nationals, means little to those who revere him. To classify human remains and mummies as scientific material is even cruder. The life and spiritual tradition of Zhanggong Zushi constructed a collective social memory over many generations of spiritual practice in a monastery in a village, but his remains conjure more than sacred memory. For devotees, the monk's remains are more than just a cultural artefact from which scholars may gather data, more than a person-with-rights, or a means for reasserting rights to cultural heritage and redressing the injustices of the past. The encased monk was reduced to a work of art when his remains crossed over into Hong Kong to be sold in Europe. Britain's relationship with China determined the status of Hong Kong and the loopholes in its legal framework continue to encourage cultural trafficking.

The processes for the return of human remains are better developed than those for stolen sacred objects, but they deserve equal attention. It has been suggested that models of good practice already in use for returning human remains could inform protocols for the return of stolen African cultural artefacts taken in colonial contexts (AFFORD Institute 2020: 3, 8, 12). The argument may be broadened yet further. Physical, biological, and forensic anthropologists and palaeopathologists could provide information about a deceased's fate or corroborate the violence of a death, while taphonomists could determine what happened to the remains. However, no generally accepted standard of investigation exists for repatriation purposes other than the orientation that human remains ought not to be used for scientific study until questions regarding origin and acquisition have been answered by provenance research (Anne Haeming's 2019 interview with Bernhard Heeb). The DMB *Recommendations for the Care of Human Remains in Museums and Collections* (2013: 57) suggest that, as soon as a context of injustice is suspected, no further research should be conducted on the human remains in question, and to focus on determining the provenance of those remains. Further, as soon as there is clear proof that human remains archived in a museum or collection originate from a context of injustice, a blanket prohibition on all further research on or with those human remains ought to be invoked. The 2021 update of the DMB *Recommendations for the Care of Human Remains in Museums and Collections* indicates that a historical context of injustice 'warrants proactively offering to return human remains to descendants of the deceased where it is possible to find them or else to those potentially authorised to decide what to do with them' (at 21).

Cross-cultural collaboration is the best method to obtain quality information about the purpose, significance, value, and provenance of ethnographic objects. It is an opportunity to take account of the beliefs and preferences of institutions and source communities (Human Rights Council Report 2020: para 48; Svestad 2012: 194ff). Without accession records or provenance documentation, it is impossible for institutions to respond meaningfully to repatriation claims when the conditions of ownership transfer cannot be clarified through research. Museums may become entangled in political agendas where the ambition is for expedient repatriations to be made.

The responses of former European colonial powers to requests for return of colonial cultural objects range from conservative attitudes that keep a safe distance from the debate to openness to requests. Some insist on long-term, revolving, or permanent loans of objects to source countries while others formulate clear policies that commit to the effective transfer of ownership and override impediments to returns. While the number of permanent, unconditional restitutions made on a case-by-case basis is growing, there are many for whom restitution and repatriation activate a fear of losing part of an institution's collection. Inaction may be preferable to confronting the role of cultural institutions in late Victorian ideologies of supremacy. Keen to limit change and risk, museums may employ every available defence against restitution claims regardless of the moral, legal, and financial risk involved (Janes 2015: 3, 22). Prioritising the relationship between an object and a collection provides national museums with a justification to discourage restitution claims.

In 1924, the Foreign and Commonwealth Office was urging its officials not to create precedents that would result in the Parthenon Sculptures' return, fearing it would put the collections in British museums at risk of being emptied. Frances Kenyon, Director of the British Museum (1909–1930), deployed the floodgates argument. He intimated that the return of the Parthenon Marbles would spark a wave of demands for return, causing the de-accession and depletion of entire collections save for locally produced artefacts (Last 2007: 137). If encyclopedic museums were denuded, they would be prevented from serving the purposes for which they were created. The spectre of the 'empty museum' prompted the promulgation of the 1963 British Museum Act. As is the case with the 1983 Heritage Act and 1992 Museums and Galleries Act, the British Museum Act limits the discretion and decision-making powers of the governing bodies of these institutions to de-accession items from their collections. Even recent policy instruments such as the British Museum Human Remains Policy 2019 stress the importance of the collections remaining intact. The Natural History Museum Human Remains Policy, dated 19 February 2019, encourages retention of all items for purposes of study and research 'for the benefit of all humankind.' A similar exhortation appears in the 2022 University Museums and Collections (UMAC) Guidance for Restitution and Return of Items from University Museums and Collections.

The fear of the slippery slope persists in political circles in the UK. Refusing one meritorious claim because others could be made in the future is hardly an example of rational debate about rightful ownership (Woodhead 2023: 337). Paradoxically, the fear that agreeing to any restitution will create a domino effect demonstrates a certain self-awareness regarding the scope of the problem in western cultural institutions and the extent of the holdings deriving from a mindset of colonial supremacy. Universal museums with institutional practices engineered to suppress petitions for restitution of stolen and illegally exported cultural material are the most vulnerable to the depletion of their collections. The fact that many artefacts in the institutions' collections could take the place of restituted objects is conveniently ignored.

1.5.2 The genealogy of legal thought

Just as genealogical research can shed much-needed light on provenance, the 'genealogy' of legal thought supports more expansive thinking about restitution and a deepening of understanding shifts in the modes of legal thought over time. A confluence of past ideas that transform at the point of convergence produces modern ideas. Earlier ideas flow together with new ideas to produce the conception that crystallises in the present. Kennedy (2010: 831) maintains that a search narrowed through time to the location of the immediate progenitors of the present encourages insight. Insight will follow if the meeting point of the temporal, the spatial, and the ontological premises of the old and new idea are understood.

Legislation is typically given prospective application only for the sake of due process or to guard against impairment of contracts; judicial rulings have retrospective application unless they will impose undue hardship upon those who have reasonably relied on an old precedent. A non-chronological argument may neutralise an opposing argument in court, and an alternate conception of time can interrupt the mimetic dynamic. Alert to the mimetic implications of methods and approaches, scholars and practitioners are better placed to cultivate an understanding of time that fosters respect for the present ways of life of cultural groups. An alternative chronosophy acknowledges that colonial relationships are not fixed in time and that complex colonial histories do not have a single, unified chronology (Bevernage 2012: ix). Non-chronological approaches can permit present values and norms to highlight problematic behaviours of the past.

The idea that ethics are bound to their era is often used to justify the deeds of perpetrators while the suffering of cultural communities is underplayed. Restitution claims hit a dead end when conceptions of time in adjudication work to the detriment of claimants in this way. The restitution of sacred ethnographical material engages not just with responsibility in a historic sense but also with societal change over time. An awareness of historical injustice in debates about the redistribution of property heightens the need to define clearly when contemporary standards are more appropriate than past approaches and practices. This necessitates determining when a certain rule or norm was adopted, examined, or applied in a location, as well as providing ethics-based reasoning for resorting to alternative chronosophies.

Differentiating between fact, opinion, and value may help not only to untangle rules and norms but also to draw out connections between the vantage point and the vanishing point of rules and norms (Van Roermund 2013: 261). The standpoint of the observer and the point where rules and norms converge, reach completion, or cease to apply, unlock ethical perspectives on the conflicts raised by time and place; the application of contemporary norms and rules; and the application of relevant rules at the time. For instance, greater certainty can be achieved by a rule whose formation has reached completion. Such rules are also easier to identify as pertinent to a claim.

1.5.3 Priorities in restitution

Collectors with access to colonial bounty removed human remains while colonial conflict raged—*pendente bello.* This exemplified the racism of the imperialist-colonialist age. The ethical implications of the ill-treatment of fellow human beings by those in power and the dehumanisation of human remains in museum collections invoke visceral arguments for repatriation. Dead or alive, the victims are witnesses to injustice and identity in a fragmented colonial historiography (Krüger 2010:

234). Restitution claims are a legal matter, but the repatriation of human remains is neither predominantly legal nor political and most cases engage predominantly with ethical considerations (Woodhead 2002: 347). Their removal will have detrimentally impacted the cultural relationship between human remains, their communities, and their system of knowledge. The unlawfulness of the misappropriation of irreplaceable human remains must weigh in on priorities and actions of repatriation processes. The repatriation of human remains from colonial contexts must take priority in alignment with human rights law (e.g., the UNDRIP). In Canada, the UNDRIP has the status of 'hard law'. The United Nations Declaration on the Rights of Indigenous Peoples Act of 2021 (SC 2021, c 14) affirms the Declaration and requires the Canadian government to draft and observe action plans for its implementation. An increasing number of ratifications of the UNDRIP confirms its potential for implementation in other parts of the world too, to help to settle claims. Governmental and institutional plans that recognise the principles of a common humanity as having top priority will foreground the repatriation of identified human remains in alignment with Article 12 UNDRIP. Identified human remains deserve more respect and dignity than other collected objects in colonial collections (Winkelmann 2020: 46).

Current national legislative frameworks evidence a growing consensus that human remains from colonial contexts should, in principle, be returned (Stahn 2023: 284). The standards related to the treatment and retention of human remains are already being applied increasingly broadly (White 2019: 91ff; Vigneron 2020: 315). The Belgian Parliament tabled a bill in 2023 that would have made the ban on the trade of human remains explicit (22 November 2023). A private member's bill was passed in France to allow for the de-accession of all Mãori tattooed human heads (Mokomōkai) held in accredited museums in France. France also adopted legislation on human remains in public collections that simplifies the law (*Loi N°. 2023-1251 du 26 décembre 2023 relative à la restitution de restes humains appartenant aux collections publiques*). Human remains less than 500 years old can be returned to their countries of origin by a decision of the Prime Minister. However, a general framework law for restitution is still being awaited.

Over the last three decades an increasing willingness on the part of western museums and states to de-accession ancestral remains demonstrates that it is possible for museum professionals to agree to respectfully repatriate identifiable human remains when the country or community of origin can be identified (AFFORD Institute 2020: 30). For instance, the National Museum of the American Indian (NMAI) guidelines presume that reasonably identifiable human remains or those culturally affiliated with Native American Indian tribes will be repatriated. This presumption respects Indigenous peoples' rights (NMAI *A Step-by-Step Guide through the Repatriation Process* 2020). French curators appealed to the moral concept of human dignity to distinguish between 'named' and 'unnamed' remains and between 'specimens' and 'persons' in the repatriations of Sara Baartman's remains and twenty Māori heads (Bodenstein & Oţoiu 2022: 14). Sara Baartman (1789–1815) was born into a pastoral Indigenous community in South Africa. Her remains were kept in the collections of the Musée de l'Homme, the former anthropological section of the National Museum of Natural History in Paris, and presented as scientific evidence of the perfect specimen of the 'African Hottentot.' In 1994 claims to have her remains returned intensified. Sara's remains were decommissioned from their status as public cultural heritage and a special law was promulgated (*Loi N°. 2002–323 du 6 mars 2002 relative à la restitution par la France de la dépouille mortelle de Saartjie Baartman à l'Afrique du Sud*).

When research results and academic expectations to conduct open research clash with community values that reserve certain knowledge for the initiated, the dignity of human remains themselves suffers. The lop-sided relationship between the rights of the cultural community and the rights of researchers, which already leans towards research, may become skewed even further.

Hailed as the first example of the return of important colonial artefacts from Sub-Saharan Africa to an African country based on a wider restitution policy, the 2018 Sarr and Savoy Report signals a radical turning point for French policy and the public role of museums in relation to restitutions on moral, rather than merely legal, grounds (in general, Campfens 2019: 94). It also resuscitated the debate across Europe. The report was a missed opportunity in prioritisation and accusations were made that its recommendations comprise 'mixed messages'. It hardly mentions immovable cultural heritage such as monuments, with the only reference being incidental mention of the 1907 Hague Convention on the Laws and Customs of War on Land (Sarr & Savoy 2018: 12). Soon the report was bogged down in political debate, museum resistance, and Realpolitik. Of the 70,000 objects in the Musée du Quai Branly-Jacques Chirac, 46,000 were acquired during the colonisation period (1885–1960) and are eligible for restitution under the terms recommended in the report. Systematic treatment of inventoried objects in a single category that encompasses culturally-sensitive, restricted sacred objects, would have provided a simpler, clearer steer for restitution and repatriation processes evolving across Europe, and could have earned the report wider endorsement.

In the earliest part of the 20th century, the dead were treated differently depending on whether they belonged to familiar groups or 'othered' groups. The dead of 'othered' groups and their cultures continued to be disrespected even when racial scientists, committed to proving the existence of a racial hierarchy, failed to produce evidence that the bones of disparate cultures had distinctive features. Displays of human remains must comply with basic standards of human decency, for their descendants, relatives, and the community that maintained a close association with the remains would wish to ensure their respectful treatment. These standards extend to ancient remains with a cultural affiliation or spiritual connection with living societies. They also have implications for repatriation policy and ethics frameworks, which do not always emphasise the importance of compliance with standards for the remains themselves, independently from the relatives and their memory of a person (Woodhead 2002: 339–340). The 2013 International Council of Museums (ICOM) Code of Ethics for Natural History Museums (para 1) reiterates and sets standards for the use, display and storing of human remains and hand-made artefacts composed of or including human remains that have the same cultural and/or spiritual significance as human remains. These materials must be treated with dignity (para 1: C, E). The origin of the material and the wishes of any descendants or other stakeholder groups must be considered (para 1: B). Display, representation, research, and/or de-accession must be done in full consultation with existing representatives of the cultural group in question. Repatriation is appropriate 'where objects still confer a spiritual and/or cultural significance, or where they can be irrefutably demonstrated as being stolen' (para 1: G). Ironically, anyone can possess, buy, and sell human body parts that were not acquired illegally and that are of archaeological or anthropological interest if they are used for transplants (Batty 2024).

In England, Wales and Northern Ireland, the Human Tissue Act of 2004 focuses on remains under 100 years old. Holding human remains that are less than 100 years old for a Scheduled Purpose (as defined in the Human Tissue Act, 2004) constitutes an offence unless a licence has been obtained from the Human Tissue Authority (British Association for Biological Anthropology and Osteoarchaeology (BABAO) 2024 Statement on the sale of human remains). Public display, including in a shop, is a Scheduled Purpose. The BABAO supports the Department of Digital, Culture, Media, and Sport *Guidance for the Care of Human Remains in Museums* (DCMS 2007) and the Advisory Panel on the Archaeology of Burials in England's *Guidance for Best Practice for the Treatment of Human Remains Excavated from Christian Burial Grounds in England* (APABE 2017). Unprotected from invasive research techniques and hardly requiring any due diligence are historic human remains more than 100 years old before the Act entered into force, and human remains taken during colonial rule. Human remains that are classified as cultural objects in national legislative frameworks may not qualify for de-accession and repatriation. Collected remains incorporated into ritual objects after inhumation and mummification may be in a similar position. Policies that homogenise all historic human remains older than 100 years treat archaeological and artefactual remains from millennia ago the same as remains that belong to modern history. There is authority for the view that homogenisation of human remains constitutes a barrier to restitution claims (Fforde et al. 2015: 44). The real barrier seems to be that of allowing museums to benefit from their past failure to keep good records on historic human remains, as this approach removes the burden of responsibility from the museum. Shifts have occurred in ethics and philosophical discourses, but the classification and racist treatment of human remains are under-researched in PrIL and other legal disciplines.

1.5.4 Material phenomena, knowledge systems, and the colonial overlays obscuring the normative

The handling of human remains is always culturally-sensitive, even when their care is anchored in ethical value systems. Whilst the remains deriving from colonial military operations speak to the sacrifices of those who were targeted, artefactual human remains, ancestral human remains, and ceremonial objects point towards the sacred at the basic level of their materiality. The intentionality of Buddha mummies manifest in the material world. Objects or materials that lie central to burial practices, pilgrimages, and rituals are more powerful in their sensory and physical realisations than virtual replications could ever be.

Traditional knowledge systems draw together all physical, mental, and emotional aspects of knowledge, data, and experience to 'find the path.' Embedded in the living entities called object-beings, spirit participates and shapes the traditions, histories, and behaviours of the people who made them (Jessiman 2017: 71; Tsosie 2010: 27). The political ascendancy of the Dutch, Portuguese, British, French, Belgian, and Germans came with military personnel, imperial administrators, colonial officials, priests, missionaries, explorers, entrepreneurs, artists, and settlers, many of whom continued living among the societies and communities who occupied the lands that had been claimed (Tuhiwai Smith 2021: 23). Museologists acknowledge that land and the distinctive approaches of Indigenous peoples to the land are interwoven with the ceremonies, customs, traditions, and languages comprising cultural heritage, and with human rights (Curtis 2014: 89–90). Native American communities connect the spiritual power of places of worship, burial, and pilgrimage to 'sacred time' and 'creation'; they experience 'being' as cyclical (Griffin 1995: 395, 397). Those dispossessed of their peoples' remains and sacred artefacts are also deprived of unique ancestral knowledge and know-how that would have helped them know themselves, and others to know them, better (Labadie 2021: para 29). Dispossessed communities of origin not only miss what is taken from them but also become unable to explain their traditions to subsequent generations (Stétié 1981: 8). There is no participation in the discussion when the negated party 'lacks language to express how he or she has been injured or wronged' or cannot express themselves in a language that the system understands (Delgado & Stefancic 2012).

The royal authority of certain objects is thought to ensure their communities' stability, protection, and survival. Among the 26 totems, statues, palace doors, and ceremonial objects returned to Benin from Paris after the publication of the 2018 Sarr and Savoy Report and the adoption of a Benin and Senegal return bill (*Loi relative* à *la restitution de biens culturels* à *la République du Bénin et* à *la République du Sénégal, Loi N°. 2020–1673 du 24 décembre 2020*), were power-figures of the kings of Abomey in Dahomey (now Benin). The statue of the voodoo god of war, Gou, remains in the Louvre still but Benin agitates for its return. Stolen or misappropriated ethnographic material and artefacts are frequently mourned by their communities. Like Gou, the power-figures of the kings are 'other-than-human-beings', called upon for guidance and counsel as embodiments of political identity and qualities worthy of transmission to present and future generations. The violence involved in their capture is poorly understood, but mimesis and the 'duel between twins' feature strongly in Dahomey's history and in their taking. King Ghézo (Dahomey's ruler between 1818 and 1858) was at war with his brother, the Yoruba Empire, and the British over the profitable trans-Atlantic slave trade. King Béhanzin (Dahomey's ruler between 1890 and 1894) was exiled by the French who installed his brother as the new King. The 'power stones' of Kwanyama, Ombalantu, and Ondonga are believed to embody ancestral spirits in what are now northern Namibia and southern Angola. The stones connect these African communities with the spiritual world, highlighting the stark differences between Indigenous societies' conceptions of heritage and those of western property law (Silvester & Shiweda 2020: 33–35). The Kwanyama stone dates from the early 17th century and the reign of King Shitenhu in the Kingdom of Oukwanyama. Believed to have fallen to earth from the outer world, it was kept in a special place and guarded by healers. Because the stone was believed to embody the power of the kingdom and the strength of its people, it played a formative role in the Kwanyama political system; it held a central place in the stone-stepping ritual for political stability which settled succession disputes between rival kings and prepared the way for the appointment of new rulers. Official reports indicate that the last Kwanyama king, Mandume YaNdemufayo, was slayed by colonial invaders from South Africa in 1917, but Mandume's descendants believe that he died by his own hand when war broke out. The Kwanyama fled because they did not know what had become of either their king or the power stone. The South Africans forbade the inauguration of a new king, and a Council of Headmen was set up to represent the people. In 1942, Vilho Kaulinge, pastor, oral historian, and special advisor to Mandume, recovered the stone from the royal family in Angola, who had taken guardianship of it. Kaulinge handed it to Erkki Laurma, a Finnish missionary, who took it to Helsinki for safekeeping in 1948. The Finnish Mission Museum displayed and looked after it, returning it to Namibia in 1995. The Kwanyama people remained without a king for seventy-nine years, but after the stone's return, a new king was inaugurated (Silvester & Shiweda 2020: 33–34).

The deep-rooted cultural meanings of the power stone as intangible cultural heritage are comparable to those associated with the Parthenon. The Parthenon Marbles are symbols, but they also stand for themselves as material objects. They evoke startling insight into mimesis and the Athenian sacrifice which the Acropolis temples embody. Restitution claims in respect of the Parthenon Sculptures are like those for the power stones and power-figures. Decontextualisation disempowers their source communities and drains them of meaning. Conceptions of property and ownership in western understandings cannot express their self-defining quality. Spiritual beliefs have importance not as derivatives of material interest, but as combinations of ideas and material interests (Begg 2011: 182). Human behaviour may be understood as the interplay between ideas and material interests, informing an actor's worldview, rather than as automatic reactions to material interests.

Repatriation requests advanced by Indigenous peoples in former colonies are predicated on meaningful interconnected considerations which vary across ancestral lines. An Indigenous ontology is the equivalent of an Indigenous epistemology. Since one's relationship to an object is more important than the thing, the relationship between the researcher and the object informs their research aims. The data extracted from objects, samples, and remains is beside the point (Wilson 2008: 73). Indigenous societies' sacred material and the systems of knowledge, including normative knowledge bound up in sacred material, are threatened by the institutions that deem the material 'unessential' to tribal survival. Holding institutions frequently get to determine whether restitution claims are 'authentic' or whether the degree of continuity between an Indigenous group and those who produced the heritage in question is sufficient to ground a claim. In many Indigenous settings, animate object-beings are used until their lifecycles come to a natural end and the artificial prolonging of their lives would fundamentally change their character. Not permitted to reach the natural end of their lives, sacred material would lose their sacred character and function in certain Indigenous communities (Parker 1990: 37).

Local traditions in China differ. Many villagers of Yangchun and Dongpu share the name Zhanggong and claim to be the descendants of the Monk Master. They regard his soul as persisting inside the mummy and believe that the blessings he transmits allow them to overcome pain and sorrow. The beliefs that Zhanggong Zushi's devotees adhere to are not suspended by the theft of the figure. Their devotional practices persist despite their beliefs being at variance with the current possessor's conceptions of the religious or cultural value of this complex material. Nonetheless, they will always pine for his material embodiment.

Patterns of exchange in source regions may support social or ethnic groups who wish to protect their heritage for future generations. The material aspect of the Potlatch ceremonies of First Nations on the Canadian Northwest Coast and American Indians of the Pacific Northwest Coast transmits beliefs that sustain not only the material but also those who produce and value the material. The material is interwoven with the knowledge that practitioners and attendees hold about births, deaths, and other important events that establish rank, social status, and ascendancy. Dance, song, ritual, and elaborate regalia mark rights and privileges, such as ceremonial names and hereditary positions.

Conceptual fragmentation at the level of the material object is evident in codes of ethics and policy guidelines that do not prioritise sacred objects as an integrated category in the context of restitution and repatriation. The 2017 ICOM Code of Ethics for Museums covers the care and display of human remains (paras 2.5; 3.7; 4.3) but does not contain any definition for sacred materials as an integrated category. This makes it harder for museums to honour the values they embody and easier to find reasons to circumvent potentially applicable protocols for the handling of sacred material. Perhaps museums are expected to define handling protocols in consultation with relevant cultural groups, but this is not made clear in the ICOM Code for Museums.

The ICOM Code of Ethics also places a duty of care on the part of museums to prioritise the retention and preservation of their collections. It suggests that trustees are obliged to safeguard the collections for the benefit of present and future generations. As a 'process,' however, museums reflect moral codes and conventions as well as social conventions, and they also reshape them (Sandell 2011: 135). Arguably, their social function extends to the movement and transfer of collection items (*International Movement for a New Museology (MINOM*) 1984 Declaration of Quebec Basic Principles of a New Museology 2010: 23–24). The ICOM Code of Ethics requires museums to take an active stance on the question of restitution. They are expected to remain prepared to initiate dialogue for the return of cultural property in an impartial manner (para 6.2). They are also expected to promote the sharing of collections with source communities or states, and to work in close collaboration with the communities of origin (para 6.1). Compliance with these ethical duties instils openness and trust. At its General Conference in Prague on 24 August 2022, ICOM took a cautious line with their definition of 'museum,' which does not make express reference to restitution claims yet challenges the confines of certain primary legal norms that preclude decisions about restitution. Discussions on the definition and redrafting of the paragraphs on repatriation (paras 6.2 and 6.3) are ongoing and are expected to be voted on in November 2025.

Guidelines and soft law that assist museums with restitution decisions for imperial artefacts and human remains, such as the ICOM and UMAC Guidance for Restitution and Return of Items from University Museums and Collections of 2022, do more than foster new museum practice. The refinement of the guidelines plays a significant role in clarifying priorities and objectives in the space between law and ethics. For instance, while institutional differences prevail, active conversations in the museum sector in Scotland give impetus to institutions' decisions. These conversations focus on a) identifying the item; b) researching its chain of ownership or possession; c) establishing its connection with the proposed recipient, be it an individual, community, or state; and d) its significance to the proposed recipient. The human rights approach of the UNDRIP shifts the focus from the legality of removal at the time (b), to the spiritual significance of an object for the people in question when present possessors cannot be held accountable for past conduct and the events that had taken place (c and d) (Articles 11 and 12 UNDRIP; Campfens 2019: 107). The 2023 Aberdeen University Museum and Special Collections, *Procedure for Responding to Repatriation Requests: Repatriation and Deaccessioning from the University Collections* refers to these considerations. The Glasgow Life Museums Policy on Repatriation and Spoliation 2022 adds the consequences of the return or retention by the possessor as an additional criterion alongside points a through d.

Sustained commitment is needed to shape a cultural discourse about the exploitative practices of colonialisation, that is appropriate for our time. This commitment was exemplified when the Chau Chak Wing Museum at the University of Sydney removed fragments of mummified bodies from public display in 2024 (Kuta 2024). It was also evident when Semley Auctioneers in Dorset, England, withdrew from sale 18 ancient Egyptian human skulls from the private museum of Augustus Pitt-Rivers, who had measured the skulls to try to define racial type. Pitt-Rivers was the founder of the Pitt Rivers Museum at the University of Oxford (Batty 2024). By participating in the trade of sacred material, auction houses fall short of best practice. By insisting on retaining possession of sacred material, and failing to represent deprived communities, museums continue to be showcases for works of art and perpetuate the dehumanising colonial discourse. Courts can usefully consider the guidance on best practice and codes of ethics that the museum sector provides (Paterson 2011: 654).

1.5.5 Traces of res extra commercium in Western European legal systems

Many European legal systems retain traces of a forgotten category of Roman law, *res extra commercium*. Under Roman law, these objects were precluded from becoming subject to private rights and their transfer in ordinary commerce due to their inherent characteristics (Thomas 1976: 136). Historically, *res extra commercium* comprised different classes of things. *Res communes* were things that belonged to everyone, such as the air we breathe. *Res publicae* were things that belonged to the government. *Res divini iuris* were subject to divine law and belonged to no one. They were outside the dominium of the sovereign: *res sacrae* (monuments, temples, shrines, things that were consecrated to the gods in ritual or used for devotional purposes); *res sanctae* (city walls or gates under the protection of deities); and *res religiosae* (tombs, burial-grounds, funerary urns, etc.). However, the right of conquest and the Roman law spoils of war doctrine permitted victors to treat consecrated items as unconsecrated and justified looting and theft. Roman law did not permit foreign territories to consecrate property either. Only the authority of the Roman people could confer the status of *res sacrae.* Consequently, foreign cultural heritage did not attract protection under Roman law. The bias against non-Romans rendered the destruction of non-Roman sacred sites irrelevant in law (Rives 2012: 165).

Considerations of convenience determined the protection of *res sacrae* in war. Over time, the technical definition of *res sacrae* ceased to matter. In the Imperial period, it was the treatment of a place that determined its sacred status more than a technical legal definition (Rives 2012: 180). Echoes of this approach are discernible in the deconsecration and sale of modern Europe's Christian churches. As a response to the dwindling numbers of parishioners and parishes, many are repurposed to meet commercial ends. In certain places, Roman law was part of the law of the land without there being any formal affiliation to the Holy Roman Empire (Hatzimihail 2021: 58). Nonetheless, a basic preclassical historical consciousness would urge anyone to realise the geopolitical difference between the Roman Empire and the contemporary world.

Dutch law offers an interesting example of a European legal system built on the precepts of Roman law, retaining the *res publicae* category of *res divini iuris* as a category to which no special rules of property law attach. The *res sanctae* category has become superfluous in Dutch law. Churches, museums, or private persons own religious objects, and the standard concept of private ownership applies to things owned by the national government or by local authorities. Such public property may be protected under special rules of written or unwritten public law (van Vliet 2006: 109, 114). Modern law provides many examples of the preclusion of certain objects from commoditisation by cultural or public legal diktat. The Greek law of 'movable monuments' (s 21(1) of the Law on the Protection of Antiquities and Cultural Heritage in General 3028/2002) provides that:

> movable ancient monuments dating up to 1453 belong to the State in terms of ownership and possession, are imprescriptible and extra commercium according to Article 966 of the Civil Code.

Export bans are imposed on finds from excavations or other archaeological research, regardless of date. Greek law stipulates that the state retains ownership and possession of these objects, which cannot be alienated by sale or adverse possession. They also enjoy the status of imprescriptibility.

Just as the legal protection of cultural heritage in Roman law was selective in practice, so is the tendency in modern European law to apply protective legal norms inconsistently. The cultural supremacy of elite social groups has unmistakable effects on the restitution discourse of former colonial powers, and an exaggeration of the role of classification in PrIL in colonial contexts would not be constructive. Judicial recognition, application and enforcement of a foreign law that expressly prescribes *res extra commercium*, is tantamount to a de facto recognition of the status of a legal class of objects and collections that could not be owned, traded, or used. However, domestic law does not always have the final word on legal classifications, and conflicts rules can defeat unpalatable state rules (Roodt 2015: 225).

Article 13(d) of the 1970 UNESCO Convention recognises the right of States Party to classify and declare certain cultural property inalienable and not amenable to exportation. When exportation has taken place, the property may be recovered. The 2012 UNESCO-UNIDROIT Model Legislative Provisions on State Ownership of Undiscovered Cultural Objects provides support for this idea. Provision 5 on inalienability states that the transfer of ownership of a cultural object deemed to be stolen under Provision 4 is null and void, unless it can be established that the transferor had a valid title to the object at the time of the transfer. States are to be encouraged to utilise the Model Provisions, especially as the 1970 UNESCO and 1995 UNIDROIT Conventions fall short of conferring full *res extra commercium* status on cultural objects. Article 3(4) of the 1995 UNIDROIT Convention exempts restitution claims for cultural objects 'forming an integral part of an identified monument or archaeological site or belonging to a public collection' from time limitations 'other than a period of three years from the time when the claimant knew the location of the cultural object and the identity of its possessor.' The *res extra commercium* status is rendered incomplete by the time limitations that remain in place.

The narrow Eurocentric strictures of *res extra commercium* and the restrictive definitions of *res sacrae* and *res sanctae* cannot contain the meaning and implications of the sacred. More deliberate and consistent recognition of the remnants of *res extra commercium* in domestic law would strengthen the legal recognition of sacred cultural property and heritage as a special, separate category of property. The next section considers gift and the explanations gift economies offer for the obligations that inhere in the sacred.

1.5.6 The role of the 'sacred' in gift economies

The anthropological dimension of the gift, counter-gift, and concomitant obligations in certain communities is pertinent to the search for a common legal basis for restitution claims in respect of cultural material. Marcel Mauss (1872–1950) published a compelling enquiry into the law, economy, and mentality of the gift in the aftermath of the First World War, in his essay on 'The Gift' ('Essai sur le Don: Forme et Raison de l'Échange dans les Sociétés Archaïques' 1925). His analysis of Polynesian, Melanesian, American Northwestern, and other Indo-European laws alongside Ancient Roman law, elevates this work above the usual Eurocentric slant of so many texts of that time. His theory on the gift encourages critical questions about the nature of 'gifts' as reproducing social relationships and, when given as tokens of loyalty by groups or persons, acting as their representatives to erstwhile occupiers in the colonial era. He also identifies a striking commonality among the different ancient societies he included in his study: They classified things according to their characteristics.

The governing structure, culture, and spiritual traditions of the communities that continue to practice Potlatch ceremonies are evident in ritual property transfers made by the host as a nourisher. The host offers gifts to the invitees. Redistribution of wealth is an integral part of the ceremony, which also demonstrates the power of leaders. Their power includes the power to destroy wealth. The social obligations of the rituals are an intrinsic part of the spiritual mechanism of the ceremony, for it is incumbent on the ceremonial participants to give gifts to the host in return. The anti-capitalist underpinning of Potlatch ceremonies was perceived as a threat by the Canadian government and the pagan implications of these rituals unsettled the Christian evangelical missionaries. This cultural expression of traditional knowledge was criminalised in 1884 (An Act further to amend 'The Indian Act, 1880', SC 1884, c 27). A major Potlatch ceremony in 1921 led to the imprisonment of several attendees, and regalia was confiscated and sold to museums and private collectors. Thefts were common at the time (Cuk 1997: 158). The ban on First Nation peoples in Canada participating in Potlatch ceremonies was only lifted in 1951. Having become part of the domestic legal framework in Canada in 2021, the Article 31 of the UNDRIP may contribute to the recognition of traditional knowledge; for now, other development needs receive priority.

The competitive dimension of Potlatch ceremonies is evident from the hierarchy they establish among the participating nobles (Mauss tr. Guyer 2016: 62–64). The normative dimension of the ceremonies prompted legal philosophical interest in the relationship between obligations and rights based on Mauss's analysis. The discourse surrounding duties can be usefully broadened to embrace a normative or philosophical discussion of the possibility for a 'free duty' to exist. Free giving is a 'true gift', which is something other than just the absence of a duty to pay back. A 'free duty to give' is categorically and qualitatively different from a duty to reciprocate. A voluntary act of giving that is unconditioned by another's right to receive and unburdened by mechanical reciprocity creates an asymmetry between right and obligation.

Mauss's gift theory provides a unique anthropological perspective on the obligations engendered by sacred material and the intangible properties of this material. Obligation is three-fold in his theory: To give a gift, to accept it, and to reciprocate, because what is given remains attached to its owner (Godelier 2002: 22, 24). This exercise in power, titles, and ranks fosters antagonisms. Clans would compete with the gifts they offered, each wishing to give so much that their gift stood apart as unrivalled. Gifts and countergifts would escalate across the entire society in a 'war of wealth' (Godelier 2002: 26–27). While the kinship networks in archaic communities (e.g., in the American Northwest, Ancient Rome, or Germanic and Hindu communities) required something to be given in return for the gift—such as an undertaking to provide social or political support to the giver of the gift—social obligations were also fulfilled through giving. The obligation to reciprocate those gifts was absolute in these gift economies; refusal would be a declaration of war. In Polynesia, not reciprocating is tantamount to losing the talisman or authority itself (Mauss tr. Guyer 2016: 61, 66). Can a similar dynamic of obligations that precede rights inspire a re-think on the responsibility to repatriate sacred cultural material?

The transference of knowledge in gift economies constitutes intangible heritage, and so does the exchange of property in begging traditions that rely on acts of gift-giving for their survival and on the communal responsibility of humans to protect (non-renewable) cultural resources. In Buddhist traditions where begging was an intrinsic part of the broader social structure based on gift and counter-gift, the support of patrons and the state hardly mattered (Faure 1994: 24). Ch'an practitioners were less susceptible to societal command and 'the vagaries of state and aristocratic patronage' than schools that prioritised clerical tutelage, monastic ritual, or scholastic training based on sutras (Sharf 2002: 6). In return for food and alms, the monks instructed the lay community on Ch'an teachings and practices. The tradition in which Zhanggong Zushi had been schooled inculcate observation, emphasise insight into the Buddha-nature of all beings, and encourage practitioners to incorporate this insight into their daily lives. The practice was undertaken for the benefit of, and as a 'gift' to, all as an offering that encouraged the sacrifice of the 'individual' to that which is 'universal.' Many Buddhist communities continue to offer instruction in exchange for donations.

Germany attempted and failed to colonise the northern part of the current Benin Republic (Effiboley 2020: 73, 75). Pieces from the Kingdom of Dahomey ended up in the permanent collection of the Dahlem Museum in Berlin. Effiboley theorises that the king, having given cultural objects to the Germans, awaited a counter-gift or the return of a gift, perhaps in the shape of military support against the French army, but he waited in vain. Effiboley poses a rhetorical question as to whether these cultural objects may still be considered a gift that the Germans can retain. Repatriation is called for because their social obligations went unfulfilled (Effiboley 2020: 73). The suggestion is that the gift framework provides a foundation for repatriation to occur when social obligations have been dishonoured.

Mauss's enquiry into the law, economy, and mentality of the gift in archaic societies conveys the plurality among the types of exchanges and modes of accounting that survive alongside capitalism. The Roman law concept of *res* acknowledged the relational quality of certain things. *Res* went beyond 'things' as 'inert beings' to include how they related to familial relationships and determined relations between people. For example, the Latin term *familia* denoted the house (the *res*) as part of the *familia* (Mauss tr. Guyer 2016: 149; Van der Walt 2018: 3, 5, 48). Mauss intimates that, in acknowledging the power of the thing in theft and in contract, Roman law was comparable to Hindu and Haida laws. Gift and exchange were *res*: By an ancient rule of law, there had to be a thing before there could be a gift, and the thing had to create obligation. The '*aeterna auctoritas*' and reciprocal obligations inherent in certain things were acknowledged (Mauss tr. Guyer 2016: 151–152). However real the connection between an object's character and the obligation it invites may be, standard legal arguments and discourses may never confirm a priority of obligation ahead of right. Therefore, it becomes important to broaden the understanding of sacred heritage and its intangible properties.

Mauss's theory renders more visible the ontological clashes that mark the ways in which different peoples and institutions relate to certain categories of material. It also exposes how narrow and object-focused the language around colonial-era loot is. The material and the intellectual, moral, and spiritual forms of exchange of the material deserve consideration; the juridical, economic, religious, aesthetic, and morphological social systems from which the material phenomena derive deserve our best attention. Mauss puts this into perspective when he makes the profound observation that deep attentiveness to human exchange could keep men from massacring each other and could support recovery from the tragedy of war (Mauss tr Guyer 2016: 11, 19, 193).

That the world is given to us and we have the ability and capacity to receive it may be palatable to many different faith traditions. Lévinas maintained that existence does not come to us as wealth to be received or accepted (Lévinas 1981: 11–12; 55, 90–93). 'Being' is lacking in specification, akin to a 'horrible neutrality.' The first encounter with existence is seeing the face of another person. Life imposes an obligation to give whatever one can, for it awaits a response. In Lévinas's conception of the origin of obligations, rights and obligations exist separately and without correlation.

Normative pluralism or plurality is typical of complex colonial contexts. Traditional ontological classifications predicated on behavioural standards of the past permeate the actions of cultural institutions. They may cause these institutions to favour decisions and policies that perpetuate the old power structures. What is more, the law of restitution and repatriation of cultural property and heritage is 'radically underdetermined' and 'indeterminate.' The singularity of events in the context of the colonial era means that each situation exceeds, or falls short of, the universals contained in the legal rule. Before it is possible to know what to do, the rule must be interpreted. However, action is always needed before all the information is available including information about the likely interpretation of the rules. Restitution claims frequently arise in contexts in which legal regulations are absent or conflicting. Claims may emerge when there are regulatory gaps; the scope of extant regulations do not match the circumstances of the case; or a conflict between legal principles is present. The uncertainty and diffusion this causes can be overwhelming, and it is often necessary to 'bridge' or reconcile facts and norms.

The timelessness of the sacred in Girard's theory challenges efforts to construct or protect 'havens for cultural imperialism' where holding institutions get to determine whether the national government consents to the return of Indigenous cultural material, or whether the material reflects cultural or religious concerns that the holding museum considers 'legitimate.' The obligations presumed by, and inherent in the 'claims' that sacred things make, resist market-oriented thinking. They can serve as a reminder that societal responsibility is at work, enabling courts to demonstrate a better understanding of the relationship between rights, duties, and obligations in restitution proceedings for private, common, and cultural property.

Obligations may precede rights in non-capitalist modes of accounting such as in many begging traditions. Obstacles to restitution inherent in primary legal norms will not disappear overnight, but the interpretation of primary and secondary legal norms may afford opportunities to make the ultimate gift of honour and respect. Secondary legal norms are rules that condition the spatial scope of application of primary legal norms or rules. They limit the temporal scope of legal rules in a way that differs from the way in which presumptions about statutory interpretation and constitutional law do this. Despite the margin of discretion available to return sacred material governance systems designed for robust resilient collective decision-making in respect of diverse commons regimes and collective goods do not always safeguard this space or permit its identification.

Elinor Ostrom's model distinguishes between operational day-to-day rules, collective choice rules for decisions about how operational rules could be changed, and constitutional rules that determine how collective choice-rules and other secondary legal norms may be changed (Ostrom 1990). This discussion has branched out into arrangements for 'cultural commons' such as art. Occasionally, primary legal rules permit cross-border application. While national in scope, the NAGPRA does not preclude cross-border transfer and its provisions may not always be conditioned by secondary legal norms. This much was demonstrated by the return of the stone ancestor T'xwelátse, stolen from the People of the River (Stó:lō) of British Columbia after more than a century at the Burke Museum in the US. The return of the Stone Being to Canadian First Nations depended on meeting the NAGPRA's preconditions that a US federally recognised tribe must make the application and prove that they are Native American, have a shared group identity that may be reasonably traced historically or prehistorically to a living tribe, and that the requested object belongs to their cultural patrimony. Originally the Nooksack community of the US Pacific Northwest Coast was part of the Stó:lō in Canada. The Nooksack brought the application under para 7(a)(1) pertaining to 'Native American human remains' and para 7(a)(5) pertaining to 'objects of cultural patrimony'. Differentiated rule-making must integrate secondary legal norms (collision norms) to facilitate international rule-making. Whereas Ostrom's model overlooks the secondary legal norms of PrIL that coordinate the application of the primary rules and the theory that informs the methods to achieve it, this study aims to integrate PrIL values and procedure at the intersection of domestic and local laws that could be pertinent to the restitution of imperial artefacts to former colonies.

In claims for the restitution of cultural material removed during the colonial era, the time factor is frequently deployed as a gatekeeper. The standard set by uniform law in this regard has a defining effect on the law in signatory states. To prepare the ground for a critical analysis of time's function in claims for restitution in Chapter 2, the structure of time is investigated next.

1.6 Chronology, chronosophy, and the fine structure of time

Historical time insists on chronological reasoning and linear timelines to capture historical reality. Under a chronological conception of historical beginnings and endings, historical injustices may be relegated to the past. Present action is not required. Ontological learning creates hierarchical knowledge, and linear time alters and colours perspectives on scientific methods of enquiry and conditions the cultural pressures to facilitate global markets and commerce. Deep, non-chronological time is the slow time which the sacred fills. The lens of historical time must be removed for it to be detected.

Western conceptions of historical time are bound to inform the institutional perspective on injustice. Its conceptual timelines may impact not only the formation of organisational structures and instruments, but also how they are perceived and interpreted. These interpretations shape how objects are defined, categorised, and treated in law. Bevernage theorises that the analytical habit of chronology conceals structural biases against the dispossessed (Bevernage 2012: 150, 168). He points out that western thought considers the relationship between history and justice as absent or distant, and therefore irreversible. Chronology favours a hierarchical history that represses the voices attesting to the violent alienation of objects and their emotional, cultural, and spiritual connections and meanings. Legal principles that do not indicate which route to follow when an object has been acquired unlawfully or unfairly confirm his suspicions. Among the complex set of rules that informs the application of the inalienability principle of French public domain is the condition that special statutory exceptions are required to enable the return of objects that are inalienable in the eyes of French law. Were it not for PrIL, the final say regarding legislative or other routes would be left to perpetrators which are states in many instances. The interesting facet is that the *lex situs* rule of PrIL can defeat unpalatable state rules (Roodt 2015: 225).

Conceptions of time affect the way in which provenance research is executed to fill gaps. It could be done either by tracking and tracing owners and transfers that make up a chain of title retrospectively, or by starting collection research with historically sensitive and potentially inaccurate suppositions that require interpretation. By working backwards through archival research and genealogies, administrative records, wills, reproductions, publications, and photographs, a provenance researcher may be able to ascertain who made, received, or owned sacred cultural material in the past. Working forwards based on this evidence might give a sense of the institutional oppression and social harm suffered at the time of the taking. Ontology works its way into the formulation of important questions and into practical approaches to research.

Judaism, Christianity, and Islam valorise historical time, whereas the cosmic symbolism in other Indigenous religions adheres to cyclical time (Eliade 1959: 110–111). Eliade points out that '[r]eligious man has given different valorizations to the same fundamental experience' (Eliade 1959: 62). This onto-epistemological difference accounts for the distinctions drawn between sacred sites and places of worship, and the inequality in the level of protection extended to Native American sacred sites compared to their western counterparts. The threat encompasses the spaces and the land in which the sacred bundles were formed and used, because ceremonies must take place in the community's concept of creation at the center of their world, which does not run on clock time. The threat faced by Native American bundle culture is linked to the narrow scope of the definition of the sacred in western culture; however, it is also precipitated by a consistent refusal to consider an alternative chronosophy.

Chronosophy is useful in epistemological studies relating to the structure of knowledge, which is confirmed by the interdisciplinary and normative study of time *sui generis*. The chronology of sequential clock and calendar time becomes secondary if the present is at the center, surrounded by the past and future. Just as objects bear the marks of time, bodies retain memories. Time and age do not diminish the imprints of threats to security and survival on the disowned and deprived in choronological time. Yet, in deep, polychronic time, potential is experienced more directly, and capability is seen more clearly, for the mechanism of language no longer gets in the way of our efforts to intuit fluid reality. Both the Buddhist metaphysician (who perceives the material realm of 'things' as 'slow-moving events' that play out over time), and the western scientific realist (who has a firm grasp on the properties of things) have the resources needed to assume the vantage point of the observer. Thus, they enter a common perspective and agree that events or processes have enough stability to be treated as things, and that all ancient cultural material that has survived through the perils of time is perishable, fragile, and unstable (Flanagan 2016: 135). Even if they cannot agree that relational and material elements inhabit 'the same order of existence,' they may find themselves in agreement that a type of property right is necessary for a restitution claim to succeed, and that certain 'things' have intangible properties that nurture and sustain community.

A consistently chronological approach to restitution claims would require the events, persons, and things that constitute that history to be treated as significant structures applied to the model of the world of a given tradition and yet, asks Libera (2011: 601), what meaning lies in the sequences of events themselves? Understanding the structure of time is more instructive than blind assumptions that ftime passes in a linear sequence. The structure of time brings into the open differences between fact, opinion, and value because it reflects more than undifferentiated fact, opinion, and value aligned with purely western, educated, industrialised perspectives (Flanagan 2016: 45–46). A study of the structure of time encourages a certain dispassion when arguments about the meanings of events become circular, as it points to the inseparability of the phenomena that occur and change over time (diachrony) and simultaneously (synchrony).

1.7 How to 'see' missing links in the provenance chain

Deprived communities and their representatives feel the impact of a missing, uncertain or incomplete provenance keenly. Producing a list of previous transfers of ownership will not bring them closure (Kößler 2018: 34, 38). Incomplete provenances omit unlawful transactions or reflect partial ownership histories. The assembly and retrieval of facts have implications for archive-building and narrative. Because a full provenance history is much harder and more time-consuming to achieve than one tailored for public consumption or commercial demands, it is crucial to establish who wrote the provenance (Mackenzie et al. 2020: 119–120, 145). The risks that attach to the pressures that bear on provenance researchers working in museums must also be appreciated. Thresholds set for provenance research in western institutions could make provenance researchers more likely to protect collections acquired through colonialism against repatriation claims (Mackenzie et al. 2020: 97). Institutions may not disclose information that comes to light. Incriminating provenance may be excluded from provenance files to avoid disgrace or return (Tythacott 2019: 365).

Monochronic provenance research that draws on the cultural values of location or religion may be hindered if information about the inner circles of the powerful has long been inaccessible in private archives and is not yet digitised or is restricted by the state under data protection laws. The events that violated persons and their heritage provide clues about the sacred inherent in material. When these clues meet across the breadth of space in time and across the ontological, dimensions of knowledge broaden. Knowledge about theft and physical violence goes beyond mere intellectual knowledge about chains of transfers of cultural heritage without consent that indicate dismemberment, smuggling, confiscation, seizure, and looting. Knowledge about theft and physical violence unlocks a new way of 'seeing' that reveals such transfers to be more than just serial recontextualisations of what was taken, or unlawful sales to be more than 'unfinished events' or 'outstanding debts' (Hicks 2021: 4).

Critical provenance insight about museum collections may also be drawn from the spiritual significance of the items and the impact of their dispossession on source communities. Best practices in restorative provenance research can shed light on conflicting and problematic documentation (e.g., Jacobs & Porter 2021: 533, 539, 543, 548). Careful and accurate representation of the beliefs and practices of the communities that produced and valued their sacred objects will restore agency to previously colonised communities.

1.8 Effects of different conceptions of time on the evaluation of past events

Profound normative change occurs with the passage of time, but the effects of different conceptions of time on the evaluation of past events give rise to many questions. Honoré rejects the idea that past events can only be evaluated against the standards of the time when it comes to just title. He argues that domestic legal rules facilitate the ascertainment of title, and when the contexts of their operation or the circumstances of their application change, or when social and moral criticism is forthcoming, the rules must be reassessed and amended (Honoré 1987: 165). Honoré considers a title valid if it is justly acquired according to the moral views prevailing at the time of acquisition, but if the views of right and wrong improve and progress over time, this validity becomes subject to review. For instance, when the moral basis of the acquisition of the enslaved and the colonies collapsed, originally valid titles lapsed, and entitlements required redistribution (Honoré 1987: 219–220). This approach negates charges of 'presentism' against an adjusted rule of intertemporal law. It can be seen in practice in Germany's governmental policy framework, which specifically enables the return of cultural objects that were acquired in a way that 'by today's legal or ethical standards is not justifiable' (*Erste Eckpunkte zum Umgang mit Sammlungsgut aus kolonialen Kontexten der Staatsministerin des Bundes für Kultur und Medien, der Staatsministerin im Auswärtigen Amt für internationale Kulturpolitik, der Kulturministerinnen und Kulturminister der Länder und der kommunalen Spitzenverbände* 13 March 2019: Principle 7, 4).

Articles 40(l) and 63(2)(i) of the Namibian Constitution of 21 March 1990 impose a legal obligation on the Cabinet and the National Assembly to actively oppose racist law, counter colonial patterns and legacies, and support those affected. These provisions share the following wording:

> to remain vigilant and vigorous for the purposes of ensuring that the scourges of apartheid, tribalism and colonialism do not again manifest themselves in any form in a free and independent Namibia and to protect and assist disadvantaged citizens of Namibia who have historically been the victims of these pathologies.

An affidavit submitted to the Namibian High Court on behalf of the Herero and Nama authorities involved in litigation with Germany cast the German and Namibian governments' application and interpretation of the doctrine of intertemporal law as a reproduction of the racist distinction between civilised and non-civilised nations and therefore racist (*Swartbooi MP et al. v Speaker of the National Assembly et al.*, HC-MD-CIV-MOT-REV-2023/00023, 20 January 2023). The court was not satisfied that all relevant documents and evidence had been placed before it [2024] NAHCMD 602.

The category of Nazi-era claims indicates that many of today's restitution cases rely on present-day norms and not on the unlawfulness of the taking at the time. The broad consensus on the 1998 Washington Conference Principles on Nazi-Confiscated Art, followed by the 2024 Best Practices for the Washington Conference Principles on Nazi-Confiscated Art, enabled several former colonial powers to overcome the obstacles posed by the time factor in restitution claims (Francioni 2024: 70–71). The principles provide redress for a continuing injustice and aim to reunite people with objects that have a specific symbolic meaning, like a family heirloom or books, artefacts, ceremonial art, and historical materials relating to Judaism that are sacred to that community (Campfens 2021: 65). The exclusion of Indigenous peoples of Africa from the community of civilised nations and the protection of international law was historical, although it lasted well into the 20th century. If such acts continue to have a harmful effect today, the historical position cannot be invoked to justify the legality of the exclusion (Campfens 2019: 89; Institut de Droit International, Resolution on 'The Intertemporal Problem in Public International Law' Session of Wiesbaden 1975: 37). Indigenous rights instruments recognise that the retention of human remains or sacred objects marks an ongoing dignity-taking that may cause spiritual harm and intergenerational trauma (Stahn 2023: 458). Campfens argues that a shift towards a human rights approach will benefit cases where present possessors cannot be held accountable for the past because the legality of removal at the time will be relegated to the background as the focus turns to the spiritual significance of an object for the people affected by its removal (Campfens 2019: 98, 106–107). Colombia's Constitutional Court that pre-Columbian Indigenous artefacts looted by gravediggers in 1890 and offered to Spain as a gift from Colombia in 1893, should not have been given to Spain, illustrates the point (*Quimbaya Treasure* case Judgment SU-649/17, Republic of Colombia, Constitutional Court, Plenary Chamber, 19 October 2017). At the time, the artefacts were seen as the relics of a dead, primitive civilisation (Losson 2022: 37). The right of self-determination of peoples, which includes the right to protect cultural objects, was held to constitute a *jus cogens* norm, which was interpreted to mean that the passage of time does not preclude any country from seeking restitution of their cultural objects. The court highlighted and rejected the manifestly unreasonable result which the time factor causes for objects acquired long before the conventional framework existed as being contrary to the *effet utile* rule. Based on the international law standards in the UNDRIP and cultural property conventions that include protections of Indigenous peoples' rights, such as the 1995 UNIDROIT Convention, the court issued an order that the Colombian president, the Ministry of Foreign Affairs, and the Ministry of Culture must take all necessary diplomatic and legal steps to pursue restitution on behalf of the Quimbaya Indigenous people. The 1995 UNIDROIT Convention is not usually interpreted as offering rights in respect of losses incurred before its implementation by States Party. This makes the order highly notable (Campfens 2019: 105). The order also demonstrates that constitutional frameworks cannot ensure a culture's survival or national recognition without additional measures in place. The scope that exists for the 1995 UNIDROIT Convention to provide this kind of support has since been more widely appreciated. The Colombian executive agencies in charge took their time to execute the order. The artefacts continue to reside in the Museo de América in Madrid but a formal request for their return was lodged by the Colombian Minister of Culture in May 2024.

Considerable scope exists to restore the law for the restitution of sacred cultural heritage, especially in relation to the principle of non-retrospectivity. The principle of non-retrospective application of treaties establishes a general rule that treaty provisions do not bind a party to any event that occurred or situation that ceased to exist before a treaty entered into force with respect to that party (1969 Vienna Convention on the Law of Treaties Article 28). The party claiming an exception must establish that the retrospective application of a treaty is warranted. In terms of cultural heritage, this is best done by adopting expansive readings of treaties such as the 1907 Hague Convention on War on Land, the 1954 Hague Convention, the 1970 UNESCO Convention, and the 1995 UNIDROIT Convention, in conjunction with provisions such as self-determination, human rights, and the rule against the use of force, which do not impose time limits regarding the removal of cultural heritage. The *Venus of Cyrene* ruling clarified that the right to self-determination includes the right to protect cultural identity and material cultural heritage associated with a sovereign state or peoples subject to a foreign government (*Associazione nazionale Italia Nostra Onlus c. Ministero per i beni e le attività culturali et al.,*

Tribunale Amministrativo Regionale del Lazio (Sez. II-Quarter) Case No. 3518, 28 February 2007; Consiglio di Stato, Case No. 3154, 23 June 2008, para 4.4; Chechi 2012: 161; Chechi 2014: 270).

The sacred is a philosophical, spiritual, and anthropological idea that guides and directs the attention of lawmakers, policymakers, and adjudicators to the 'obligations' it conveys. These obligations are normative effects that are congruent with the rule of law and the idea of the 'rechtsstaat'—the use of the protections that law extends to citizens against the all-intrusive claims of power and render it unavailable for arbitrary abuse (Krygier's Adam Smith Lecture 10 June 2024). Every empire qualifies as the antithesis of a constitutional state in which the law constrains the exercise of governmental power. This stark reality prevents the simple retrospective application of human rights doctrine, however.

Article 11 of the 1970 UNESCO Convention addresses the export and transfer of cultural property 'under compulsion arising from foreign occupation to its rightful owner', which is to be considered illicit, but the temporal scope of this instrument leaves the provision's application within the discretion of former colonial powers. The *Quimbaya Treasure* case held that the non-retroactive application of the 1970 UNESCO Convention and other instruments was not an absolute rule (para 5.5). Overzealous judicial activism in respect of the retrospective application of contemporary standards on the return of cultural objects and the 'shaky constructions of jus cogens' in the *Quimbaya Treasure* case elicited criticism, however (Stahn 2023: 462). When considering retrospective application of law in a concrete case, one must also consider how evolved the law was at the time of application (Zeidler 2016: 191). Nonetheless, the statutory construction rule that legislative changes apply prospectively cannot mean that 'imperial law' values must continue to reign supreme; that courts must uphold the fragmented and dichotomous approach to law that marked the colonial era; or that the occupation decrees that declared the property of persecuted peoples as state property must inform every contemporary decision about that property.

The 'true' lawgivers are said to be those who interpret the law, not those who draft them. Judicial interpretation of duties imposed under constitutional law provides norms that could fill crucial gaps for restitution claims. For instance, Germany was held accountable to a Brazilian family for the unlawful behaviour of a German submarine during the Second World War. The German submarine torpedoed the *Changri-lá*, a fishing boat in Brazil's territorial sea, killing a member of the family. The family lodged a compensation claim for material damages and non-pecuniary losses in a Brazilian court (*Karla Christina Azeredo Venâncio da Costa and others v Federal Republic of Germany, Federal Supreme Court*, Judgment ARE954858/RJ of 23 August 2021). While the court of first instance upheld Germany's jurisdictional immunity for acts of war, Brazil's Federal Supreme Court held that, based on the Constitution, wrongful acts committed by foreign states in violation of human rights do not enjoy immunity from jurisdiction in Brazil. The case was remanded to the lower court, and following a challenge by the federal public prosecutor, the Brazilian Supreme Court clarified that state immunity is to be denied only when the human rights breach at stake occurred within the national territory (*Karla Christina Azeredo*

Venâncio da Costa e Outro v. República Federal da Alemanha, ARE 954858/RJ, Judgment of 23 May 2022).

Aims and methods are outlined next.

1.9 Aims and methods

Employing textual and discursive modes of expression, this study aims to rectify the most prevalent optical delusions of colonial thinking to restore PrIL's depth dimension in restitution claims to sacred heritage looted and trafficked during the colonial era. It relies on law and ethics approaches that restore the capacity of cultural material to challenge or decenter discourses, and argues that, for the law of restitution to be 'restored' to a fully functioning state in respect of claims for the return of colonial-era and Indigenous cultural property disputes, the normative framework must be integrated around the 'sacred,' constructs of time, the ethic of PrIL, and the intangible heritage.

A broad-based definition of the sacred was the focus of the preceding work, *Restitution of Cultural Property and the Law*, and a summary was offered in this Chapter. To further improve the normative environment for restitution and restore the law for the restitution of sacred cultural material, an alternative chronosopy deserves consideration in restitution claims. The time dimension of legal norms encourages us to see and observe the structures we impose on time when called upon to clarify rights, obligations, procedures, and standards. Therefore, new ways of seeing complex cultural material must be matched with new observations on the legal rules and norms that condition the 'vanishing point' of restitution claims (e.g., prescription conflicts, statutes of limitation conflicts, interpretations of the principle of intertemporality). In addition, attention must be drawn to PrIL's capacity for coordination within and between legal systems, and its potential to accommodate alternative chronosophies.

In pursuit of restoring the law for the restitution of sacred material, among other things by enlisting PrIL to help to achieve this, this study proposes that fewer distinctions are to made and that the inexorable fragmentation of separate disciplines resisted. Where necessary, it goes back to medieval and early modern conflicts that may cast more light on substantive policies pursued by colonial law and the international legal order that superimposed itself on the law of the forum.

However carefully PrIL doctrines are contextualised, the approach one adopts towards history may foster conceptual oppositions. To recreate the past with the eyes of the present is different from using the past to explain the present. Furthermore, 'pedigree history' may be employed in many different ways: 'dialectic,' 'opposition,' 'quest,' or 'narrative' (Hatzimihail 2021: 79–92). Because the history of PrIL doctrine stands apart from general European legal history and remains separate from developments in jurisprudence, private law, the international system, or legal theory, scope exists to weaponise its history. An historical narrative may be used as an 'insidious argumentative weapon' (Hatzimihail 2021: 84, 91; also 110, 135). However, it is paramount to establish better ways for these claims to be heard on their merits.

The absence of a cross-disciplinary unifying point that offers a common legal basis for restitution and repatriation claims for material that was looted and trafficked during the colonial era creates opportunities to resist acknowledging that legal claims brought by source communities in respect of sacred cultural material already point to a legal basis for restitution of sacred cultural material taken during the colonial era. The basis need not be sought in the intricacies of an internationally wrongful act, *jus cogens*, the principle of self-determination, or in so-called 'non-binding' obligations, for the common ground on which the legal basis is found reveals itself in the nature of the material; its sacred qualities impart an elemental intuition about the violent impulses in society. The myths that disguise the injustice of the status quo usually determine the duties identified and the responsibilities assumed, but when that injustice is made evident, the 'ground' on which action must be taken is revealed (Wolff 2021).

Single-issue scholarship will not provide adequate support for a study of historical restitution claims that necessitates a closer look into the ontology, epistemology, axiology, and methodology of different cultural paradigms and their capacity to yield common ground. Inter-disciplinary engagement with aspects of 'normativity,' the sacred, and constructs of time is necessary. The 'normative' as well as knowledge about norms and their effect is implicit in the materiality of the sacred. This study aims to distil the knowledge concerning the obligations that inhere in the knowledge of what connects law, ethics, and the spiritual conceptions and practices of different communities around the world, to support restitution claims for human remains and looted sacred cultural heritage that bear the imprint of colonialism. The concern is not so much with 'new theoretical models' or 'new forms of returns,' but rather with a deeper understanding of the characterisation of these legal disputes that is anchored by a legal-theoretical perspective on the complex relationship between law, ethics, and PrIL as a model of ethics. The potential characterisations of a 'moral' claim, a 'property' dispute, a 'wrongful' international act, a 'human rights' violation, or a violation of 'humanitarian' law indicate that adjustment of the restitution argument could secure a more unified basis for restitution claims involving this cultural material. This knowledge is a much neglected question of our time. To arrive at PrIL as an ethic, it must undergo 'defragmentation' to clarify what may be achieved at the intersection between public values and policies geared to the safeguarding of cultural heritage, and PrIL tools and legal governance strategies.

Museums find it challenging to establish and maintain contact with their collections. They also struggle to identify what communities consider sacred, and to set priorities, as discourses on the return of cultural heritage do not always accommodate or accurately capture the sacred. Western epistemology relies on linear forms of knowledge and scientific paradigms predicated on doing and having. These methods validate only certain data and experiences (Stewart-Harawira 2005: 35–36). They locate the sacred in historical moments and cultural styles that condition the expressions of religious life (Eliade 1959: 62–63). The separation of epistemology from ontology assumes an inherent difference at a metaphysical level between human and nonhuman, subject and object, mind and body, matter and discourse (Barad 2003: 829). This insight relativises the priorities conferred by the epistemology of western museal practice. In an Indigenous world view, the sacred is all-encompassing. For example, the authority to keep and care for sacred bundles protects and permits the generational transmission of cultural knowledge and spiritual information. To transmit intergenerational knowledge within communities, it is crucial to reactivate and relearn Indigenous systems of knowledge associated with sacred bundle culture by putting the bundles back on the ceremonial circuit. The discrete elements that constitute the sacred bundles fulfil other functions, but restoring context to the decontextualised intangible cultural heritage requires more than viewing individual pieces in isolation (Simpson 2009: 122, 124).

The term 'sacred cultural property and heritage' is adopted throughout because it is inclusive of ceremonial and funerary objects, human remains, and spiritual artefacts unethically removed during the colonial era (Human Rights Council Report 2020: 88). It embraces complementary features associated with both tangible and intangible aspects of material inherited from past generations, maintained in the present, and bestowed upon future generations. This language is far from perfect. Legal ownership in the western tradition is based on the rules, principles, and tenets of domestic property law and international law. Few legal systems have specific rules or exceptions for sacred heritage. Separate and different positions are reached in private law, PrIL, PublIL, cultural heritage law, and uniform law embodied in pertinent conventions and secondary European Union (EU) law. The tension between 'property' and 'heritage' is exacerbated by the disconnect between domestic and international law. This situation creates exclusionary effects in international heritage law on account of its hostility towards the conception and language of 'property.' Domestic law, however, relies heavily on 'property' as a category to implement international legal obligations with respect to heritage. Narrowing the focus to national cultural property produces gaps in conceptions of responsibility, just as isolating legal disciplines does. Furthermore, the gaps and contradictions in the patchwork of treaty law that aims to provide relief for dispossessed owners are notable. International instruments fall short of protecting the full range of cultural material that attests to the sacred core of a community, as the treaty regime was not designed for historical colonial takings. Concepts of 'cultural property' and 'heritage' developed in response to imperial ambitions. The secular world often lumps in the sacred with these umbrella terms or treat it in such specific terms that sacred cultural material not specifically associated with Indigenous peoples is excluded. For instance, the definition in Article 1(f) of the 1970 UNESCO Convention refers to 'objects of ethnological interest,' whereas Article 4(c) is concerned with the protection of cultural property at the domestic level. The format of the definitional section pre-determines the nature of the cultural material that qualifies for protection as part of the cultural heritage of each state, namely cultural property acquired by ethnological missions, if it was acquired with the 'consent of the competent authorities of the country of origin of such property.'

The extent to which PrIL supports dispute resolution and ethical judgment in the interrelationship between legal systems in cultural heritage law is not a new topic. PrIL fits the epistemic model of an adjudicator applying rules and norms to prevent and resolve conflict. Secondary legal norms for the transfer of property in PrIL have a relational dimension; the *lex situs* rule takes account of the location of the property and the people residing there (Roodt 2015: 225ff). A relational ethic requires flexibility. Arguably, more flexibility is required in claims to sacred heritage because relationships formed around the sacred are nonlinear. Courts interpret and apply rules that require direct, concrete engagement with foreign law in international civil litigation. PrIL rules and methods facilitate decisions on the effects of problematic behaviours that cannot be territorially limited, e.g., determining whether courts located in the place where the misappropriated objects are found, are competent to decide on claims. Alongside the adjudicatory responsibilities of developing the law and the court's duty to avoid unjust or absurd applications of otherwise valid norms, adjudicators must also resolve disputes where the ruling norms come from outside the domestic legal system or from a foreign legal system (Bix 2011: 57). The fragmentation of the landscape of culture and law makes it hard to navigate. PrIL's reach extends to questions such as which state's courts are competent to hear a case or what legal system governs the time limitation for bringing the claim. It is designed for complex legal questions set in a legal pluralist context but not everyone agrees that PrIL offers a feasible course of action (e.g. Chechi 2014: 84–98; 244–249, 292, 296ff). Chechi has argued in favour of a composite body of rules or *lex culturalis* that would affirm the uniqueness of cultural property and exclude ordinary PrIL rules that are conceived for business transactions involving ordinary goods from disputes that involve cultural property (Chechi 2017/18: 272). The vantage point adopted in this study is different. It is intentional in considering internal (national) and external (international) conflicts of legal norms and in outlining the difference which a common conception of the sacred can make in jurisprudence and policymaking. More specifically, this study argues that PrIL's common principles are of acute relevance to questions of justice, as they offer considerable value in broadening claimants' pathways and access to justice. PrIL makes connections between the forum and the personal and factual circumstances of a case. It has a deep capacity for interdisciplinarity within the interlocking network of domestic, provincial, national, regional, international, and transnational norms, as its aspiration is for 'global justice.' Its connectivity renders it a rich testing ground for new theories, methods, and frameworks for the resolution of disputes over contested ownership and restitution that take account of normativity in property transfer. More importantly, normative conflicts create opportunities to consider the meaning and effects of globalisation, which other legal disciplines do not (Muir Watt 2016: 400–401).

The law cannot always confirm that certain behaviour is either lawful or unlawful in a single uncomplicated answer. Insisting on definitive answers before understanding the complexities of colonial-era claims risks miscasting the legal and political complexity (Banu 2022: 391). The indeterminacy of the law—a radical underdetermination as opposed to an overdetermination—must be acknowledged (Hurley 1989: 28). When normative clashes play out on the global stage, rules and norms interact in sophisticated ways. Since primary legal norms are subject to territorial limitations, they do not have extra-territorial effect, and by themselves, they cannot provide a complete sense of how legal norms operate in space. Against this backdrop, an original and tailor-made method for this study is to consider how the normative effects of mimetism may be countered at the intersection between primary legal norms, secondary legal rules, and common principles of PrIL. To what extent can secondary legal norms accommodate the ontological paradigms that may clash in relation to complex cultural material? PrIL's capacity to condition the depth dimensions of primary legal norms and conflicts rules at the intersection of local law and colonial law begs for reappraisal. The study also reflects on new technologies at the cross-over of intellectual property rights and PrIL. Technologies with the potential to combat the lack and loss of documentary proof of ownership of illicitly traded antiquities may render the physical locations of ancient artefacts less important than PrIL methods allow for.

The method adopted in this inquiry proceeds with the evaluation and revaluation of laws and lawmaking, adjudication, decisionmaking, and policymaking by abstract concept and exemplification. It combines the critical perspective on the sacred of anthropological theory with the time space and depth dimensions of PrIL in internal conflicts that arose during the colonial era. The material frame of reference helps to communicate the effects of pertinent decisions, norms, rules, and principles on communities and individuals in ways that other frames of reference cannot. For this reason, case studies have been carefully selected to highlight gaps and blind spots in dispute settlements, policy, and practice in Greece, Britain, parts of North America, Southern Africa, China, and Hong Kong.

The tug-of-war over the Parthenon Sculptures obscures a clear understanding of the implications of the connection between the restitution claim and the inherent sacrality of the Parthenon Temple whose architecture survives to this day. What this means for the obligations that sacred cultural property and heritage engender needs to be determined. The discourse conditions the attitudes of the public and of government officials towards restitution (AFFORD Institute 2020: 19). It sets the tone for restitution debates more broadly, and its ramifications 'spill over' onto other dispossessed communities. The dispute appears to be dissimilar from the claim for the artefactual encased human remains of Zhanggong Zushi in every way, and yet both disputes are concerned with sacred cultural property in competitive colonial contexts. Both claims are linked to the colonial era. Lord Elgin's colonial networks in the Ottoman Empire made the extraction and trade of the Sculptures possible while the Zhanggong Zushi mummy case links the influence of colonial powers in global trade with the postcolonial illicit antiquities trade.

Just as implicitly agreed practices of knowledge can be made explicit through a re-unification of the Parthenon Sculptures with the material in Athens that would see some of their sacred qualities restored, litigation at the interface between domestic and international law may anchor the arguments in value-rationality and balance competing values.

The monk Zhang Qisan readied himself for the 'next stage of existence' by the rites of the Ch'an School of Buddhism and, having been trained up to control the manner and timing of his death, gave himself to the ritual of self-sacrifice for his spiritual community. The most convincing scholarly interpretations of the depictions on the Parthenon frieze is the human sacrifice of Parthenos for the victory of Athens (e.g., Connelly 2014). Neither Athens nor Yangchun village can disprove the legality of the acquisitions of their cultural material. In both instances legal battles have reached a stalemate with their opposing sides. The characterisation of the mummified monk as a 'smaller, slightly gruesome, Chinese version of the Elgin marbles' rings true (Hooper & Plafker 2017). The quotation highlights the material complexity that lies central to these disputes. The self-mummified monk is as rare and complex as the Parthenon Sculptures. He represents the values of his community and provides comfort to the villagers, while the Parthenon Sculptures are valued by the people of Greece as their heritage and their place in world history. The element of sacrifice is common to the communities who produced this heritage. The villagers have a genealogical succession story in which the Zhanggong Zushi mummy is a central figure, just as the Parthenon Sculptures evoke the genealogical origins of Athens (Roodt 2024b). Greece maintains that ownership never passed to the British government and therefore never to the British Museum. What passed is simply possession and bad title, which the passage of time alone cannot make good. The acquisition of the Parthenon Sculptures was an illegal act with falsified permissions, and therefore they should never have left the Parthenon. Legally, the Sculptures never ceased to belong to Athens (Titi 2023: 137, 232). The British Museum refutes this and insists that they would have been destroyed in Athens had they been left there. The Chinese village communities insist their Buddha statue was stolen, while the dealer refutes this with allegations that the mummy he bought was a different one. Athens, Yangchun and Dongpu feel their respective losses as part of their cultural identities. Legal ownership and control of their cultural heritage help them develop and preserve this identity. Both disputes bear all the markings of 'hard cases,' the outcomes of which cannot be predicted with certainty. Both examples call for effective approaches to conflict and normative pluralism, and for some form of 'justice.'

To pave the way for a new normative narrative that restores the law in relation to the restitution of sacred cultural material, the technical hurdles encountered by both Greece and the Chinese villagers require assessment. Jurisdictional problems prevented the case for the return of the Parthenon Sculptures from reaching the merits in the European Court of Human Rights, one of the organs established under the European Convention on Human Rights in service of the aim to encourage the development of Europe's cultural identity and diversity. *Syllogos ton Athinaion v United Kingdom* (Application No. 48259/15, First Section, 31 May 2016, ECHR 23 June 2016) demonstrates the problematic interplay between historical events and legal mechanisms and strategies that rely on the time factor to frustrate restitution claims. The Parthenon Sculptures' removal took place 150 years prior to the UK signing up to the European Convention on Human Rights in 1951, just a few years after the United Nations General Assembly adopted the 1948 Universal Declaration of Human Rights. In the Netherlands, the Amsterdam court was not amenable to reaching the merits stage of the claim to the Zhanggong Zushi mummy. To enable the intangible cultural heritage carried by the sacred to be protected, the hurdle of formalistic denial of standing needs to be surmounted. However, the Amsterdam court cited technicalities that absolved it from having to consider the proprietary basis of the restitution claim and any possible exceptions. To decide a restitution claim on its merits, a certain reconciliation must occur between law and ethics. Yet, the standards set in international conventions for the transfer of cultural property were not considered. The Dutch collector was given the protection of technical defences that shielded him from accountability.

Restitution claims frequently fail to identify sacred cultural property and heritage and overlook the fact that they engender obligations. The most immediate consequence of this failure is that critical questions about provenance are not raised when they should be. The implicit practices of legal knowledge are profound, and yet they routinely escape the attention of legal scholars, practitioners, and adjudicators. Riles suggests that legal doctrine or tacit knowledge practice that is assumed to be obvious to everyone, becomes imperceptible (Riles 2005: 981, 1018). The capacity of the law for restitution and remembrance becomes discernible if the implicit is explicitly debated. The prospects for restoring the law become more immediate.

The structure of the argument Greece advances when claiming the Parthenon Sculptures confirms the importance of making explicit the dimensions of property and ownership, the implications of the sacred on the taxonomies of private and public law, as well as the effects of the passing of time on claims for restitution. To succeed with an argument that the theft of the mummified monk had broken the centuries-long chain of title and custody the Puzhao temple in China must likewise confirm its title based on property ownership. Where civil claims are based on PrIL rules and the principles of property transfer the claim to have property returned is a restitution claim rather than a repatriation claim (Last 2007: 131).

The reasoning that there comes a point when history must be laid to rest facilitates the argument against restitution. It features even in the context of Nazi-era takings. Domestic law did not always entertain the idea that old wrongs required rectification. Scrutiny was reserved for events from the relatively recent past and the problems of the past were avoided (Moran 2019: 425–426). Among the numerous doctrines developed to limit the reach of domestic and international law to relatively recent history is the expiry of time periods under statutory limitations rules. Any effort to delineate the past and present in absolute terms introduces complications for restitution cases, for they exist in a dynamic relationship (Bevernage 2012: x).

1.10 Outline

Facts concerning the sacred and the 'normative' are interdependent categories of thinking. Their interdependence produces moral and legal obligations. The gaps, cumulative effects, and connections between fundamental legal norms cannot be pre-judged, but the normative thrust of mimetism can be countered by legal strategies that take account of ethical standards and by ethical guidelines that take account of law.

The so-called 'non-legal' factor in western conceptions of law and art history—the sacred—already carries normative meaning in Indigenous communities. Many examples bear this out, including stones that carry the authority of kings. This normative effect is not widely understood in the West, and yet sacred cultural heritage resists mummified understandings of the nature of the responsibility for this material. The critical framework which Girard's theory provides for the concepts, criteria, guidelines, policies, and soft law is useful because its conception of the sacred does not hinge on any one model of ethics. This ensures wider relevance. Furthermore, the theory of the sacred does more than identify which material is to be prioritised. Its anthropological insights cast the import, export, and sale of ethnographic material in private and museum collections in a broader context.

To restore the law of restitution, the nature of the material and the provenance research that supports restitution must be given room to breathe. Attending to the complex nature of sacred material does not undermine the moral argument at the heart of the reunification debate in the way 'western exceptionalism' is permitted to do. As a unified point for the social and human sciences that counters the mindless replication of colonialist ideas, the sacred facilitates the identification of the residual strands of colonial arguments that have become entangled in the discourse. The theory behind the mechanism that controls society's mimetic impulses and behaviour lays the groundwork to critically analyse 'responsibility' in normative ethics in colonial-era restitution discourse. This aspect is important because confusion concerning the normative effect of law and ethics befuddles decisions and policy on restitution and repatriation. In moral philosophy and ethics that challenge rules, legal judgments, theories of legal knowledge, and policy frameworks, the distinction between what has, and what lacks normativity is fundamental. A firmer grasp on normativity must amalgamate the random efforts to constrain the normative thrust of mimetism in European legal and policy frameworks. When circular and self-serving discourses attribute normative effects to mimetism and brutality, the special function of the sacred in society is obscured. For instance, if a government's consent is required to proceed against it in the International Court of Justice (ICJ) the normative effect of mimetics receives a boost.

Chapter 1 dissected the relationship between the sacred and the 'normative.' It raised questions about the ethics of sacred property and heritage and considered broader anthropological insights that clarify legal tenets and non-legal factors that weigh in on decisions about restitution. The basis, nature, and scope of the 'obligation' to return material from museums and private collections were investigated. Chapter 2 provides a fresh perspective on the time factor in claims. It highlights the structure of time and the adjudicatory scope for an alternative chronosophy in interpretations of the time factor that permits restitution claims to be heard on their merits. Whereas Chapter 2 considers the space time dimensions of normative conflicts, Chapter 3 considers the depth dimension and the contribution which PrIL could make to a more holistic and comprehensive theory of responsibility and responsiveness in the domain of the law of restitution. Chapter 4 maps out a coherent theory of responsibility to help adjudicators and policymakers steer the course through sophisticated normative precepts that govern the domains of the tangible and intangible. Secondary legal norms and common rules of PrIL are instrumental in affording the sacred the recognition it deserves.

Bibliography

7th Report of the House of Commons Select Committee on Culture, Media and Sport *Museums: Acquisition and Return* <https://publications.parliament.uk/pa/cm199900/cmselect/cmcumeds/371/37102.htm>

Aberdeen University Museum and Special Collections. 2023. *Procedure for Responding to Repatriation Requests: Repatriation and Deaccessioning from the University Collections* <https://www.abdn.ac.uk/collections/about/policies-167.php>

Advisory Panel on the Archaeology of Burials in England. 2017. *Guidance for Best Practice for the Treatment of Human Remains Excavated from Christian Burial Grounds in England* (APABE 2017) <http://www.archaeologyuk.org/apabe/pdf/APABE_ToHREfCBG_FINAL_WEB.pdf>

Alexandrowicz, Charles Henry. 1967. *An Introduction to the History of the Law of Nations in the East Indies (16th, 17th and 18th Centuries)* Oxford: Clarendon Press.

Anghie, Antony. 1999. 'Finding the Peripheries: Sovereignty and Colonialism in Nineteenth Century International Law' *Harvard International Law Journal* 40(1): 1–80.

Arts Council England. 2022. *Restitution and Repatriation: A Practical Guide for Museums in England*, 5 August 2022 <https://aim-museums.co.uk/guidance-restitution-repatriation-released-arts-council-england>

African Foundation for Development (AFFORD) Institute. 2020. *Return of the Icons: The Restitution of African Artefacts and Human Remains Project Mapping Report* compiled by Paul Asquith.

Banu, Roxana. 2022. 'Teaching by Historicising Private International Law' *International Journal of Law in Context* 18(4): 383-392.

Barad, Karen. 2003. 'Posthumanist Performativity: Towards an Understanding of How Matter Comes to Matter' *Signs: Journal of Women in Culture and Society* 28(3): 801–831.

Batty, David. 2024. 'Dorset Auction House Withdraws Egyptian Human Skulls from Sale' *The Guardian*, 1 May.

Begg, Mohammed Rashid. 2011. *A Weberian Analysis of Afrikaner Calvinism and the Spirit of Capitalism* DPhil Thesis, University of Stellenbosch.

BELatina Daily. 2024. 'Colombia Sent a Formal Request to Spain to Return Gold from Their Quimbaya Treasure Joining the Move to Decolonize International Museums' <https://belatina.com/colombia-sent-a-formal-request-to-spain-to-return-gold-from-their-quimbaya-treasure-joining-the-move-to-decolonize-international-museums/>

Bevernage, Berber. 2012. *History, Memory and State-Sponsored Violence. Time and Justice* London: Routledge.

Binns, John. 2017. *The Orthodox Church of Ethiopia: A History* London: Bloomsbury Publishing.

Bix, Brian H. 2011. 'Radbruch's Formula and Conceptual Analysis' *American Journal of Jurisprudence* 56: 45–57.

Bix, Brian. 2015. 'Rules and Normativity in Law' in Michał Araszkiewicz, Paweł Banaś, Tomasz Gizbert-Studnicki & Krzysztof Płeszka (eds.) *Problems of Normativity, Rules and Rule-Following, Law and Philosophy* Switzerland: Springer 125–146.

Bodenstein, Felicity & Damiana Oţoiu. 2022. 'Introduction' in Felicity Bodenstein, Damiana Oţoiu & Eva-Maria Troelenberg (eds.) *Contested Holdings: Museum Collections in Political, Epistemic and Artistic Processes of Return* New York: Berghahn Books 1–20.

Bollée, Sylvain. 2019. 'Thoughts on the Dallah Case: The Hypothesis of the Indeterminacy of the Legal System' in Horatia Muir Watt, Lucia Bíziková, Agatha Brandão de Oliveira & Diego P. Fernández Arroyo (eds.) *Global Private International Law: Adjudication without Frontiers* Cheltenham: Edward Elgar Publishing 342–349.

British Association for Biological Anthropology and Osteoarchaeology (BABAO). 2024. Statement on the Sale of Human Remains <https://babao.org.uk/babao-statement-on-the-sale-of-human-remains/>

British Museum. 2019. Human Remains Policy <https://www.britishmuseum.org/sites/default/files/2019-10/Human_Remains_policy_061218.pdf>

Bruncevic, Merima. 2021. *Regulating Transnational Heritage: Memory, Identity and Diversity* London: Routledge.

Butt, Daniel. 2009. *Rectifying International Injustice: Principles of Compensation and Restitution between Nations* Oxford: OUP.

Byrne, James G. 2015. *Factors Determining the Repatriation of Cultural Heritage from Museums; the Place of Cultural Rights in British Museums Practice* Master Thesis, SOAS University of London.

Campfens, Evelien. 2019. 'The Bangwa Queen: Artifact or Heritage?' *International Journal of Cultural Property* 26(1): 75–110.

Campfens, Evelien. 2021. *Cross-Border Title Claims to Cultural Objects: Property or Heritage?* PhD Thesis, Leiden University (Meijers-reeks Eleven).

Chechi, Alessandro. 2008. 'The Return of Cultural Objects Removed in Times of Colonial Domination and International Law: The Case of the Venus of Cyrene' in *The Italian Yearbook of International Law Online* 8(1): 159–181.

Chechi Alessandro. 2012. 'The Role of Domestic Courts in Resolving Restitution Cases: Unveiling Judicial Strategies for Culture-Sensitive Settlements' in Marc-André Renold, Alessandro Chechi, Anne Laure Bandle (eds.) *Resolving Disputes in Cultural Property* Genève: Schulthess 147–173.

Chechi, Alessandro. 2014. *The Settlement of International Heritage Disputes* Oxford: OUP.

Chechi, Alessandro. 2017/2018. 'When Private International Law Meets Cultural Heritage Law: Problems and Prospects' *Yearbook of Private International Law* 19: 269–293.

Childress III, Donald Earl. 2011. 'Introduction' in Donald E Childress III (ed.) *The Role of Ethics in International Law* Cambridge: CUP 1–8.

Conaty, Gerald T. 2015. 'The Development of Museums and Their Effects on First Nations' in Gerald T. Conaty (ed.), *We Are Coming Home!: Repatriation and the Restoration of Blackfoot Cultural Confidence* Athabasca, Edmonton: AU Press 37–69.

Connelly, Joan Breton. 2014. *The Parthenon Enigma: A Journey into Legend* New York: Alfred A. Knopf.

Coody Cooper, Karen. 2008. *Spirited Encounters: American Indians Protest Museum Policies and Practices* Lanham, Maryland: AltaMira Press.

Cuk, Natalie. 1997. '"Carrying the Battle into the Form": Repatriating First Nations' Cultural Artifacts' *Dalhousie Journal of Legal Studies* 6: 157–186.

Curtis, Neil. 2014. '"A Welcome and Important Part of their Role": The Impact of Repatriation on Museums in Scotland', in Louise Tythacott & Kostas Arvanitis (eds.) *Museums and Restitution: New Practices, New Approaches* Burlington: Ashgate 85–104.

Department of Digital, Culture, Media and Sport. 2007. *Guidance for the Care of Human Remains in Museums* <https://www.gov.uk/government/publications/guidance-for-the-care-of-human-remains-in-museums>

Delgado Richard & Jean Stefancic. 2012. *Critical Race Theory: An Introduction* 2nd ed., New York University Press.

Descartes, René. 1937. *Vertoog Over de Methode* (tr Helena C. Pos) Amsterdam: Wereldbibliotheek.

Dutch Council for Culture. 2021. *Policy Vision on Collections from a Colonial Context* (Advies over de omgang met koloniale collecties) Den Haag <https://www.raadvoorcultuur.nl/documenten/adviezen/2020/10/07/advies-koloniale-col-lecties-en-erkenning-van-onrecht>

Edge, Peter W. & M.C. Rajan. 2020. 'Sacred Sites and State Failures: A Case Study of the Babri Masjid/Ram Temple Dispute in Ayodhya' in Jahid Hossain Bhuiyan & Darryn Jensen (ed.) *Law and Religion in the Liberal State* Oxford: Hart Publishing 217–232.

Effiboley, Emery Patrick. 2020. 'Reflections on the Issue of Repatriation of Looted and Illegally Acquired African Cultural Objects in Western Museums' *Contemporary Journal of African Studies* 7(1): 67–83.

Eliade, Mircea. 1959 (tr Willard R Trask). *The Sacred and the Profane, The Nature of Religion* New York: Harcourt, Brace and Co.

Erste Eckpunkte zum Umgang mit Sammlungsgut aus kolonialen Kontexten der Staatsministerin des Bundes für Kultur und Medien, der Staatsministerin im Auswärtigen Amt für internationale Kulturpolitik, der Kulturministerinnen und Kulturminister der Länder und der kommunalen Spitzenverbände 13 March 2019.

Evans, Matthew T. 2003 'The Sacred: Differentiating, Clarifying and Extending Concepts' *Review of Religious Research* 45(1): 32–47.

Faure, Bernard. 1994. *The Rhetoric of Immediacy: A Cultural Critique of Chan/Zen Buddhism* Princeton, NJ: Princeton University Press.

Flanagan, Owen. 2016. *The Geography of Morals: Varieties of Moral Possibility* Oxford Scholarship Online.

Fforde, Cressida, Ormond-Parker Lyndon & Paul Turnbull. 2015. 'Repatriation Research: Archives and the Recovery of History and Heritage' in Ruth Redmond-Cooper (ed.) *Heritage, Ancestry and the Law: Principles, Policies and Practices Dealing with Historical Human Remains* Leicester: Institute of Art and Law 39–59.

Frigo, Manlio. 2023. 'Restitution of Cultural Property and Decolonization of Museums: Issues of Consistency Between Fulfilment of Legal Obligations, Ethical Principles and Identity Links' in Laura Pineschi (ed.) *Cultural Heritage, Sustainable Development and Human Rights: Towards an Integrated Approach* London: Routledge.

Forbes. 2013. 'British Museum Sold Benin Bronzes', a 6 June 2013 update of an article first published on 3 April 2002 <https://www.forbes.com/2002/04/03/0403conn.html>

Foundation Melina Mercouri <melinamercourifoundation.com/en/oxford-union-june-12-1986>

German Lost Art Foundation. 2019. *Provenance Research Manual* <https://www.bibliotheksverband.de/sites/default/files/2020-12/Provenance%20Research%20Manual.pdf>

German Museums Association (DMB). 2013. *Recommendations for the Care of Human Remains in Museums and Collections* Kassel, April 2013 <https://www.museumsbund.de/wp-content/uploads/2017/04/2013-recommendations-for-the-care-of-human-remains.pdf>

German Museums Association (DMB). 2021. *Guidelines: Care of Human Remains in Museums and Collections* Berlin, June 2021 <https://www.museumsbund.de/wp-content/uploads/2021/07/dmb-leitfaden-umgang-menschl-ueberr-en-web-20210625.pdf>

German Museums Association (DMB). 2021. *Guidelines for German Museums: Care of Collections from Colonial Contexts* 3rd ed., April 2021 <https://www.museumsbund.de/wp-content/uploads/2021/03/mb-leitfaden-en-web.pdf>

Girard, René. 2010. *Battling to the End: Conversations with Benoit Chantre (Studies in Violence, Mimesis, and Culture)* (tr Mary Baker 2007) East Lansing: Michigan State University Press.

Glasgow Life Museums. 2022. *Policy on Repatriation and Spoliation* <https://www.glasgowlife.org.uk/media/lzgca2tq/glasgow-life-museums-spoliation-and-repatriation-april-2022.pdf>

Glenn, H. Patrick. 2011. 'The Ethic of International Law' in Donald E. Childress III (ed.) *The Role of Ethics in International Law* Cambridge: CUP 246–270.

Godelier, Maurice. 2002. 'Some Things You Give, Some Things You Sell, but Some Things You Must Keep for Yourselves: What Mauss Did Not Say about Sacred Objects' (tr.

Nora Scott) in Edith Wyschogrod, Jean-Joseph Goux & Eric Boynton (eds.) *The Enigma of Gift and Sacrifice* New York: Fordham University Press 19–37.

Grabar, Oleg. 1988. 'A Sense of the Sacred: The Values Enshrined in Holy Places' *The UNESCO Courier* 8: 27–31.

Griffin, Rayanne J. 1995. 'Sacred Site Protection Against a Backdrop of Religious Intolerance' *Tulsa Law Journal* 31(2): 395–419.

Haeming, Anne. Interview with Bernhard Heeb, 'Schädel mit Würde Behandeln' *TAZ* 13 September 2019.

Hai, Mariam. 2013. 'Selling the Sacred: An Examination of Sacred Objects in Legal Contexts' *DePaul Journal of Art, Technology & Intellectual Property Law* 24(1): 193–217.

Hance, Clea. 2020. 'The Interaction Between Intangible Cultural Heritage and Human Rights' in Marie Cornu, Anita Vaivade, Lily Martinet & Clea Hance (eds.) *Intangible Cultural Heritage under National and International Law: Going Beyond the 2003 UNESCO Convention* Cheltenham: Edward Elgar Publishing 81–96.

Hatzimihail, Nikitas E. 2021. *Preclassical Conflict of Laws* CUP online.

Heffter, August Wilhelm. 1844. *Das Europäische Völkerrecht der Gegenwart* Berlin: E. H. Schroeder.

Hicks, Dan. 2021. *Necrography: Death-Writing in the Colonial Museum*, British Art Studies 26 February Issue 19 3–6.

Hobbes, Thomas. 1651. *Leviathan* Minneapolis: First Avenue editions.

Honoré, Tony M. 1987. *Making Law Bind: Essays Legal and Philosophical* Oxford: Clarendon Press.

Hooper, John & Ted Plafker. 2017. 'The Body in the Buddha' *The Economist*, 4 May.

House of Commons, Culture, Media and Sport Committee, Cultural Objects: Developments Since 2000. First Report of Session 2003-04. H.C. 59.

Howes, Hilary. 2020. 'Germany's Engagement with the Repatriation Issue' in Cressida Fforde, Timothy McKeown & Honor Keeler (eds.) *The Routledge Companion to Indigenous Repatriation* London: Routledge 83–100.

Human Rights Council Report, *Repatriation of Ceremonial Objects and Human Remains under the UN Declaration on the Rights of Indigenous Peoples*, A/HRC/45/35 21 July 2020.

Hurley, Susan L. 1989. *Natural Reasons: Personality and Polity* Oxford: OUP.

ICOM Code of Ethics for Museums. 2017. <https://icom.museum/wp-content/uploads/2018/07/ICOM-code-En-web.pdf>

ICOM Code of Ethics for Natural History Museums. 2013. <https://icom.museum/wp-content/uploads/2018/07/nathcode_ethics_en.pdf>

Institut de Droit International, Resolution on 'The Inter-temporal Problem in Public International Law' Session of Wiesbaden, 11 August 1975 <https://www.idi-iil.org/app/uploads/2017/06/1975_wies_01_en.pdf>

International Movement for a New Museology (MINOM) 1984 Declaration of Quebec Basic Principles of a New Museology 2010: 23–24.

Jacobs, Jordan & Benjamin W. Porter. 2021. 'Repatriation in University Museum Collections: Case Studies from the Phoebe A Hearst Museum of Anthropology' *International Journal of Cultural Property* 28(4): 513–550.

Janes, Robert R. 2015. 'Prologue' in Gerald T Conaty (ed.) *We Are Coming Home!: Repatriation and the Restoration of Blackfoot Cultural Confidence* Athabasca: AU Press 3–20.

Jessiman, Stacey R. 2017. 'Object and Spirit Agency: The G'psgolox Poles as Mediators within and between Colonized and Colonizer Cultures' in Paul Basu (ed.) *The Inbetweenness of Things: Materializing Mediation and Movement Between Worlds* London: Bloomsbury Academic 59–78.

Kennedy, Duncan. 1991. 'A Semiotics of Legal Argument' *Syracuse Law Review* 42(1): 75–116.

Kennedy, Duncan. 2010. 'Savigny's Family/Patrimony Distinction and its Place in the Global Genealogy of Classical Legal Thought' *The American Journal of Comparative Law* 58(4): 811–841.

Koskenniemi, Martti. 2017. 'Introduction: International Law and Empire–Aspects and Approaches' in Martti Koskenniemi, Walter Rech & Manuel Jiménez Fonseca (eds.) *International Law and Empire: Historical Explorations* Oxford: OUP 1–18.

Kößler, Reinhart. 2018. 'Imperial Skulduggery, Science and the Issue of Provenance and Restitution: The Fate of Namibian Skulls in the Alexander Ecker Collection in Freiburg' *Human Remains and Violence: An Interdisciplinary Journal* 4(2): 27–44.

Kreps, Christina F. 2003. *Liberating Culture: Cross-Cultural Perspectives on Museums, Curation, and Heritage Preservation.* London: Routledge.

Krüger, Gesine. 2010. 'Moving Bones: Unsettled Histories in South Africa and the Return of Sarah Baartman' in Sebastian Jobs & Alf Ludtke (eds.) *Unsettling History: Archiving and Narrating in Historiography*, Frankfurt/Main: Campus 233–250.

Krygier, Martin. 2024. 'Well-Tempered Power: "A Cultural Achievement of Universal Significance"' Adam Smith Lecture, 10 June 2024, University of Glasgow.

Kuta, Sarah. 'Australian Museum Removes Mummified Body Parts from Display' *Smithsonian Magazine*, 30 April 2024.

Labadie, Camille. 2021. 'Decolonizing Collections: A Legal Perspective on the Restitution of Cultural Artifacts' *ICOFOM Study Series* 49(2): 132–146.

Last, Kathryn V. 2007. 'Cultural Pluralism and the Return of Cultural Heritage' in Stephen Tierney (ed.) *Accommodating Cultural Diversity* Burlington: Ashgate 123–143.

Lemkin, Raphael & William Schabas. 2008. *Axis Rule in Occupied Europe: Laws of Occupation, Analysis of Government, Proposals for Redress* 2nd ed., Clark, NJ: The Lawbook Exchange, Ltd.

Lévinas, Emmanuel. 1969 (tr Alphonso Lingis) *Totality and Infinity: An Essay on Exteriority* Pittsburgh, PA: Duquesne University Press.

Lévinas, Emmanuel. 1981 (tr Alphonso Lingis) *Emmanuel Levinas, Otherwise Than Being, or, Beyond Essence* The Hague: Martinus Nijhoff.

Libera, Zbigniew. 2011. 'History and Culture: Problems of Cultural Anthropology and Historical Anthropology' *Anthropos* 106(2): 597–602.

Liu, Zuozhen. 2017. 'Will the God Win?: The Case of the Buddhist Mummy' *International Journal of Cultural Property* 24(2): 221–238.

Lixinski, Lucas. 2019. *International Heritage Law for Communities: Exclusion and Re-Imagination*, Oxford Scholarship Online.

Lixinski, Lucas. 2024. 'Religious Heritage and the Law' in Lucas Lixinski & Lucie K. Morisette (eds.) *The Routledge Handbook of Heritage and the Law* London: Routledge 473–488.

Losson, Pierre. 2022. *The Return of Cultural Heritage to Latin America: Nationalism, Policy, and Politics in Colombia, Mexico, and Peru* London: Routledge.

Lyotard, Jean-François. 1988. *The Differend: Phrases in Dispute* (tr George Van Den Abbeele) Minneapolis: University of Minnesota Press.

Mackenzie, Simon R.M., Neil Brodie, Donna Yates & Christos Tsirogiannis. 2020. *Trafficking Culture: New Directions in Researching the Global Market in Illicit Antiquities* London: Routledge.

Maine, Sir Henry. 1861. *Ancient Law* London: JM Dent & Sons Ltd.

Markby, Sir William. 1905. *Elements of Law, Considered with reference to Principles of General Jurisprudence* 6th ed., Oxford: Clarendon Press.

Mairesse, François. 2019. 'The Sacred in the Prism of Museology' *ICOFOM Study Series* 47(1–2): 15–22.

Mastalir, Roger W. 1993. 'A Proposal for Protecting the "Cultural" and "Property" Aspects of Cultural Property under International Law' *Fordham International Law Journal* 16(4): 1033–1093.

Mauss, Marcel. 2016. *The Gift: Expanded Edition Selected, Annotated, and Translated by Jane I. Guyer* Chicago, Illinois: Hau Books.

McHugh, Conor, Jonathan Way & Daniel Whiting. 2018. 'Introduction' in Conor McHugh, Jonathan Way & Daniel Whiting (eds.) *Normativity: Epistemic and Practical* Oxford: OUP 1–13.

Merryman, John H. 1988. 'The Retention of Cultural Property' *University of California Davis Law Review* 21(3): 477–513.

Miles, Margaret M. 2011. 'Still in the Aftermath of Waterloo: A Brief History of Decisions about Restitution' in Peter Stone (ed.) *Cultural Heritage, Ethics, and the Military* Suffolk: The Boydell Press 29–42.

Moran, Mayo. 2019. 'The Problem of the Past: How Historic Wrongs Became Legal Problems' *University of Toronto Law Journal* 69(4): 421–472.

Muir Watt, Horatia. 2014. 'Future Directions?' in Horatia Muir Watt & Diego P. Fernández Arroyo (eds.) *Private International Law and Global Governance* Oxford: OUP 343–382.

Muir Watt, Horatia. 2016. 'Jurisprudence Without Confines: Private International Law as Global Legal Pluralism' *Cambridge Journal of International and Comparative Law* 5(3): 388–403.

National Museum of the American Indian. 2020. *A Step-by-Step Guide through the Repatriation Process* <https://americanindian.si.edu/sites/1/files/pdf/repatriation/NMAI-Repatriation-Guidelines-2020.pdf>

Natural History Museum. 2019. Human Remains Policy, 19 February 2019 <https://www.nhm.ac.uk>

Neidhardt, Alberto Horst. 2018. *The Transformation of European Private International Law A Genealogy of the Family Anomaly* PhD Thesis, European University Institute.

Oost, Tabitha I. 2018. 'Restitution Policies on Nazi-Looted Art in the Netherlands and the United Kingdom: A Change from a Legal to a Moral Paradigm?' *International Journal of Cultural Property* 25(2): 139–178.

Ostrom Elinor. 1990. *Governing the Commons: The Evolution of Institutions for Collective Action* Cambridge: CUP.

Paterson, Robert K. 2011. 'Heading Home: French Law Enables Return of Maori Heads to New Zealand' *International Journal of Cultural Property* 17(4): 643–652.

Parker, Patricia L. *Keepers of the Treasures: Protecting Historic Properties and Cultural Traditions on Indian Lands: Report on Tribal Preservation Funding Needs submitted to Congress* National Park Service, United States Department of the Interior, The Branch 1990.

Paul, Joel R. 1988. 'The Isolation of Private International Law' *Wisconsin International Law Journal* 7(1): 149–178.

Riles, Annelise. 2005. 'Taking on the Technicalities. A New Agenda for the Cultural Study of Law' *Buffalo Law Review* 53(3): 973–1034.

Rives, James. 2012. 'Control of the Sacred in Roman Law' in *Law and Religion in the Roman Republic* Leiden: Brill 165–180.

Robertson, Geoffrey. 2019. *Who Owns History?: Elgin's Loot and the Case for Returning Plundered Treasure* Hull: Biteback Publishing Ltd.

Robson, James. 2003. 'A *Tang Dynasty Chan Mummy [Roushen] and a Modern Case of Furta* Sacra? Investigating the Contested Bones of Shitou Xiquian' in Bernard Faure (ed.) *Chan Buddhism in Ritual Context* London: Routledge 151–178.

Rogero, Tiago. 2024. 'Indigenous Leaders Frustrated Despite Cloak's Return to Brazil After 300 Years' *The Guardian*, 16 July.

Roodt, Christa. 2015. *Private International Law, Art and Cultural Heritage* Cheltenham: Edward Elgar Publishing.

Roodt, Christa. 2024a. 'Cultural Heritage and Property Law' in Lucas Lixinski & Lucie K. Morisette (eds.) *The Routledge Handbook of Heritage and the Law* London: Routledge 157–172.

Roodt, Christa. 2024b. *Restitution of Cultural Property and the Law: Complex Colonial Histories* London: Routledge.

Saldukaityte, Jolanta. 2019. 'The Place and Face of the Stranger in Levinas' *Religions* 10(2): 67–79.

Sandell, Richard. 2011. 'On Ethics, Activism and Human Rights' in Janet Marstine (ed.) The *Routledge Companion to Museum Ethics: Redefining Ethics for the Twenty-First Century Museum* London: Routledge 129–145.

Sarr, Felwine & Bénédicte Savoy. 2018. *The Restitution of African Cultural Heritage: Toward a New Relational Ethics* <https://www.about-africa.de/images/sonstiges/2018/sarr_savoy_en.pdf>

Shapiro, Daniel. 1998. 'Repatriation: A Modest Proposal' *New York University Journal of International Law and Politics* 31(1): 95–108.

Sharf, Robert H. 2002. *Coming to Terms with Chinese Buddhism: A Reading of the Treasure Store Treatise* Honolulu: University of Hawai'i Press.

Shepherd, Lois. 2003. 'Face to Face: A Call for Radical Responsibility in Place of Compassion' *Saint John's Law Review* 77(3): 445–514.

Silvester, Jeremy & Napandulwe Shiweda. 2020. 'The Return of the Sacred Stones of the Ovambo Kingdoms: Restitution and the Revision of the Past' Special Issue on Sensitive Heritage: Ethnographic Museums, Provenance Research, and the Potentialities of Restitutions (Philipp Schorch ed.) *Museum and Society* 18(1): 30–39.

Simpson, Moira. 2009. 'Museums and Restorative Justice: Heritage, Repatriation and Cultural Education' *Museum International* 61(1–2): 121–129.

Smith, Annie. 2022. *Creating and Applying an Ethical Framework for Nigeria's Claims to the Restitution of the Benin Bronzes: What are the Moral Obligations of Western Museums?* Hons Dissertation in History of Art (Unpublished), University of Glasgow.

Soirila, Pauno. 2022. 'Indeterminacy in the Cultural Property Restitution Debate' *International Journal for Cultural Policy* 28(1): 1–16.

Spitra, Sebastian M. 2021. 'The Administration of Culture in International Law since the 19th Century: A New Historical Narrative' *University of Vienna Law Review* 5(1): 121–158.

Stahn, Carsten. 2023. *Confronting Colonial Objects: Histories, Legalities, and Access to Culture* Oxford: OUP.

St Clair, William. 1998. *Lord Elgin and the Marbles* 3d ed., Oxford: OUP.

Stétié, M. Salah. 1981. 'The View of UNESCO's Intergovernmental Committee' in Irene Staunton & Murray McCartney (eds.) *Lost Heritage: A Report of the Symposium on the Return of Cultural Property, held at the Africa Centre, 21 May 1981* London: Commonwealth Arts Association.

Stewart-Harawira, Makere. 2005. *The New Imperial Order: Indigenous Response to Globalization* London: Zed Books.

Sugarman, David. 2015. 'From Legal Biography to Legal Life Writing: Broadening Conceptions of Legal History and Socio-Legal Scholarship' *Journal of Law and Society* 42(1): 7–33.

Svestad, Asgeir. 2012. 'What Happened in Neiden? On the Question of Reburial Ethics' *Norwegian Archaeological Review* 46(2): 194–222.

Thielecke, Carola & Michael Geißdorf. 2021. 'Collections from Colonial Contexts: Legal Aspects' DMB *Guidelines for Care of Collections* Berlin: German Museums Association 153–164.

Thomas, Joseph Anthony Charles. 1975. *The Institutes of Justinian: Text, Translation and Commentary* Amsterdam: North-Holland Publishing Company.

Thomas, Joseph A. C. 1976. 'The Sale of Res Extra Commercium' *Current Legal Problems* 29(1): 136–149.

Thompson, Janna. 2003. 'Cultural Property, Restitution, and Value' *Journal of Applied Philosophy* 20(3): 251–262.

Titi, Catherine. 2023. *The Parthenon Marbles and International Law* Switzerland: Springer.

Tsosie, Rebecca. 2010. 'Who Controls Native Heritage?: "Art," "Artifacts," and the Right to Cultural Survival' in James A.R. Nafziger & Ann M. Nicgorski (eds.) *Cultural Heritage Issues: The Legacy of Conquest, Colonization, and Commerce* Leiden: Brill 1–36.

Tuhiwai Smith, Linda. 2021. *Decolonizing Methodologies: Research and Indigenous Peoples* 2nd ed. London: Zed Books.

Tythacott, Louise. 2019. 'Problems, Practices, and Politics of Provenancing Objects from China's Yuanmingyuan' in Jane Milosch & Nick Pearce (eds.) *Collecting and Provenance: A Multidisciplinary Approach* Lanham, Maryland: Rowman & Littlefield 359–370.

University Museums and Collections (UMAC). 2022. *Guidance for Restitution and Return of Items from University Museums and Collections* <https://ocm.iccrom.org/documents/umac-guidance-restitution-and-return-items-university-museums-and-collections>

UNESCO Guidance Note for Inventorying Intangible Cultural Heritage under the 2003 Convention for the Safeguarding of the Intangible Cultural Heritage <https://ich.unesco.org/doc/src/50279-EN.pdf>

UNESCO Intangible Cultural Heritage Inventory <https://ich.unesco.org/en/lists>

UNESCO-UNIDROIT Model Legislative Provisions on State Ownership of Undiscovered Cultural Objects 2012 <https://www.unidroit.org/english/documents/2012/study70a/s-70a-main-e.pdf>

US Department of State. 1999. *Washington Conference Principles on Nazi-Confiscated Art, Released in connection with The Washington Conference on Holocaust Era Assets, Washington, DC, 3 December 1998.*

US Department of State. 2024. *Best Practices for the Washington Conference Principles on Nazi-Confiscated Ar*t, *Washington, DC,* 5 March 2024.

Van den Berge, Lukas. 2018. Rethinking the Public-Private Law Divide in the Age of Governmentality and Network Governance: A Comparative Analysis of French, English and Dutch Law *European Journal of Comparative Law and Governance* 5(2): 119–143.

Van der Walt, Johan. 2018. 'The Origins of Legal Obligations: Towards a Fundamental Phenomenology of Moral and Legal Obligation' in Daniel Matthews & Scott Veitch (eds.) *Law, Obligation, Community* London: Routledge 35–70.

Van Roermund, Bert. 2013. *Legal Thought and Philosophy* Cheltenham: Edward Elgar Publishing.

Van Vliet, Lars P.W. 2006. 'The Boundaries of Property Rights: Netherlands National Report 2006' in Sjef van Erp & Lars van Vliet (eds.) *Netherlands Reports to the Seventeenth International Congress of Comparative Law: The Principles of the Law of Restitution* Utrecht: OUP.

Veraart Wouter & Laurence Winkel. 2011. 'An Introduction to Dilemmas of Post-War Restitution in Europe' in Wouter Veraart & Laurence Winkel (eds.) *The Post-War Restitution of Property Rights in Europe. Comparative Perspectives* New York: RVP Press 1–10.

Vigneron, Sophie. 2020. 'The Repatriation of Human Remains in France: 20 Years of (Mal) practice' *Santander Art and Culture Law Review* 6(2): 313–339.

Vrdoljak, Ana F. 2008. *International Law, Museums and the Return of Cultural Objects* Cambridge: CUP.

Weber-Sinn, Kristin & Paola Ivanov. 2020. '"Collaborative" Provenance Research – About the (im)possibility of Smashing Colonial Frameworks' Special Issue on Sensitive Heritage: Ethnographic Museums, Provenance Research, and the Potentialities of Restitutions (Philipp Schorch ed.) *Museum and Society* 18(1): 66–81.

Weikart, Richard. 2003. 'Progress through Racial Extermination: Social Darwinism, Eugenics, and Pacifism in Germany, 1860–1918' *German Studies Review* 26(2): 273–294.

Wheaton, Henry. 1866. *Elements of International Law* (Eighth edition, edited, with notes by Richard Henry Dana, Jr.) London: Sampson Low, Son & Co.

White, Liz. 2019. 'Conflicts Over the Excavation, Retention and Display of Human Remains: An Issue Resolved?' in Stuart Campbell, Liz White & Suzie Thomas (eds.) *Competing Values in Archaeological Heritage* Switzerland: Springer 91–102.

Wilson, Shawn. 2008. *Research is Ceremony. Indigenous Research Methods* Halifax & Winnipeg: Fernwood Publishing.

Winkelmann, Andreas. 2020. 'Repatriations of Human Remains from Germany—1911–2019' Special Issue on Sensitive Heritage: Ethnographic Museums, Provenance Research, and the Potentialities of Restitutions (in Philipp Schorch ed.) *Museum and Society* 18(1): 40–51.

Wolff, Jonathan. 2021. 'Injustice in the Real World', Dudley Knowles Lecture in Political Philosophy Delivered at the University of Glasgow, 1 February.

Wood, Philip. 2016. *The Fall of the Priests and the Rise of the Lawyers* London: Bloomsbury Publishing.

Woodhead, Charlotte C. 2002. 'A Debate Which Crosses All Borders – The Repatriation of Human Remains: More than Just a Legal Question' *Art Antiquity & Law* 7(4): 317–347.

Woodhead Charlotte C. 2023. *Caring for Cultural Heritage: An Integrated Approach to Legal and Ethical Initiatives in the United Kingdom* Cambridge: CUP.

Zeidler, Kamil. 2016. *Restitution of Cultural Property: Hard Case, Theory of Argumentation, Philosophy of Law* Gdańsk: Gdańsk University Press.

2 Normative conflicts

2.1 Introduction

'Hard' cases are those in which it is difficult to identify a single appropriate response to questions of interpretation, creation, application, applicability, and observation of the law. They invite multi-normative perspectives. The Parthenon Sculptures (taken from a sacred monument that commemorates the genealogy of Athens) and the encased mummified monk (artefactual remains taken from a temple built in honour of the monk where his descendants continue to hold devotional rituals), pose challenges in the private and public spheres—at the material level and at the level of the status and significance of what constitutes 'cultural property' for the immediate community and wider group. The cultural and religious arguments employed go beyond claims for personal property. The disputes resonate with claims to other cultural heritage that embodies knowledge and group identities that manifest in material creations.

Colonial looting poses complex questions for primary and secondary legal norms alike. Private and civil law, administrative, constitutional, and criminal law supply the primary rules, principles, mechanisms, and language by which restitution claims are operationalised. Satisfactory answers will not be found at the level of the primary legal norms of any single legal system alone. In the colonial era, pertinent tenets of customary law were unobserved at the time of removal or were deemed inapplicable. Consequently, the source community's legal claims contemporaneous with the removal would have gone unacknowledged. Inevitably, the approaches which colonial courts adopted to resolve internal (personal) conflicts of law affected the norms, obligations, and practices surrounding the sale of objects under value and the sale of stolen objects. When national and international legal frameworks do not consider traditional or customary legal systems in relation to applicable tenets of relevant customary law, imperial law is presented as 'unequivocal' and 'impervious'. How do we establish what the 'imperial law' or the 'colonial law' was in the locations in issue? How do we determine the appropriate applicable law in cases where mixtures of European law, international law, Private International Law (PrIL), Indigenous law, customs, and Islamic law exist, for instance? Choice-of-law rules derive from the legal diversity among states. While they may aim to enable the same results to be reached regardless of which country ends up as the forum in an international case, the pursuit of international

DOI: 10.4324/9781003583967-2

uniformity of decision—where the same concrete case is treated in the same way and produces the same outcome—is not every court's priority (Hatzimihail 2021: 38, 198). Many courts insist that PrIL problems are to be conceived from the viewpoint of a given state's courts and legal system, but in complex colonial contexts, PrIL's contribution lies in promoting peaceful co-existence. To this end, adjudicators and court officers are to fulfil their tasks in a spirit of mutual respect and cooperation (Struycken 2009). Martin Wolff adopted the view that PrIL rules should be drawn up in an international frame of mind and those responsible for developing such rules should aim 'to establish rules they can reasonably wish to see introduced by the lawgivers of other countries' (Wolff 1944: 16). Batiffol's idea was that the PrIL framework coordinates the different legal systems and competing rules claiming application, to promote the formation of international society and forge mechanisms that support orderly co-existence (Batiffol 1956: 311–335). His understanding was that PrIL goes beyond 'ordination,' and finds its true purpose in 'coordination.'

Whereas legal obligations that give effect to claims to sacred cultural property and heritage may vary across different states, social and ethical pressures work globally. Inconsistency in the outcomes of cross-border disputes draws attention to PrIL and its aspiration towards global justice. PrIL's peacemaking role is undeniable, but it would be naïve to think it is immune to xenophobic and chauvinistic arguments. General principles and propositions make up the common structure of PrIL argument. These principles condition primary norms as well as conflicts rules. Decisional harmony is a requirement of justice in external conflicts, but the greater the divergence between conflicts systems, the more elusive it is. Local populations' views about their governments and the place held by European imperial law provide different perspectives.

Rules and norms that indicate correlations in cultural, social, and economic interests could contribute to the integration of law and ethics, which is an important task for the future. The restoration and evolution of restitution law implies the integration of liability, responsibility, and obligation, which cannot be achieved solely at the level of the primary legal norms. The question about the status and place of customs, beliefs, and practices in Indigenous society, as well as its structure and organisation, remains critical today (Byrne 2015: 11).

Normative uncertainty over precisely *which* rules and norms apply to the spatial and temporal itineraries of the objects and collections looted, stolen, seized, or removed by colonial masters under duress deserves systematic treatment. The assumption that hybrid colonial law applied to non-European nations overlooks the dimension of 'internal' conflicts of law and the rulings of colonial courts when normative systems were overlapping in specific cases. The interaction between laws and the conflict of laws is frequently glossed over in studies that are predicated on the replacement of the precolonial legal orders by a European international legal order. Is it accurate to think that the application of alternatives to the law of the metropole in settler colonialism contexts was superseded or suppressed in the spaces in which legal norms took effect? Rejecting the precolonial history of the laws that could have been applied makes way for the argument that wartime looting was not illegal at the time, and therefore restitution cannot be legal. Such postcolonial constellations render it is necessary to investigate whether uncodified customary international law continued to have application and to critically evaluate whether it is appropriate to apply time limits to plundered cultural property. Roeland Kollewijn, a Dutch PrIL scholar who specialised in contacts between different civilisations in 'western and non-western law,' posed the question of whether PrIL can bring forth new principles, norms, and theories appropriate to the interplay between fundamentally different laws, values, and cultures (Kollewijn 1951: 307ff). Kollewijn took issue with the widespread assumption that there was no legal system in place within the so-called 'uncivilised' populations (Salomon 1889: 193–194). He was adamant that the dynamic nature of PrIL does not automatically accord priority to the metropolitan system of law in colonies adhering to plurality of law and that no standard could measure whether one legal system is higher or better than another. His important insight was not widely shared, however.

The colonial overlays and undercurrents of law that enabled the bypassing of normative conflicts are problematic aspects of research in the field of international law. Plural normative orders give rise to questions of incompatibility, partial indeterminacy, and where marriages and civil partnerships receive legal recognition in some countries but not in others, 'limping' relationships (Bollée 2019: 343, 346). Studying the approaches that were enlisted to rationalise the unquestioned preference for the law of the metropole in commercial cases sheds light on attempts to lend legitimacy to colonial approaches after the fact. Examples from the British and German colonies confirm that the procedural reasoning of colonial courts amounted to an unprincipled procedural *fait accompli*. Yet it is possible to devise a theory that explains their approach, namely that normative pluralism was managed based on jurisdictional competition. Procedural practices that enlisted PrIL's self-limiting boundaries in ways that worked hand-in-glove with Public International Law (PublIL) also reveal a streak of adjudicatory competitiveness.

Chapter 2 starts with an outline of the space time dimensions of normative conflicts and highlights how they manifest in internal conflicts. It pieces together the obligations engendered by the sacred and the juridical framework of exception. The internal and external dimensions of PrIL must be considered to determine when the principles of conflict of laws operating in an external dimension can shed light on the issues, and when those governing conflicts in their internal dimension would be more helpful.The time factor in claims for the restitution of cultural material removed during the colonial era is a troublesome aspect regarding which a fresh perspective is urgently needed. The standards set by uniform law have a defining effect on the law in signatory states and calls for explanation.

2.2 Conflict of laws arising 'externally' and 'internally'

Orthodoxy has it that legal norms compete in the inter-spatial dimension. When non-unified or dissimilar legal systems interact to regulate a particular private-law relationship in the same space or geographic area, there is the prospect of a clash. Pluralism and conflicts have ancient links. In ancient Greece, relations among different political groups were hostile, but an international community of the Hellenes developed over time. The idea that foreigners deserved specialised treatment took root (Taubenschlag 1972: 1–55). Despite isolated descriptions of conflicts law phenomena in antiquity, the ancient Greek and Roman worlds did not produce a conflicts structure in the law. No law of the conflicts of laws developed to authorise the application of foreign law to foreign cases. The legal treatment of foreigners was differentiated in the Ptolemaic era. A text on contract found on one of the ancient Fayoum Papyri indicates that specialised courts with special laws existed for racial groups within a political community. Disputes concerning contracts drawn up in Greek form between Egyptians and Greeks who had established colonies in Egypt had to be tried before the chrēmatistai (the Greek courts), while contracts in Egyptian form went before the laokritai (the native courts) (Yntema 1953: 301). Much later, courts in the city-states of Florence, Bologna, and Modena were obliged to consider each other's customary and business rules or statutes. Jurists added their notes on the demarcations within the scope of these statutes to authorative legal texts. Their notes show that they expected the law of the forum to yield a solution but their musings also spurred the development of theories and conflicts systems to identify which substantive national law should apply to conflicts between national and regional substantive laws.

A secondary legal norm in the form of a rule that determines that a particular legal system applies is a choice-of-law rule. These rules of PrIL are designed to settle normative conflicts between private individuals or collectivities (or states acting to protect ownership interests) with reference to the applicable legal system. For instance, in a dispute over ownership of property in which the law of Greece gives title to X but the law of Finland gives title to Y, the primary legal norm is the decision of the law of Greece to give title to X or the law of Finland to give title to Y. Whether it is the law of Greece or the law of Finland that should determine title in a particular instance, is a type of secondary legal norm, or a 'norm of competence' (Mills 2009: 19). Secondary legal norms govern which legal systems' rules apply and when, or what the scope of a particular right might be. A similar method applies to identify the court(s) competent to hear the case. A secondary legal norm determining the limits of jurisdiction and enforcement of judgments regulates whether the court in Greece or in Finland can enforce a judgment delivered in France by exercising physical power over a person or seizing their property (Mills 2009: 229, 239).

Conflict of laws may arise 'externally' when crossing international state borders. PrIL's international vantage point brings into view the competition between legal systems and legal norms belonging to different legal systems. The perspectives on those legal problems diverge, for PrIL assumes the existence of a complex mix of competing values and interests in cross-border relationships that are simultaneously connected to multiple jurisdictions (Banu 2022: 384). A dispute that requires a choice to be made between the legal systems of two political units or politically distinct countries, such as South Africa and France, is clearly about an international and external conflict when claimants are domiciled or habitually resident abroad.

International conflict of laws rules govern disputes that implicate more than one territorial system of law, yet '*the body of law that aims to resolve claims involving foreign elements*' does not require a state or international border (Yntema 1953: 299; Okoli & Oppong 2020: 3–7). Conflicts can arise 'internally' within one state with differences in jurisdiction and law. Rules may conflict internally with other rules that apply in the same district, country, or legal unit, and a state's general central legal system may conflict with a local set of legal rules that operate within the same political unit. One of the questions arising in respect of colonial contexts, namely whether claimants could argue and present evidence about which law ought to govern their case, remains theoretical to some extent as the colonised would rarely be free to make use of the courts, but it is essential to grapple with the theory to better understand the realities of the time. Conflicts of law were inevitable in the interaction of the legal norms of a colonial power and its colony. A dispute about the removal of property that necessitated a choice between the law of the metropole and the former colony required a court to consider the potentially applicable laws and judicial practice. Questions about normative conflicts that were 'internal' to Empire in the late 19th and early 20th century draw on the theory and practice of interspatial collisions between legal systems and precepts. Normative conflicts in a colonial context would in theory have to be accounted for in claims for the return of a culturally specific object to a territory within one state as legal norms accumulated and clashed within the same 'colonial space' even if the personality of the tribal personal laws of African and Asian colonies would not be considered in the way that statehood functioned for PrIL purposes.

Establishing the personal law of people was a means of resolving internal conflict of laws situations in civil cases concerning status in African colonies. Where a local administration of justice existed prior to colonisation and a new social order had to be created, the interpersonal law doctrine attributed a personal law based on a person's nationality, domicile, habitual residence, tribal affiliation, or religion, which may have been a matter of choice or not (Jiménez 2019: 442). The law governing substantive private-law relationships in 'internal' conflicts may be based on a personal law that attaches to the subject because of their religious denomination and not because of their connection with a territorial unit based upon, e.g., their domicile or habitual residence within that territory. For example, Greeks living in Egypt have their personal and family matters regulated by the law of the Greek Orthodox Church; the Muslim population in Greece has its personal and family matters regulated by Islamic law. An interpersonal conflict may arise between the private law rules of the various denominations, between the general law of the country and Indigenous law, or between different renditions of African customary rules.

The concept of personal law is reflected in the notion that a person carries the law that governs their affairs and their property along with them when they move from place to place (e.g., Huber 1686 *Heedensdaegse Rechtsgeleertheyt* 1.3.51 on the adage *mobilia sequuntur personam* of Roman-Dutch law). The challenge of conflicts 'internal' to Empire but 'external' in a postcolonial sense draws attention to the nationalism-parochialism that supplanted cosmopolitan ideas about normative conflicts and the bodies that were set up for these disputes. It also imparts clues about religious divisions. For instance, the division between Greece and the new successor state that emerged when the forces of Turkish nationalism defeated the Greek army in Anatolia in 1922 reflects the line between Christianity in Europe and Islam in the Middle East.

In the 19th century, the principles of conflict of laws operating in an external dimension and the conflicts occurring in their internal dimension were considered different in character. Internal conflicts continue to be set apart when defining PrIL's scope today (Struycken 2009: 189–192, 194–195; Siehr 1994: 147–161, 182–202). Some commentators prefer to keep the delineation simple and designate 'internal conflicts' as outside the purview of PrIL rules (e.g., Last 2007: 128, 131). Socialist commentators predicted that the problem of external and internal legal conflict would disappear with the spread of socialist legal systems across the world (e.g., Szászy 1974: 323). Supporters of the codification movement do not foresee collisions between national laws and Indigenous law because they expect lawmakers to promulgate laws to minimise the potential for collisions.

There is an age-old question about which rules to apply to determine if, or when, an object has a sacred character or whether it can be lost. This question belongs squarely in the PrIL domain, where adjudicators face an apparent choice between civil law and the internal rules of the various religious societies such as canon law. Various denominations will have private law rules that may compete with the general law of the country and/or with Indigenous law or different renditions of African customary rules. The normative knowledge of the colonised subjects never 'surfaced' in practice. Indigenous governing structures did not codify or publish their customs regarding burial grounds, sacred places, or funerary and sacred objects. Islamic and Ethiopian law texts exist, but most African law was unwritten custom which gradually garnered binding force through popular usage. Consequently, when domestic law and imperial law could have claimed application alongside each other, the local customs and traditions that prevailed in property transactions and contracts were either suppressed or neglected. 'Intercustomary' law conceivably developed from the interpersonal laws regime (Hatzimihail 2021: 75).

It would be unreasonable to 'infer' that customary laws 'authorised' the removal of their cultural heritage under duress or permitted forcible removal (al Attar et al. 2009: 321). Traditions orally transmitted by elders used to be overlooked in relevant guidelines under the Native American Graves Protection and Repatriation Act (NAGPRA). Only written and cartographic documentation concerning territory and property was recognised and accepted. The revised procedural framework for NAGPRA encapsulated in the Final Rule to improve its implementation that took effect on 12 January 2024 expects the claimant to gather as much information as possible. Where written records are inconclusive or unreliable, claimants may submit evidence in other forms, e.g., evidence derived from oral tradition, folklore, or archaeology (clause 3.4). Aboriginal perspectives on legitimate acquisition and transfer of title prioritise oral testimony as proof of ownership, but little is gained if these perspectives do not carry weight in a western court (Last 2007: 133).

In the mid-19th century, the medieval theory of *conflictus legum* was in decline and its rejection as a theoretical base caused legal uncertainty. No substantial methodological novelties emerged from continental Europe to minimise inconsistency in the outcomes of cross-border disputes. English scholars did not come up with adequate explanations for contradictory precedents in cross-border matters in English law either (Neidhardt 2018: 156, 207–208). The acute need to reorganise the conflict of laws made fertile soil for a new paradigm to take root in the second half of the 19th century. Elite German jurist Friedrich Carl von Savigny (1779–1861) published his *System of the Modern Roman Law* (*System des heutigen römischen Rechts*) in eight volumes between 1840 and 1849. He proposed a highly influential theoretical model for PrIL based on a fundamental postulate of natural law: That every legal subject has a place and every legal question and solution to a problem derived from this place (Hatzimihail 2021: 21). Savigny's new paradigm localised the legal relationship in space and embraced the conceptual correlation of rules and social categories. PrIL's transformation from a method of legal interpretation to an autonomous discipline was complete (Hatzimihail 2021: 354). PrIL's new 'classical' paradigm took hold between 1869 and 1873, a few decades after the publication of Savigny's ideas (Hatzimihail 2021: 95).

The Sarr and Savoy Report foregrounds 'new cultural relations based on a newly reflected upon ethical relation' (2018: 29). At first blush, PrIL seems unable to achieve new ethical relations because it elevates the application of the technical dimension of legal knowledge and foregrounds the 'technical' more than other legal subjects do (Riles 2005: 1029). Does PrIL's internal and external modes accommodate mummified thinking and discrimination based on ethnic origin and race? Banu adopts the view that PrIL is apathetic towards the ills of colonialism. She ascribes this stance to PrIL's close association with PublIL prior to its splitting into discrete disciplinary branches. She asserts that PrIL's formalism and its objective of neutrality in litigated cases mean that the consequences of racial inequality across legal frameworks are seldom challenged (Banu 2018: 7–8).

In the years between 1920 and 1945, US scholars drew attention to the distinction between 'material contacts' or connecting factors and the balancing of 'policies' and 'interests' (Hatzimihail 2021: 175). The focus on 'material contacts' combines with formalism to promote a supposed neutrality that makes it possible to ignore questions of social justice in transnational contexts. A 'value-neutral' stance will promote a blinkered view of injustice, which will inhibit PrIL's engagement with justice amid the pressures exerted by many new global forms of social, cultural, and legal pluralism (Roodt 2007a: 79; Oppong 2007: 677–719).

Because the complexities of PrIL's relationship with global legal pluralism are not widely understood, pluralist thinking has sought to identify foundations of legal authority beyond the bounds of the state. Various brands of legal pluralism are flourishing and eclipse PrIL (Muir Watt 2016a: 393). 'Rule formalism' is a contributing factor in rendering PrIL disinterested in the colonial question. A general preference for rules over standards takes hard rules at face value rather than looking deeper to general principles as the foundation of the system (Hatzimihail 2021:

176). Recourse to rules is always an attractive option when faced with normative uncertainty.

The normative function of PrIL plays out at different levels. It is evident at the level of relations between states and in the choices regarding international governance it is expected to make, and also at the level of relations between individuals and in the choices to be made regarding private-law governance (Hatzimihail 2021: 168–169, 204–206). Lixinski submits that blurring the public-private divide is the only way to attain objectives directed by the values attributed to global public goods. He calls for PrIL's tools of engagement and governance strategies to stop 'hiding in their own shadow' (Lixinski 2018: 27–28). PrIL jurisdiction is a tool of legal governance in the protection of cultural heritage that has potential to control the supply-and-demand of cultural heritage (Lixinski 2018: 27; Roodt 2015: 345; Gillies 2015: 295ff). In classical conflict of laws PrIL's multilateral and unilateral methods, which are distinct formal categories of legal rules, were tools for 'international governance'. Ideas about the conflict of laws have always depended on immediate relationships and affiliations, as well as broader international norms. The PublIL approach has predominated since the 17th century but when Savigny's approach wrought a switch from unilateralism to multilateralism, the relationship among sovereign states was thrust into the foreground. In an age in which democracy and its support for equality are in peril, PrIL's failure to fulfil its governance function cannot be justified. The resolution of normative conflicts demands the development of sharper legal tools of global governance. Contemporary PrIL supports a certain vision of globalisation that aims to reconcile public policies with conflicting individual choices (Hatzimihail 2021: 216). This is contemporary PrIL's vision of 'international governance.' The governance functions and strategies of PrIL express themselves in the ways in which secondary legal norms and methods condition the time space depth dimensions of the application of primary law and of conflicts rules. Individuals may 'alter the equation' of the state laws applicable to them by relocating or using contractual and testamentary stipulations (Hatzimihail 2021: 459–460).

The conflict of laws could apply equally to disputes arising between regional customs and cities as well as disputes between states, and attention turned to private law (Struycken 2009: 203). While Wheaton's *Elements of International Law* (1866) draws no distinction between PublIL and PrIL, detailed, state-directed choice-of-law rules appeared in the 19th century (Glenn 2011: 248). Clashes between public economic legislation and private interests provoke international disputes between private bodies, indicating that PrIL and public law are not sharply delineated even if contemporary PrIL remains firmly attached to the public-private divide (Struycken 2009: 194–195).

Savigny did not subscribe to individual liberty, nor did he adopt a libertarian perspective on private law above all else. Instead, he foregrounded the relationship between different types of rules and basic categories of social life. He relied upon PrIL's association with private law to increase the agency of individuals in the transnational realm and counter state-centered premises. This 'relational internationalist' perspective conceives of individuals in relation to the other parties in a private law relationship and with the communities in which that private law relationship is embedded, as well as with broader humanity (Banu 2018: 9, 291–292). Private law-focused theories of the 19th century were more nuanced than state-centered theories in the sense that they were attuned to the way in which individuals pursue claims in particular courts as part of their quest for integration in various communities. They took seriously the fiduciary duties which courts have toward the litigating parties and their responsibility to weigh the interests of domestic and foreign parties equitably (Banu 2018: 8–9). The portrayal of a more relational, socially constituted image of the individual point to various dimensions of responsibility and respect individuals owe to one another and the communities in which they operate. Analogising PrIL to private law led authors like Savigny to develop premises to focus on a relationship instead of an isolated individual; draw from extra-legal social expectations as much as from the law; justify the application of foreign law to individuals; and respect inter-personal equality (Banu 2018: 292).

Banu contends that the 'relational internationalist' perspective is no longer part of the contemporary PrIL memory bank, as it has been misunderstood and overlooked. For sacred cultural property and heritage, the level of embeddedness of private law relationships into a community is pivotal in the framework of justification for the application of any law. PrIL cannot afford to operate in isolation from private law in this field. Geographical connecting factors as well as policies of the laws regulating private law relationships must be analysed. This is not sufficient, however, since PrIL can ill afford to operate in isolation from PublIL. The view that sovereign states make up the international system in which relations are modelled on conflicting private law leaves no scope for a vision of international law that effectively reduces injustice. Uncritical engagement with the state-centered premises of PublIL in disputes concerning material removed during the colonial eras is a dead-end street. The ways in which interspatial law could contribute to the progress of international law remain under-researched because of the artificial split in international law that left PublIL unable to offer solutions for 'internal conflict of laws.' The discursive framework around which internal conflicts are structured receives more scholarly attention thant it gets.

Banu urges scholars to engage with historical variations of the PrIL-PublIL relationship and move beyond an individualistic conception of the individual in relation to rights, legitimate authority, and the cosmopolitan dimensions of PrIL. Superficial observations about the historical alignment invite mindless replication of the structural connection between PrIL and PublIL that prevailed in the 19th century. It is an insufficient response to the colonial question (Banu 2018: 291). She encourages contemporary scholars who wish to pursue a reconnection between PrIL and PublIL and a new relationship between them to study the history of the association and, in particular, the perils of the limitations of the 19th-century state-centered theory when agitating for social justice reform (Banu 2018: 292).

Understanding the relationship between PrIL, PublIL, and international cultural heritage law with this caveat in mind puts paid to the supposedly neutral or apolitical perspective ascribed to PrIL. Clusters of treaties and regimes, as well as different types of normative materials, make room for private regulation within the scope of international law. PrIL scholars do not have to remain out of touch with the political edge that attaches to studies of empire and imperialism (Koskenniemi 2011: 2).

2.3 PrIL as battleground

The present state of PrIL is a battleground of competing and antithetical ideas from across time about territorialism and personalism (i.e., the territoriality of laws and the personality of laws), unilateral and multilateral choice-of-law methods, and the opposition between particularists preferring territorialist solutions in national conflicts systems and the universalist aspiration of a uniform system of conflict of laws rules referred to as the nationalist-internationalist opposition. Opposing conceptions are in evidence at the level of doctrine, formal sources, and ideology (Hatzimihail 2021: 78–79, 139–171). PrIL's evolution has yielded no grand objective.

The relations of public and private law, including soft law, also invite examination. A report prepared by the ILC Study Group (*Fragmentation of International Law* 2006: 100, 102) emphasises the risks attached to promoting PrIL's close association with private law and neglecting PrIL's interaction with public law. The main risk is that of norm reductionism in international law discourse. The importance of avoiding norm reductionism has been studied in human rights discourse (David 2020: xvi, 145–154). Henry Wheaton explained the core function and purview of PrIL as the application of foreign laws with consideration of public utility, necessity, comity and mutual convenience of states, provided that their application does not contravene prohibitory enactments (Wheaton 1866: paras 79–80). Wheaton's description of PrIL's function alludes to overlapping jurisdiction or regulatory authority between 'sovereign' states. If secondary legal rules 'allocate' transnational private law claims among national legal systems and affect regulatory authority, PrIL operates between states as public law (Mills 2009: 45, 209).

The modes of legal reasoning in Duncan Kennedy's model—classical, socially oriented, contemporary—are forms of legal thought anchored in legal rationalism. The distinction between public and private law was the central way of organising legal rules in the genealogy of Classical Legal Thought (CLT) (Kennedy 2010: 831; Hatzimihail 2021: 26). All western legal systems reflect this distinction and rationalistic ordering of the legal universe. CLT achieved prominence in international law in the late 19th and early 20th centuries and it matches the doctrinal developments in PrIL (Muir Watt 2014: 358). Savigny's *System* refigured CLT (Kennedy 2010: 811, 833, 835). The *System* incorporated the structure of Roman private law (the *Roman corpus juris*) and adopted as its basis the doctrines of 18th-century jurisprudence found in notions of German natural law theory and Kant's legal philosophy. The 'conceptualist legal apparatus' of this systematisation and its rationalism had the potential to support the colonial enterprise because classical PrIL revolved around a horizontal system of sovereign states and set out to manage the legal diversity between them (Hatzimihail 2021: 131). The classifying or pigeonholing of the scenario into the appropriate legal class or category permits the relevant jurisdiction or choice-of-law rule to be selected. The process of seeking to allocate a certain legal issue to a PrIL category supplies the connecting factor to be employed. CLT's dichotomies neatly excluded certain communities and peoples from legal mechanisms, concepts, principles, and rules. It is fair to say that characterisation also had this potential, therefore. The way in which the legal subject matter is organised into categories allows a glimpse into the general conflicts theory of whoever designed the system in question (Hatzimihail 2021: 181).

CLT facilitates a close understanding of the types of rules that counteract social, economic, and cultural disadvantages and stereotypes, as well as rules that do not have this power. The legal distinctions drawn between family and market can be helpfully contextualised by reference to CLT. In turn, the *System* established family law as a unifying category of private law and advanced the family/patrimony distinction as a basic principle inhering in the law that governs any legal relationship. The mechanistic 'adaptability' of the *System* rendered it workable for pretty much everyone regardless of grounding premise—natural rights believers, utilitarians, idealist philosophers, and social Darwinists. It did not matter whether the proposition entailed freedom, natural rights, historical spirit, utility, or adaptive 'fitness' as doctrinally; the PrIL machine was supposed to run on 'legal logic' alone and practically 'ran by itself' (Kennedy 2010: 837). This feature heightened PrIL's appeal to all 19th-century schools. Savigny also held fast to the view that law, in a broad sense, does not necessarily make moral claims. He considered PublIL an imperfect positive law for 'correlative rights, obligations and expectations' which cannot be unilaterally determined (Banu 2018: 296). History can support a critical and politically conscious provenance, and PrIL theoryunderscore the relational dimensions of secondary legal norms.

PrIL's adaptability and CLT's exclusion made it possible to invoke and sustain a passive, value-neutral argument even when the application of PrIL's tenets promoted social and economic discrimination.If jurisdiction cannot be established, no scope arises to air arguments about the moral repugnancy of the free and unencumbered circulation of human remains and body parts proven to stem directly from genocide. Meanwhile, the juridical framework of circulation of cultural goods will continue to expand. This framework is acknowledged in national constitutional law (e.g., constitutional guarantees of cultural rights and the protection of cultural heritage within states); the circulation (and loan) of heritage objects and collections (which depends on rules that ensure access to justice with a view to the settlement of normative conflicts); private and commercial law rules governing the circulation of cultural assets (e.g. versions of market overt principles); rules that embody protections of municipal criminal and civil law for cultural assets; rules governing their export, import or transfer; and proprietary and other PrIL rules. Upon reaching the question of applicable law, it will become apparent how a substantive argument concerning transactions and repatriation can obstruct the adjustment of the traditional boundaries between PrIL's territorial and cultural dimensions.

To liberate legal norms from the orthodoxy that perpetuates 'value-neutrality' PrIL's methods and approaches to the time space dimensions of primary legal norms and conflicts rules as well as PrIL's relationship with global legal pluralism need to shift. PrIL's function plays out not only inter-spatially but also at different levels in the horizontal coordination of legal frameworks, rules, norms, principles, and choices. More than just legal doctrine and the underlying patterns of legal reasoning in case law or legislation are at stake amidst this plurality. Attacks on cultural heritage in times of armed conflict have been banned under PublIL, but the over-abundant literature on the topic of restitution and repatriation of cultural material offers remarkably little guidance for weighing up the arguments about colonial-era removals of cultural heritage. The spill-over of such arguments into PrIL invites a philosophical appraisal of its legal-theoretical foundations and underlines the need to consider its depth potential for the restoration of the law of restitution for complex colonial contexts. The relevance of PrIL's methods and approaches outside of inter-national, or infra-state contexts corroborates its depth potential (discussed in more detail in Chapter 3).

The layer of complexity added by the problem of grievous historic wrongs implores legal systems to venture into unfamiliar territory. The scope of reparative justice renders outcomes unpredictable. Practices such as the involuntary removal of Indigenous children from their parents, operationalised through the instrument of the law in the 20th century, are widely condemned today. Reparative justice touches on liability in criminal law; accountability of regimes that transitioned to democracy, truth and reconciliation commissions, state responsibility, the rights of victims of grievous violations of fundamental human rights to restitution, reparations, and other remedies in international law. It reaches into the international humanitarian law of armed conflicts and international criminal law (Manacorda 2011: 25). Moran theorises that demands for reparatory justice are steadily eroding the notion that the past is beyond law's reach (Moran 2019: 425–426). The doctrines that determine the outcomes of claims in the Indian Residential Schools cases or those brought by the Herero and Nama for economic and legal recognition of slave labour, and confiscation and expropriation of land and tribal property, may affect claims for the restitution of cultural material. In instances where such deeply troubling aspects of survivors' compensation claims for historic wrongs are at stake, normative leverage exists to activate the juridical framework of exception to the circulation of cultural goods. A strong PrIL response to the violent looting and theft that occurred during the colonial era can follow if ethical norms could suspend the application of ordinary commercial rules, shift PrIL categories, and justify the non-application of procedural protections in claims for damages and restitution. Dismantling the frivolous distinctions and dichotomies that prevent a strong response can also activate defragmentation of the law and re-integrate the 'internal' and 'external' conflicts affecting erstwhile colonial territories in PrIL.

PrIL's development will be delayed if tendencies to replicate and venerate past power structures were to continue. Ironically, excluding PrIL from efforts to address the law's colonial undercurrents will only increase the risk that a colonial mindset will prevail in 'internal conflicts.' Yet treating legal norms as if they remain 'at war' will not uncover disintegrating pathways to restitution. The space time dimensions of normative conflicts and the obligations engendered by that intangible heritage must find their proper place.

2.4 The space time dimensions of normative conflicts in colonial contexts

Descriptive commentaries on case law and codifications far outnumber interrogations of the theory and methods of PrIL (Muir Watt 2014: 363). Yet PrIL must be freed from the mummified thinking that consigns it to joining other vestiges of the pre-global age (Muir Watt 2016a: 399; Muir Watt 2016b: 341).

Norms evolve and shift in positive law (*lex*), principle (*jus*), and at the intersection between rules and principles (ethics). Disagreements arise in legal circles over the issue of ownership of cultural property and heritage that cannot be settled to everyone's satisfaction. A conflict that arises between primary legal norms can be resolved by introducing an exception clause or declaring one of the rules invalid. Principles do not lose their validity in the same way. When principles conflict, one of the prima facie relevant principles will simply take precedence over other principles that recede. To be resolved, arguments of principle and policy assume more than just recourse to the (settled legal) traditions of an ethical community. Another point of reference is needed (Habermas 1996: 208–210).

It so happens that irreconcilable differences arise across property laws in many jurisdictions (Lixinski 2019a: 62, 63). The choice-of-law technique determines which legal system's property law norms apply, when they apply, as well as the scope of authority of the court hearing the case. As a body of law, PrIL reflects ideas of justice that may differ from those of the court called upon to identify the 'applicable law.' It confronts the question of which law applies in international cases where applicable legal systems may have different conceptions of justice, or of which legal system qualifies as good, adequate, and just (Struycken 2009: 224).

As a legal theory on legal conflicts in the interspatial and intertemporal dimensions, and the external and internal planes, courts use PrIL to ascertain the content of the foreign law, accurately 'describe' the legal problem, and 'decide' international disputes by applying those norms correctly. PrIL offers a philosophy of the interrelationship between legal systems (and, therefore, legal cultures) and how this intersection is to be treated. To justify the application of a foreign law, the consideration that secondary legal norms give to the space time and depth dimensions of the law in complex colonial contexts may be usefully considered.. Time and space shape our involvement with the world, even if direct study of these phenomena challenges and eludes us (Canales 2015: 220). A different time, era, and context is not a haven from which to relativise injustice.

2.4.1 Establishing temporal and substantial jurisdiction over 'sacred' cultural property and heritage

In a class action brought against Germany on behalf of members and descendants of the Ovaherero and Nama in US courts, human remains were in issue. The claimants alleged that the Museum of Ethnology in Berlin sold skulls and body parts from the private collection of Felix von Luschan to the American Museum of Natural History (AMNH) as part of a commercial transaction. Attempts to establish jurisdiction in the US courts relied on the PrIL pillar of jurisdiction and on satisfying the substantial commercial contact requirement in US law (*Rukoro et al. v Federal Republic of Germany* No. 17 CV 62-LTS (SDNY 2019) 5–6, 23). A sale of bones would satisfy the requirement of German commercial activity, but the mere presence of Herero and Nama remains in the AMNH in New York was considered insufficient to confer subject matter jurisdiction under the exceptions for commercial activity and takings in the Foreign Sovereign Immunities Act of 1976 (*Rukoro et al. v Federal Republic of Germany* 2d Cir. 2020 21). The implications of the interface between colonial takings and international cultural heritage law deserve to be worked out more systematically to preclude unintended opportunities for unethical behaviour from arising. Commodification of human remains may allow the free market to flourish, but this approach has an incalculable cost for the legal system. A presumption that repatriation efforts do not entail a substantial commercial contact with the US or a causal connection with the AMNH for purposes of a jurisdiction ruling facilitates the display of looted sacred material in the US and allows the normative effect of mimetics to flourish. A 'liberal jurisprudence of power' must be cultivated to resist such effects and permit PrIL's jurisdictional rules to engage with the juridical framework of exception (Kostal 2005: 454).

Jurisdictional problems also arose in the only adjudicatory intervention in the Parthenon Marbles dispute to date, *Syllogos ton Athinaion v United Kingdom* in the European Court of Human Rights (EurCtHR). An non-governmental organisation (NGO) posing a hypothetical question on Greece's behalf proved to be insufficient to establish jurisdiction. The Athenians' Association is an advocacy group active in the field of protection and maintenance of the monuments and works of art connected with the history of Athens. It filed the first legal bid for restitution of the Parthenon Sculptures. All the claims were held inadmissible *ratione materiae* (i.e., based on subject matter), and the case was dismissed *ratione temporis* (i.e., by reason of the time pertaining to the subject under consideration). The sculptures were removed from the Parthenon Temple approximately 150 years before the UK ratified the European Convention for the Protection of Human Rights and Fundamental Freedoms. To bring the claim within the temporal jurisdiction of the EurCtHR, the claimant argued that the UK's refusal to engage in mediation or undertake return constituted a continuing act that violated the human rights of the Athenians' Association, its members, and ancestors (sub 'The Law'). The complaint was ruled 'inadmissible as incompatible *ratione materiae* with the provisions of the Convention and its Protocols.' The underlying grievance or cause of action was identified by the EurCtHR as the alleged unlawful removal of the Sculptures by Elgin's men, requiring retrospective application of European Convention on Human Rights. The Convention expressly prohibits the retrospective application of national and international laws (Article 7). There was no opportunity to raise the standard of protection that existed in ancient Greek law for architecture, friezes, and sculptures that were embedded in the Parthenon Temple, for the case never reached the merits. The impact of colonial thinking on sacred cultural property and heritage was beyond the jurisdictional scope of the Court.

The Convention text makes no reference to property. Case law on the violation of Article 1of the 1952 Protocol, which outlines the right to protection of property and the ongoing effects of colonialism, leaves scope for finding that the continuing retention of the Parthenon Sculptures constitutes a continuing act. Notwithstanding the expropriation of property years before Greece acceded to the ECHR, the application of Mr Papamichalopoulos and other landowners in *Jean Papamichalopoulos and Others v Greece* (Application No. 14556/89, ECHR 5 March 1991) remained admissible and the EurCtHR accepted jurisdiction. In *Syllogos*, the Court focused on the date on which the dispute started. It stopped short of basing its ruling on non-retrospectivity in the framework of human rights. Instead, it circumvented hearing the merits of the claim by declining its competence to consider the merits of the lawsuit. Ultimately, the human rights thrust of the claim in *Syllogos* (that continuing possession by the British Museum constituted an ongoing violation of Greece's rights) could not suspend the power hierarchies of the colonial era.

A successful claim would depend on Greece filing a suit against the UK on its own behalf and asking the EurCtHR to extend its understanding of the ECHR to include 'a new human right' that is not apparent from the text. The EurCtHR was not convinced that a general right to the protection of cultural heritage exists, however. The argument would have to be that the discrete rights guaranteed by the ECHR, when considered in the aggregate, imply a right to cultural property, or that there is a penumbra of extratextual rights in the ECHR text that comes within its purview, and that the right to cultural property is a part of the aggregated rights and is enforceable against states (Wadsworth 2023: 143, 145). Thus far, the EurCtHR has not recognised the right of protection of cultural heritage as an active right, that is, a right that can support a claim as opposed to a defence. It does not recognise 'an individual universal right to the protection of one or another cultural heritage' (*Ahunbay and others v Turkey* Application No. 6080/06, Decision, 29 January 2019, para. 25; Titi 2023: 208). Wadsworth denies that any realistic option exists for Greece to institute proceedings in an international forum that would be declared admissible, as there is no international court with both jurisdiction over Greece and the UK and the power to compel return. Threats of compulsory litigation are impractical, as they cannot exert diplomatic leverage. Wadsworth also criticises the dismissal of Greece's lawyers when the desired diplomatic results proved elusive as a game of 'brinksmanship' (Wadsworth 2023: 129).

Commentators have not canvassed the 'PrIL pathway' of international civil litigation for this dispute. Having declared that it is not interested in taking the dispute to court, Greece would not be amenable to it but considering such a scenario as a theoretical possibility can contribute to new thinking on policy-formulation and promote the law's coherence. PrIL techniques can be conceived as tools for structuring one's thinking about dispute resolution in the context of the removal of sacred material from complex colonial contexts.

2.4.2 The procedure/substance distinction

What constitutes form and substance signifies a determination of what should fall under the domain of PrIL and conflicts discourse and what falls outside it. However, this is seldom defined in express terms, and juristic opinions fluctuate.

Jacobus Balduinus proffered that courts apply their own procedural law in international civil litigation because they cannot be expected to be familiar with foreign court procedure (e.g., Hatzimihail 2021: 114). Modern Greek jurists adopted the view that, although local substantive law must be used as the starting point for obvious reasons, the foreign law applicable in each case should be decisive if its distinctions are not contrary to Greek public policy (Nicoletopoulos 1948–1949: 461). Sir John Salmond, former judge of the Supreme Court of New Zealand, defined procedure as the branch of the law which governs the process of litigation in civil and criminal proceedings (the means or mode of proceeding courts use to give effect to foreign-created rights) and is supposedly governed by the law of the court that hears the dispute. All the rest concerns the purposes and subject-matter of the litigation, which is substantive law. Substantive law is supposed to be concerned with the ends sought by the administration of justice (Salmond 1966: 461–462).

When characterising certain requirements as formal (procedural) or substantive, it is widely understood that 'form' has a different meaning when foreign institutions are involved in conflicts cases than it does under substantive forum law in domestic trials (Hatzimihail 2021: 184). Because proceedings may be suspended or dismissed prior to hearing the substantive arguments, it matters a great deal where adjudicators draw the line between procedure and substance. The delineation is disputed in the law of prescription, statutes of limitation, burden of proof, procedural rules of evidence, and remedies (e.g., Garnett 2012; Roodt 2007b: 357ff). The EurCtHR has classified rules on limitation periods as 'procedural,' that is, as secondary rules that do not define the substance of offences and penalties, but that set preconditions for the assessment of the case in question (*Previti v Italy* (Dec.) No. 1845/08, ECHR 12 February 2013: para 80). While it is theoretically possible to draw sharp lines between substance and procedure, Salmond cautions that the dividing line cannot be taken to exist in any preordained sense. His observations foreshadow the impact of the mode of the proceedings on their substance (Cook 1941: 191). The practical operation of many rules of procedure is equivalent to rules of substantive law (Salmond 1966: 462). Some commentators would say that it makes a difference whether the legal relation itself is at the core of the dispute resolution instead of the remedies (Hatzimihail 2021: 189). However, since rights and remedies are inseparably connected, it does not work to ascribe the distinction to the difference between them. For instance, one's right to give evidence on one's own behalf shows that a right can be procedural in nature. Furthermore, the rules defining the remedy are frequently part of substantive law; the rules as to the measure of damages and those declaring what damage is actionable belong to substantive law. The advantages of treating the foreign law of limitation as substantive have been elaborated at length. In the European Union (EU), for instance, the law applicable to non-contractual obligations confirms a relatively wide scope of the law applicable and this tempers forum dominance (Regulation (EC) No 864/2007 ('Rome II') Article 15). Procedural characterisations strengthen the role of the *lex fori* in international civil proceedings. Carving issues away from the category of procedure can limit the reach of the *lex fori*. This insight would suggest that, in disputes over sacred cultural material with colonial-era provenance, a shift is needed at the frontiers of international civil procedure. Shifting the delineation between procedure and substance in these cases could result in a reappraisal of the rationale of a PrIL rule or principle.

2.4.3 Conferral of standing to sue in adjudication to argue the merits of ownership

Any object or property could potentially have an action brought against it, and not just a sacred cultural object. The civil forfeiture (*in rem*) case against a Cambodian sandstone sculpture, removed from a temple at Koh Ker and illegally brought to the US, is an example involving a sacred object (*United States v A 10th Century Cambodian Sandstone Sculpture Currently Located at Sotheby's in New York, New York*, Stipulation and Order of Settlement, 12 Civ. 2600 (GBD), 12 December 2013).

The dispute over the ownership of the Parthenon Marbles prominently illustrates how western understandings of ownership can impose upon sacred objects that once belonged in temples. Churches, Hindu idols, and various sculptures have frequently sued—or have frequently been sued—in their own name (e.g., *Autocephalous Greek-Orthodox Church v Goldberg & Feldman Fine Arts Inc* 717 F Supp 1374 SD Ind 1989). An extraordinary depth of insight into the problem posed by *locus standi* in claims for restitution or repatriation can be found in the English Court of Appeal's affirmation of the trial judge's ruling in *Bumper Development Corporation v Commissioner of Police for the Metropolis* ([1991] 1 W.L.R. 1362; [1991] 4 All E.R. 638 (C.A.)). A Canadian oil company with a sizable art collection lost title to a bronze temple idol that had been dug up by a local Indian labourer in Pathur, Tamil Nadu, in 1976 and sold to the corporation in London. The Metropolitan Police seized it on suspicion of theft during appraisal and conservation procedures undertaken by the British Museum. The police adduced evidence that the statue had metallurgical qualities, termite mounds, and soil like that of other statues known to have originated from a certain location in India (Forrest 2010: 146). The Pathur community understood the proceedings as the deity itself participating in the court process through the idol. The Court of Appeal upheld the ruling of the court of first instance, that the ruined Hindu temple and its idols possessed legal personality under Tamil Nadu law. It recognised that the temple could sue or be sued in the English courts by virtue of Indian law, even though the temple would not be recognised as having such legal personality under English law. The CA concluded that the finding was in accord with 'the comity of nations' and not contrary to English public policy. The Indian parties associated with the temple then pursued the recognition and enforcement of the two English judgments in the courts of Canada. The Court of Queen's Bench of Alberta found the English judgments persuasive and applied the comity of nations principle. It rejected the corporation's opposing argument against enforcement of the English judgments, that the temple lacked standing and that the judgment of the English court was contrary to the public policy of Canada (*India v Bumper Development Corporation* (1995) 171 AR 166 (QB) paras 74–76). The corporation's attempts to establish a right under Canadian law to compensation for having to surrender possession of the sculpture failed (Paterson 1996: 331). The question of whether an entity may be the subject of litigation 'may result in a liability being imposed or not imposed under local law which would not have occurred under the law of the place of the entity's formation.' This will necessarily affect parties' rights and duties (Garnett 2012: para 5.08). Proceeding to the merits of restitution claims based on property ownership gives the opportunity to attend to distributive and corrective justice within a private law relationship.

Justice and international judicial comity implore adjudicators to hear the merits of restitution claims, but courts in locations on the demand-side of the trade in cultural objects have denied human remains legal personality and standing to sue in restitution proceedings (e.g., *Na Iwi O Na Kupuna I Mokapu v Dalton* 894 F Supp 1397 D Haw 1995). International judicial comity could ensure greater attunement with a relational internationalist perspective that extends to third parties and the various communities affected by the private law relationships implicated in these cases (in general, Banu 2018: 303). The International Law Association Committee on the Participation in Global Cultural Heritage Governance, Resolution 01/2022, acknowledges the need for guidance on the removal of possible obstacles to standing for collective claimants to cultural heritage and the possible harmonisation of legal personality for NGOs active in the field of the preservation of cultural heritage.

A natural or legal person would likely be accorded standing to sue but procedural evaluations may preclude cultural relics from being accorded standing in western courts. A court with a formalist approach to the substance/procedure dichotomy in international civil litigation will likely interpret 'procedure' expansively and substance more narrowly, so that the law of the court is more likely to find application than potentially applicable foreign law. Comity may support the conferral of legal standing so that the case may proceed to the merits, but a court may prefer to decide differently based on its discretion if it is most convenient for them to do so (Last 2007: 131). Even when religious societies or other groups have the requisite authority to bring a suit in their country of origin, courts elsewhere may decide differently. The village committees faced this situation in the Amsterdam District Court. In China, committees typically exercise ownership rights to land collectively owned by village peasants on behalf of the villagers (Article 61(1) of the Property Rights Law of the People's Republic of China of 2007). No judicial notice was taken of this fact by the Amsterdam District Court when it made a ruling on the village committees' standing (*Village Committee of Yangchun and Dongpu v Oscar van Overeem* 2018).

The classification of legal rules, facts, or the cause of action into categories to determine the 'applicable law' in PrIL is not an overriding concern in the preliminary stage of the proceedings, but it may colour the thinking of the adjudicators. The custodians of a mummy classified as cultural property may be granted standing whereas a mummy that is classified as human remains may not because direct family members would need to approach the court. The Amsterdam court characterised the dispute as one of ownership involving an object but the technical basis of the ruling released the court from having to consider the proprietary basis of the restitution claim (Liu 2017: 231). With the denial of the right to proceed with the villager committees' action for recovery, the court also by-passed having to consider the merits of the restitution claim or engage with the vexing question of provenance. A formalistic approach to the question of standing depletes substantive normativity in a way that is reminiscent of the domination of 'form' over substance in colonial settings (Glenn 2011: 252–253).

2.4.4 Jurisdictional conflict in parallel litigation

Because adjudicatory proceedings in different states have legal authority in the jurisdiction of the ruling court, concurrent litigation in multiple locales at the same time makes it harder to reach finality in a case. PrIL techniques to control this include rules on finality, rules of priority, and consolidation of related proceedings (McLachlan 2009: 59ff). In the case of the Yangchun and Dongpu village committees responsible for the care of the temple built in honour of Zhanggong Zushi, a lawsuit was initiated in China when the villagers became fearful that their restitution claim might be barred when time ran out to lodge a claim. Proceedings were instituted in December 2015 (Liu 2017: 223). The Intermediate People's Court in Sanming took almost five years to make its ruling public. By the time it did so, the village committees had also instituted proceedings in the Amsterdam District Court in the Netherlands. Proceedings against van Overeem and his companies to return the Buddha statue commenced in May 2016. The Sanming Intermediate People's Court ordered van Overeem to return the stolen relic to the two village committees, which the court considered competent to pursue their cross-border claim as active holders of ownership rights on behalf of the villagers (San Min Chu Zi 2020). The group litigation in the Netherlands in 2017 did not yield a similar result. Anticipating a ruling from the Amsterdam District Court on the spatial conflict as to which of the two laws applied, the Dutch collector argued that Dutch law conferred good title on him. Several factors torpedoed the villagers' claim. In 2018, a ruling was issued that the case could not proceed to the merits (*Amsterdam District Court, Village Committee of Yangchun and Dongpu v Oscar van Overeem* 2018).

In 2022, the Higher People's Court in Fujian Province confirmed the Sanming Intermediate People's Court's ruling. It held that the mummified monk was a stolen and illegally exported cultural relic that could be characterised in multiple ways given that it contains human remains and was made up of other materials that have been worshipped for centuries. It highlighted that the Buddha mummy embodies traditional customs and imprints of relics from the southern Fujian regions. The court determined that the villagers' 'imprint' of the Zhanggong Zushi statue was a special emotional, cultural, religious, and historical relationship of ownership.

By virtue of this relationship, its return was necessitated by the facts and the law, its historical origins and cultural traditions, and factors such as moral ethics and religious beliefs (*Oscar van Overeem, Design & Consultancy Oscar van Overeem B.V. v Yangchun Village and Dongpu Village Committees*, Fujian Province Higher People's Court, 2021 Min Min Final No. 302, 19 July 2022: sub 'On the issue of ownership'). Van Overeem was instructed to return the Buddha mummy to the village committees.

Since property rights are protected in the law of tort/delict and in property law, claims for the restitution of stolen property may either be based on rights *in rem* or on tortious liability. Neither one of these causes is tailored to cultural property as such. Property law arguments and their implications for imperial artefacts reclaimed in trans-border contexts require analysis for this reason and should not be taken to suggest that justice is located exclusively in the equality of variables such as income, resources, and property rights.

Scholarly opinions differ on the cause of action in Sanming Intermediate People's Court. Some sources indicate it was the law of tort while others refer to property (Chen 2022: 281; contra Liu 2017: 223). The court applied Chinese law to resolve the dispute and endorsed the argument put forward by the village committees that stolen property cannot be acquired in good faith under Chinese property law (Min Min Final 2022: sub 'Trial court ruling' (c)). Application of the good faith criterion was suspended based on the due diligence standard set by the 1995 UNIDROIT Convention. The Sanming Court held that embedded human remains do not qualify for good faith acquisition in view of the deep moral and ethical considerations that apply to them (Min Min Final 2022: sub 'Trial court ruling' (c)). While no duty arises for a possessor in the position of a good faith third party in Chinese law, the sale of a stolen object to a third party can lead to recovery and return by law enforcement authorities to the original owner or the fiscus if the original owner cannot be found (Article 106 Property Rights Law of the People's Republic of China, No. 62, 2007). An owner would be entitled to recover property that has been alienated to an assignee or that was disposed of by a person unauthorised to do so. Chinese judicial practice does not generally permit the good faith acquisition of cultural relics as limited merchantable goods (Liu 2017: 231). The court's line of thinking demonstrates awareness that the material is complex and more than just a cultural relic.

Claimants may request the recognition of obligations arising under foreign law or the enforcement of judicial orders issued by a foreign court. A court's recognition and application of a foreign judgment presents an opportunity to surmount the spatial limitations of a particular legal system's application and to promote decisional harmony. It is a condition for enforcement that the judgment was rendered by a 'convenient forum.' The legal outcomes reached in one jurisdiction would then have effect in another jurisdiction.

Apart from the dealer's submission that he bought a different statue and not the Zhanggong Zushi statue—a claim advanced in Amsterdam—the claims were based on the same facts. A Dutch court may be asked to recognise and apply an earlier Chinese judgment. In the hypothetical instance where a Dutch court considered it appropriate, it may decide that the Chinese court is the *forum loci delicti*—the court where the delict was committed—but in proprietary actions, it would likely give preference to proceedings in the place where the defender is domiciled (Liu 2017: 234). A Dutch court may recognise and enforce foreign judgments without full re-litigation on the merits of the case if they meet the requirements including finality, fairness, and not being contrary to the public policy of the Netherlands. A further requirement relates to the compatibility of foreign judgments either with a prior judgment rendered by a Dutch court in a dispute between the same parties, or with a foreign judgment in a dispute between the same parties, concerning the same subject matter and based on the same cause of action, provided it is also capable of being recognised in the Netherlands (Koppenol-Laforce et al. 2017).

In the claim for the return of the Zhanggong Zushi statue, the villagers did not attempt to have the final ruling enforced in the Netherlands. Article 431 of the Dutch Code of Civil Procedure requires the existence of a treaty for the mutual recognition and enforcement of civil judgments or European regulation facilitating the enforcement of foreign judgments within the territory of the Netherlands. No treaty exists between China and the Netherlands. Consequently, a favourable judgment obtained by the claimants on the substance of the case in China, rendered in accordance with Chinese law, would likely be subject to full re-litigation in the Netherlands in new proceedings on the merits. In a conflict of litigation in this factual complex, comity cannot achieve its broad aim of controlling competing outcomes.

2.4.5 Pluralism of conflicts methods: Multilateral and unilateral

Traditional choice-of-law rules are multilateral in the sense that they designate the applicable law in abstract terms regardless of whether this leads to the application of forum law or of another legal system (Hatzimihail 2021: 152). Multilateral conflicts rules co-exist with mandatory rules ('rules of immediate or necessary application') that can accommodate substantive rules that delimit their own spatial reach, whether personal or territorial. The starting point of the conflicts problem is the 'type of situation,' which the rule links to either an individual legal rule or a comprehensive legal system taken as the 'law' (Hatzimihail 2021: 154). The purpose and content of mandatory rules impart a spatial reach (rules *ratione materiae*) as well as a spatial criterion (rules *ratione loci*) (Guedj 1991: 667ff). Mandatory rules determine the scope of application of the forum's own law as a unilateral, ex post device. Other examples are found in autonomous fields, e.g., uniform rules and international business law. The rivalry between international business law and PrIL is ongoing (Hatzimihail 2021: 21, 25, 88).

PrIL's unilateral and multilateral rules co-exist alongside escape devices. In the EU, standards in respect of the law applicable to contracts have taken on the status of escape rules (Hatzimihail 2021: 175). A more universally applicable example is the public policy exception, which may result in a derogation from multilateral aprioristic rules.

2.4.6 Space time and location

When laws from different legal orders potentially apply to the same dispute in the same space, a problem of 'conflict of laws' may arise. PrIL provides a method to determine if the rules of the court or the rules of the foreign legal system will prevail when legal norms vie for application in space. A PrIL lens helps to identify the layers of restitution claims that may invite the application of public and private laws, of international and domestic laws, or of different contradicting domestic laws that compete for application. PrIL resembles a philosophy rather than a negotiation about the interrelationship between legal systems. Spatial perspectives on title claims in adjudication point to the foreign elements in cross-border cases and how they affect decision-making. As indicated at the outset, PrIL rules and methods guide adjudicatory attempts to ascertain the content of the foreign law to settle a dispute; describe the legal problem and the contents of the law as accurately as possible; and correctly apply those norms to decide the dispute in question. The process of pinpointing the legal system that has the most significant relationship with the issue in a transnational case includes a decision as to whether a given rule, issue, or set of facts should be regarded as fitting into a particular category. Choice-of-law categories mirror those of national or domestic law: Obligations, property, contract and so on. The cause of action is allocated according to spatial contacts inherent in the facts, such as e.g., the habitual residence of the person, the seat of the contract, the place where a delict occurred, or the location (*situs*) of the (corporeal) property. Few states have a specific or special choice-of-law rule for cultural property, and fewer still for enshrined human remains. Most jurisdictions resort to the residual secondary PrIL rules when there is no uniform law in the form of a convention that binds the States Party in cross-border restitution claims. On the understanding that the issue is proprietary, international civil claims for restitution are based on PrIL rules and principles relating to property transfer (Last 2007: 131; Roodt 2019: 347). Put differently, if a claim for return or a declaration of ownership is characterised as a proprietary claim in the (external) conflict of laws, the secondary legal norm that determines the applicable law is the law of the place where the property was situated at the time of transfer, or the *lex situs*. 'The law where the thing is situated' is the *lex situs* (D'Avout 2017: 1429–1436). This rule governs transactions constituting, transferring, or ending real rights in both movables and immovables. The *lex rei sitae* connects the legal question to the legal system that would supply the legal norms that would settle the question. As the spatial contact, it connects the issue to a specific legal unit in space—the location, whose legal system will then determine the issue. The connecting factor points to the governing law among potentially innumerable applicable private law rules (Muir Watt 2014: 371).

Modern civil law systems and common law systems alike favour the *lex situs* as the choice-of-law rule regarding all property. Examples are found in the 2010 Law Applicable to Foreign-related Civil Relations of the People's Republic of China (Article 37) and in Chapter 2, Section 1, Book 1 of the Greek Civil Code of 1946 (Articles 12 and 27). The generally accepted rule that the form of a transaction creating or transferring real rights is governed by the law of the place where the thing is, also forms part of Greek law.

The collision between laws from different locations or jurisdictions may be likened to a war between norms in space. The function of PrIL is to manage this pluralism on the horizontal plane (Muir Watt 2016a: 394). An international dispute involving cultural goods, or a transaction or event involving such goods, may be classified as proprietary in nature and treated as a restitutionary claim if it is seen to be concerned with the creation, content, exercise, and transfer of property rights, and the law of the state where the object is located at the time of transfer may be applied to resolve it. This would denote the category 'property transfer.' The juridical framework of circulation assumes that 'transfer' is an acquisition for value (e.g., sale, exchange, bequest, bequest by exchange, pledge, rights *in rem*, descent, delivery, auction, commission, gift, and gift by exchange). Choice-of-law rules for external conflicts are generic and do not take account of the special nature of cultural heritage. The rule for transfers of movable property, while specific in respect of the location that indicates applicable law, is unspecific as to the material it applies to. The *lex situs* rule determines the scope of the right to property but does not encourage adjudicators to look out for the nature and cultural significance of material that is being claimed. The classification of the rules, facts, or cause of action affects the result for choice-of-law, and frequently also the outcome of the case.

Public international law does not create property rights. It fulfils its role on a different plane to decide which of various, potentially conflicting, municipal rights it will protect. As part of international law, the *lex situs* rule has internationally binding effect (Staker 1987: 251). The comparative importance of intangibles has increased and poses challenges to the *lex situs* rule (Hatzimihail 2021: 181).

National courts supply different answers on the decisive moment for the *lex situs* rule. French courts favour the law of the location on the day of the claim. British courts favour the law of the country where the artefact was situated when it was acquired by its current owner. Another possibility is the so-called 'special connection' solutions, which aim to identify the legal system with the closest link to the situation in dispute. Application of the legal system with the closest link may lead to the recognition and application of the statutes of the place of origin of a stolen cultural object (*lex originis*) (Labadie 2021: para 17). The *lex furti* (the law of the place where the property was located when the theft occurred) and the *lex originis* (the law of the place where the monument is situated) have been formulated as alternatives to the *lex situs* rule.

The authority of rules of law over legal relations has limits in time which may interfere with efforts to identify the applicable law in a dispute. Inter-temporal conflicts will be discussed next.

2.4.7 The limits of legal rules in time

Savigny explained that the collision of two rules in respect of time could be approached by making one of two possible adjustments. To settle the boundary between the rules, a new rule that alters the earlier rule that has authority over that rule could be adopted. Alternatively, the legal relation of the person or transaction may be adjusted (von Savigny & Guthrie 1869: para 34, 4). In a leading article by Jan Grodecki published in 1959, he argued that PrIL's choice-of-law rules are devoid of any 'temporal dimension' and that the 'law' designated in a choice-of-law rule can only mean the current law. This current law sets temporal limits for its operation which, according to expert evidence, the courts of the foreign country in question would apply to the same set of facts at the time of reference. He identified three theoretical ways an adjudicator could solve the problem of supervening changes in applicable law: They could refuse to take account of the change; apply the rules of statutory interpretation that bind adjudicators in their own court; or consult the transitional law of the governing legal system (Grodecki 1959: 64–65). Changes in the law that purport to have retrospective effect may raise conceptual challenges, which transitional rules may overcome (Liu 2016: 93).

Transitional rules are applied in English courts as well as in courts in Europe. The hypothetical scenario of a claim to return the Dunhuang manuscripts from the UK to China is instructive on the operation of transitional rules in PrIL. This most important collection of Buddhist scriptures ever found was hidden in the Library Cave at the ancient cave temple complex of Mògāo in China. The Library Cave was one of 735 caves cut into a cliff for Buddhist meditation, each with Buddhist painted sculptures, murals, wooden architecture, relics paintings, wall coverings, statues, and steles. It housed fifteen cubic metres of manuscripts and paintings dating from the 4th to 11th century. A claim for the restitution of the manuscripts would likely proceed in a Chinese court, but if brought before an English court, the claim would likely be ruled out of time. Traditional Chinese law did not contain prescription or statutory limitation rules. Rules of this kind were considered contrary to traditional Chinese morality. Under contemporary Chinese law, limitations may apply, but Chinese courts will not initiate the application of limitations rules; a plea to this effect must be entered. Claims regarding damage to state property are not subject to any limitation period unless commercial management has been delegated (Art 170, Opinion for Trial Use of the Supreme People's Court on Questions of Implementation of General Principles of Civil Law of the PRC). In an hypothetical case before an English court, the relevant transitional rule would be found in Chinese civil law. For cases accepted after 1 January 1987, if the civil conduct occurred before 1987, the laws and policies that applied at the time of the conduct, when the Dunhuang manuscripts were transferred, will apply. The rule states that if there is no concrete provision in the law of the time nor a clear rule, then the General Principles of Civil Law may be applied by analogy, meaning contemporary Chinese law could potentially apply. Contemporary Chinese civil law includes the administrative rule that no valid title passes for stolen state-owned property or cultural relics (Liu 2016: 94, 97). The application of the governing law identified by the choice-of-law technique of PrIL presents a choice between the application of only the substantive legal rules of the foreign legal system, and the application of the entire foreign system, including its transitional rules. The latter that are formed when legislation is enacted that restricts the application of an old law or revokes existing legal rights to correct past mistakes will invite the application of more recent laws in transnational disputes. Evidently, the operation of the transitional rules of PrIL may be conducive to the restitution of sacred cultural material.

Former colonies' courts may apply transitional rules if precedents exist that clarify the temporal scope of a transitional rule. A transitional clause in a constitution or a contract may permit a law of a later date to be invoked if, at the time of removal, the rule was obscure. Constitutional or other rules that condition or limit the temporal scope of legal rules or presumptions about statutory interpretation may need to be consulted (Morris 1966: 422; Liu 2016: 93).

Transitional rules are significant for our purposes since they can modify the application of those choice-of-law rules. They determine the reach of the applicable provisions through time, but the corrections will only take effect with a view to the future. When PrIL is called upon to determine the area of operation of a rule of law after the localisation of the connecting factor has changed, the adjudicator faces a choice between the space dimension and the temporal dimension. Grodecki suggests that the space dimension will predominate (Grodecki 1959: 58). The approach adopted by the Sanming Court confirms this. The court pinpointed the moment when the Buddha mummy was stolen from the temple (the *lex furti*) and held that Chinese law governed ownership. The time at which the legal fact occurred was not interpreted as the time of the first transaction, the last transaction, the exhibition, or the commencement of legal proceedings. The court considered the relevant legal fact to be the theft and applied the law of the place where the property was located when it was stolen. The court's interpretation was guided by the purposes and objectives of the 1970 UNESCO and 1995 UNIDROIT Conventions to protect cultural property and promote the return of illicitly trafficked cultural property (Min Min Final 2022: sub 'On issues concerning the applicable law'). This policy approach was considered appropriate despite the actual dates of the transactions and ratifications of pertinent conventions. Had the Dutch court evaluated the merits of the restitution claim in respect of the Zhanggong Zushi mummy, it would have had to consider the apparent non-retrospective application of pertinent cultural property and heritage conventions. The Netherlands issued implementation legislation for the 1970 UNESCO Convention on the Means of Prohibiting and Preventing the Illicit Import, Export and Transfer of Ownership of Cultural Property in 2009 (Uitvoeringswet UNESCO-verdrag 1970, Staatsblad 2009, no. 255; incorporated into the Dutch Heritage Act of 2016). The 1995 UNIDROIT Convention was signed but never ratified by the Netherlands. However, the most important features of the 1995 UNIDROIT Convention apply as domestic Dutch law in full alignment with EU secondary law (Directive 2014/60/EU on the Return of Cultural Objects Unlawfully Removed from the Territory of a Member State and amending Regulation (EU)). This route is known as the UNESCO-plus option, because the UNESCO Convention is implemented, and the due care standard set in the EU Regulation is incorporated into domestic law.

The application of the *lex furti* facilitates return of stolen cultural property, whereas application of the law of the place where the post-theft sale had taken place, the law of Hong Kong, would invoke the market overt principle. This principle was revoked in England in the Sale of Goods (Amendment) Act of 1994, but it continues to confer title to stolen or looted goods upon sale, thereby protecting buyers of stolen or looted goods from claims for the return of stolen cultural heritage from China (Hong Kong Sale of Goods Ordinance s 24 ('SOGO'); in general Yap 2008). The SOGO still effectively enables title laundering by helping collectors establish clear title if the intermediary purchases property in accordance with the market they attended if they had acted in good faith. 'Purchased in Hong Kong' is widely understood to be coded language for 'illegally obtained' (Gallagher 2017: 489). Applying a relaxed dispensation for trade in cultural property, the place where the transaction occurred legalises the trade in stolen cultural property (Min Min Final 2022: sub 'Trial court ruling' (b) and sub 'On issues concerning the applicable law'). Other transit jurisdictions besides Hong Kong also accommodate versions of market overt or leave it unqualified (e.g., Article 194 Japanese Civil Code; Article 799 Mexican Civil Federal Code).

The UNCITRAL Convention on Contracts for the International Sale of Goods, commonly known as the Vienna Convention, took effect in Hong Kong on 1 December 2022. It permits parties to international sale of goods contracts governed by Hong Kong law to expressly disclaim any application of the Vienna Convention and New Sale of Goods (United Nations Convention) Ordinance (Cap. 641) to their sale (see UNCITRAL Convention Article 6). This legislation does not replace the market overt principle, however. The rule of law in Hong Kong has been compromised and arbitrary governmental power can no longer be effectively reined in. British judges resigned their positions at the court of final appeal as a result (Hawkins 2024). The effect of judges of the colonial powers continuing to sit in former colonial territories on questions such as which law ought to apply to resolve disputes, remains critically under-researched.

Crimes against cultural property and heritage must be seen in a broader context that encompasses questions relating to ownership, title, restitution, de-accession, disposal, relocation, liability, and respect for sacred cultural material and artefactual and ancestral human remains. Attempts to hold a state responsible for the crimes committed by a previous regime raise perennial questions of ethics, politics, and law (Zeidler 2016: 207). The forum may decline to extend recognition to foreign retrospective laws on public policy grounds, either by virtue of PrIL or PublIL (*Estate of Feivel (otherwise Faivel) Pikelny (Ex parte Max Pikelny and Others*) (unreported), The Times, 30 June and 1 July 1955 (1955)). The House of Lords declined to recognise a Nazi decree going back to 1941, which sought to strip German Jews of their German nationality (*Oppenheimer v Cattermole* [1976] AC 249). Non-retrospectivity encourages interpretations to the effect that the rules on state succession in the context of decolonisation do not give rise to any obligation to return cultural objects removed from the colonised territory by the former colonial ruler, let alone by a third country, and cannot provide a basis for restitution claims (Lubina 2009: 141; Jakubowski 2015: 140). The problem of conflict of laws in time—the temporality in PrIL—ceases to be one of private law alone in matters of state succession. Treaties concluded with territories in Africa after the reconfiguration of 1885 in the 'Congo' or 'Berlin' Act did not enable state succession to cultural property and archives. Later, former colonial powers and their museums insisted on excluding cultural objects from the principle of state succession in the 1983 Vienna Convention on the Succession of States in Respect of State Property, Archives, Debt as well (Vrdoljak 2008: 200; Byrne 2015: 11). Importatntly, however, a state governed by the rule of law may legitimately bring criminal proceedings against those who have committed crimes under a former regime that was in power prior to the state succession. The courts in the state that succeeded the former regime take the place of courts that existed previously and they may interpret and apply the law in force at the material time in the light of the principles governing a state subject to the rule of law (*Streletz, Kessler and Krenz v Germany* [GC] Application Nos. 34044/96 and 2 others, ECHR 2001-II paras 74, 77–83; *Vasiliauskas v Lithuania* [GC] Application No. 35343/05, ECHR 20 October 2015 paras 158–159). State practice that tolerates or encourages acts that have been deemed criminal offences under national or international legal instruments will not protect those who have acted with impunity under the ECHR.

2.5 Trafficking and title laundering

Some national laws reserve high standards only for specific categories of objects and for persons with specialist knowledge (Italian Civil Code Article 1147). Some legal systems transpose treaty obligations as questions of risk of damage, compensable damage, loss, or injury, whereas others focus on strengthening the seizure and confiscation powers of the state or attempt to balance adequate substantive protection with procedural guarantees of fair process to third parties acting in good faith and their property rights (Manacorda 2011: 45). A more stable regime is in place in Belgium, where the rights of dispossessed owners of movable goods are extended (Book 3 (Property Law) of the Belgian Civil Code, entry into force 1 September 2021). Original owners may reclaim a stolen or lost object from current holders within three years of a theft or loss without having to reimburse the purchase price to current holders who bought the object at auction or from a trader in the art market.

Given the legal diversity prevailing in this area, the application of proprietary conflict rules may facilitate the title laundering of objects or collections stolen, looted, or illegally exported from places under former colonial rule on the demand-side of the international art trade. Title is 'laundered' if a court permits a good faith purchaser who bought from a thief or from a seller who lacks authority to sell to gain title upon conclusion of the transaction. The difficulty of tracking smuggled objects that move through transit states renders alternative sources of law, such as conventions, more appropriate than the *lex rei sitae* choice-of-law rule. Since the *situs* of goods in transit is unknown, there is no relevant ascertainable court to which this matter can be referred, and the forum is likely to apply its own law (Schoeman et al., 2013: para 152). Problems arise when the fact that the goods are being trafficked remains undisclosed at the time proceedings are raised.

Under the *lex situs* rule, the time of the transfer of movables assumes importance. However, where theft and looting weigh in on the facts of the case, the juridical framework of exception would take wrongful removal as the relevant moment. It is hardly a secret that the *lex rei sitae* encourages laundering of stolen art through jurisdictions that give generous protection to good faith purchasers. The juridical framework of circulation and that of exception differ and function independently. Because most cultural material removed during the colonial era is located in the territories of the former colonial masters, and location is such a crucial connecting factor in the choice-of-law rule for the validity of transfers of property in PrIL, the choice of applicable law can be skewed in favour of European law, while the law of the place where the material was taken or where the source community is based is left unaccounted for.

No order for restitution was given in *Winkworth v Christie Manson and Wood* ([1980] Ch 496) because the aspects that pointed in the direction of the juridical framework of exception were not considered to be sufficiently compelling (Roodt & Carey Miller 2013: 1ff). The court settled for the application of Italian law to determine the validity of the sale of stolen netsuke in Italy without considering that Italian law functioned to 'filter' title in the circumstances of the case. The court did not consider that 'transfer' in the conflicts rule could encompass conversion and theft. The unintended consequence of the court's readiness to support trade and exchange was to ensure the circulation of the stolen netsuke. Tainted titles can be laundered through norms protecting good faith purchasers in 'intermediary' or 'filter' states or through the expiry of limitation periods, and then sold to private individuals, institutional collectors, or established art trade companies (Council of Europe, *Explanatory Report to the Council of Europe Convention on Offences relating to Cultural Property*, 19 May 2017: para 31). If the defender is a non-EU domiciliary, the question arises as to which forum guarantees the right to a fair trial and has a sufficient connection with the property in question. It remains an open question whether the *Winkworth* court would have been more amenable to applying the public policy exception if material that is neither exchangeable nor replaceable, such as artefactual human remains, had been at issue.

Common conflict rules that defer to global markets cannot refocus PrIL's function in relation to cultural trafficking and title laundering. Mechanisms are needed to restrain the law's deference to the commercial imperatives that predominate in the art trade. To this end, the juridical framework of exception must be brought into the open to protect the intangible value of smuggled material. This framework is constituted by international humanitarian law of armed conflicts, international criminal law, and rules regarding offences relating to cultural property and heritage. If the juridical framework of exception remains unacknowledged, and its public policy underpinnings unarticulated, the public policy exception will not be deployed as needed and the standard classifications in PrIL will preclude value-based substantive arguments.

The PrIL rule for the validity of the 'transfer' of colonial artefacts to colonial agents, caretakers, and archaeologists—the law where the artefacts were situated before they were removed, applied as the law of the place where the artefacts were located at the time of the 'transfer'—facilitates global trade and exchange of goods, objects, ideas, and more on the marketplaces and art markets of the world. In the regional setting of the EU, the objective of market integration is to facilitate commerce and remove barriers created by having to manage diversity (Ruiz Abou-Nigm 2019: 384). The extended application given to general commercial law rules in ownership claims means that claims arising from the illicit trafficking of cultural objects brought by dispossessed or deprived owners frequently fail when the validity of the transfer of valuable stolen cultural objects is disputed. The finding of the Amsterdam District Court that the village committees lacked legal personality was an implicit prioritisation of the commercial and proprietary interests in cultural objects above their sacred nature and character, and a value choice in favour of the jurisdictional framework of circulation over the framework of exception. Decisions based purely on technicality and procedure preclude any interrogation of the title laundering mechanism at work in antiquities sales in Hong Kong. In many other instances ordinary rules governing transfers tend to apply in the absence of special conflict rules and uniform law. Purchasers on global markets rely on the unpredictability of a colonial provenance for reassurance instead of their due diligence (Stahn 2023: 48). Yet global trade cannot serve as a rationale for the evolution of normativity in PrIL in colonial contexts. In the context of colonial-era removal of cultural heritage, the connotations of 'circulation' are, and deserve to be, perceived as a 'vice' (Effiboley 2020: 70). The juridical framework of circulation enhances the effects of liberal capitalism and economic expansion. Social and moral responsibility frequently give way to this framework.

While the circulation of ethnographic material may be a function of commerce, assumptions that sacred material and human remains must be permitted to circulate erode PrIL theory and PrIL adjudication and practice. If the framework of exception is applied, the *lex furti* can govern the question of legal title and ensure a just outcome. Being unclear as to which framework to invoke, or when, will mean justice in normative conflicts is out of courts' reach.

2.6 Uniform standards for the illicit trafficking in culture

Firming up control over present-day illicit trafficking of sacred cultural material are the standards laid down in the 1970 UNESCO and 1995 UNIDROIT Conventions. States Party to the 1970 UNESCO Convention undertake to prohibit the import of cultural property stolen from a museum, a religious or secular public monument, or similar institution in another State Party after the Convention enters into force for the States concerned, provided the property is documented in the inventory of that institution. A State Party may seek return of illegally exported, removed, or stolen cultural property imported into another State Party, if it is listed in the inventory of a museum or a religious or public monument, after the Convention's entry into force in both States. The unfortunate reality is that, by their nature or by virtue of the conditions in which they are protected, sacred property and religious artefacts privately owned by monasteries, temples, churches, or other monuments are uniquely vulnerable to illegal trafficking (European Commission DG Home Affairs, *Study on Preventing and Fighting Illicit Trafficking in Cultural Goods in the European Union*, October 2011: 21; Schneider 2016: 151). The Holy Doors of

St. Anastasios, which used to separate the sanctuary from the nave in the Orthodox Church of Cyprus, fell into the hands of traffickers between 1974 and 1980, for example. The decade-long delay before the Kanazawa College of Art in Japan returned them in 2021 was due to the absence of evidence in the form of an inventory or images, which would have been crucial to pursue a legal claim (Giorgallis 2023: 166–167).

Article 5 of the 1995 UNIDROIT Convention empowers a Contracting State to request the court or other competent authority of another Contracting State to order the return of a cultural object illegally exported from the requesting State's territory, but leaves crucial questions concerning intangible cultural heritage unanswered. The legal standard exemplified in Article 4 is that stolen cultural objects are to be returned if an owner claims return. Another one of the conventions' stronger points is its attempt to define 'lawful transaction.' Article 4 confers an autonomous meaning on 'due diligence' to ensure that cultural objects and heritage can be bought or sold lawfully, while aiming to narrow the scope for trafficking in stolen cultural objects and for the misuse of good faith defences. It pinpoints the generic moment at which the possessor's diligence is assessed (which differs across legal systems) at the compensation stage when restitution is indicated. The definition of due diligence is captured in a list of 'common minimal legal rules' or objective factors such as price, mode of payment, database checks, and documents accompanying goods. Courts are expected to assess the criteria and circumstances within the scope of Article 4 in combination (Roodt 2024: 565–566, 570–576). Buyers and possessors are often unaware that they must undertake investigative steps to ascertain the veracity and accuracy of all provenance information prior to purchase, or that they must return stolen cultural objects to dispossessed owners if their conduct falls short of the due diligence test. Certain events *ought* to heighten judicial scrutiny of a buyer, dealer, or collector's due diligence. These events include civil unrest in the country of origin, looting in the source area of the antiquities, opaque histories, and false, inconsistent, or misleading provenance of antiquities; sales by exposed and named unethical dealers, forgers, and anyone willing to sell forgeries; and red flags of the Nazi era and colonial era. An abbreviated provenance tends to accompany objects' entry on the art market and many art market participants do not share known information about the chain of ownership.

The principal representatives of internal art markets and antiques fairs in Europe and the US, such as the European Fine Arts Fund, lobbied fiercely against ratification of the 1995 UNIDROIT Convention by any host state of the big art fairs (Prott 2009: 202). There is a slow but steady growth in the signatures and ratifications needed for a concerted international effort to uphold due diligence standards and procedures.

For disputes concerning artefacts that were misappropriated before the UNESCO Convention entered into force—i.e., nearly all of the claims presented today—a new possessor gains valid title after a good faith acquisition or merely by the passing of time (Campfens 2021: 174). Since the UK did not ratify the 1995 UNIDROIT Convention, it relies on the common law standard for property law. 'Common law' is generally understood as the 'law of England and the United

States in as much as these systems are unchanged by statutes or special doctrines.' The common law differs in crucial aspects from the uniform standard by assuming the owner transacts in good faith. A court applying English law may need to consider the *nemo dat* rule of English law, that no one can give what they do not have. The rule casts a shadow over the British Museum's title and the 1816 Parliamentary process. A court applying Greek law, on the other hand, may struggle with the historical timeline of the principle of state ownership of antiquities between the fall of Constantinople in 1453 and the legal uncertainty concerning state ownership from 1801 to 1833. The Greek vesting law only took effect decades after Elgin's team took the Marbles.

The 'disconnection clause' in the 1995 UNIDROIT Convention on Stolen or Illegally Exported Cultural Objects (Article 13 para. 3) enables the so-called 'UNESCO-plus' option. It permits Contracting States which are EU Members to apply the internal rules of the EU in their relations with each other, instead of the Convention's provisions, whose application coincides with that of EU rules (ILC Study Group Report 2006: 61). In a hypothetical case in a court in Amsterdam, the global 1995 UNIDROIT Convention would be considered alongside the sphere of application of the interregional Directive 2014/60/EU, both of which form part of Dutch law but are effective only after the illegal exportation had occurred. If it is accepted that the scope of application of these legal instruments did not pose hurdles for the sake of argument, the possessor would be expected to provide proof of his due diligence at the time of purchase. At the very least, the court would consider the character of the parties, the price, the mode of payment, whether databases for stolen art had been checked, and whether the exporter had obtained a proper permit from any of the organisations designated by the State Administration of Cultural Heritage in China.

2.7 Complications for justice in internal/external conflicts in colonial settings

While structured as tools for resolving disputes, PrIL techniques structure one's thinking about transnational disputes (Ruiz Abou-Nigm 2019: 366–267). 'Interspatial law' opens the door to plural values. 'Hybrids' occur and are accommodated, for courts can accept that no foreign claim (or indeed, institution) will be given effect in another forum in the exact same way that it would in a court in its own territory. Ideally, an informed debate about values, the direction they provide to correcting the historical injustices of the past in the present, and the theoretical questions arising on the structural level will be possible. An understanding of the interspatial application of law, and how the application of Indigenous law was repressed, supports the 'unlearning' of a colonial mindset. However different the applicable law may be from its own, the court 'accepts' the application of the foreign law provided the threshold of tolerance is not crossed (Muir Watt 2016a: 400).

Interspatial conflict among competing laws is evident between western and non-western laws on the domestic and international planes. In a traditional, external 'conflicts of law' paradigm, assertions of authority by entities other than the state do not constitute 'law'—the judgment on legitimacy is conducted ex ante. In a pluralist paradigm, however, there are no *a priori* judgments that exclude claims of non-state law to govern and the conclusion is different (Muir Watt 2016a: 401). The increased visibility of non-state authority and heterogeneous forms of law-making contributes to the intensifying crisis in the legitimacy of PrIL. Positivist conceptions of what law is add to the pressures mounting on the conflicts paradigm, including in the world of international commerce (Hatzimihail 2021: 5). The challenges of title laundering and cultural trafficking loom large, more especially when complex colonial histories veil the dynamics bound up in their origins.

2.7.1 Customary law in 'internal' conflicts

The origin of normative pluralism has been sought in the conflicts and overlaps between social spaces and ordering in the 19th century (Oh 2018: 427–429). Not every Asian state embraced the plurality of normative orders when the West espoused legal pluralism, leading Oh to conclude that westerners developed another set of rules for interacting with non-western nations (Oh 2018: 420, 424). However, new primary, substantive rules cannot always explain what happened when Europeans colonised Africa. The phenomenon of conflicting normative structures deserves more in-depth reflection in colonial contexts. After all, it was possible to circumvent practical engagement with a law that is 'foreign' to the court designated to issue the ruling. The lens we use to look at legal foundations and legal practices must keep track of the application and non-application of different domestic systems of law in the lifetimes of people and their cultural heritage.

Courts in the colonial territories developed views on which law should apply to resolve disputes in each individual case, but the delineation of jurisdiction in the colonial era encouraged structural bias in their evaluation of the suitability of local Indigenous law (Bennett 1980: 133–134). British judges acted as final arbiters of customary law, often without having access to relevant information on the customary law of the communities they were responsible for. Their knowledge was second-hand at best. They were entitled to request evidence of disputed or questionable rules *mero motu*, but their perceptions coloured the application of Indigenous law (Thielecke & Geißdorf 2021: 157). To stabilise societies in the territories of the colonies, the courts considered it necessary to maintain the elevated status of the received legal systems to maintain social order and peace and promote their plans regarding commercial trade.

Any authentic administration of customary law in colonial spaces would require adjudicators to take account of constant and imperceptible changes in shifts in customary law rules, for they derive from social practice. This did not happen in the British colonies. When legal norms with inter-personal application conflicted, British court officials would make use of 'connecting factors' to identify the governing law. Race was the personal factor by which an artificial separation of cultures was maintained under relevant colonial policies. Theory has not caught up with the detrimental effects of this approach essentially because the approach was disguised (Bennett 1980: 131). A theoretical framework premised on jurisdictional competition and adjudicatory dominance offers a convincing explanation for the treatment of customary law in former British colonial territories.

The received systems of European law were reserved for application to white officials or settlers, while customary law was exclusively applied to Africans and relegated to a secondary position. State authority to predetermine the race of persons compounded the disadvantages for the local population. Whereas it was permissible in some colonies to change one's personal law, in Africa this freedom was curtailed. African nationalists resented the basic inequality in reserving 'European' law and suppressing 'non-European' law, which contradicted the national ideals held by independent African governments. Legislation eroded the space in which customary law operated (Bennett 1980: 133–134). The compliance checks associated with the standards of the rule of law further undermined the substance of customary law (Grenfell 2013: 159). Former British colonies like South Africa and Nigeria introduced the so-called 'repugnancy proviso' through the received English law in the 19th century. It required that no rule of customary law should be recognised if it is 'repugnant to natural justice or morality.' It functioned as an exclusory rule. Although the repugnancy proviso applied in a very different context than the public policy exception in PrIL, it raised very similar problems to those presenting when the external public policy rule is applied in PrIL (Leslie 1977: 117–118). Most African states repealed their repugnancy provisos upon achieving independence because it used foreign standards to assess the validity of African customary rules and was considered a remnant of colonialism. In South African law, the Law of Evidence Amendment Act of 1988 treated African customary law in the same way as it did foreign law in certain respects (South African Law Commission, Issue Paper 4 Project 90 1996: 33). Section 1 of the Law of Evidence Amendment Act set out relevant choice-of-law rules but made the application of customary law subject to a repugnancy proviso. It was repealed by the Justice Laws Rationalisation Act 18 of 1996. Today, South African courts apply customary law subject to the 1996 Constitution and any legislation that sets out the sphere of operation of Indigenous customary law systems. Difficulties remain with proving the content of the customary law rules and applying them as they were intended to be applied.

In the wake of the Berlin Congress, the Protectorate Act of 1886 granted the Kaiser authority to regulate and govern the newly developing German colonial territories without the involvement of the parliament (Thielecke & Geißdorf 2021: 155). Section 4 provided that the law of the German Reich applied to the local population only if the Kaiser decreed so, but no such decree was issued. The local customs and traditions continued to govern the private law relationships of local peoples although Imperial decrees were passed on various individual issues. Colonial officials enjoyed wide discretion to formulate and pass their own laws and to consult judges in their district or province. This introduced a risk of prejudice that rendered the law unpredictable. German law applied in most 'mixed legal disputes' that arose between local and non-local people, including commercial trade disputes. Germany attempted to engage private commercial law to resolve internal conflicts between western law and customary law but their efforts caused complications. For example, the German government left the regulation of overseas trade and land acquisitions to private commercial and colonial trading companies. They negotiated land ownership and other rights with local rulers and made use of one-sided 'contracts.' The representatives of the local population had limited knowledge of the European legal concepts that featured in 'letters of protection' issued to colonial trading companies and in private 'land purchases.' Sacred material and ethnographic collections were illegally acquired from locals and sold.

Western concepts of property rights follow the Eurocentric blueprint based on individual ownership. Societies that value individuals cannot confer absolute property rights. As soon as any right impinges on another's legally protected interests, limitation is called for. This tension between ownership and obligation is the 'essence of property.' Obligations to other owners, non-owners, and the community ensure that property rights function in ways that shape social relationships in just and defensible ways (Singer 2000: 204, 207–209). The responsibility to protect cultural property would lodge with the community under customary law. The communal ownership attached to sacred objects, shrines, and intangibles is in many respects incommensurable with individual ownership. These rights are embodied collectively and are not (permanently) transferable. Colonial administrations and private European 'buyers' conceded on occasion that certain legal rights could not be sold or transferred, demonstrating awareness that the communal property status of certain material hindered transfer into private custody and ownership where the European civil law code conception of ownership did not prevail (Thielecke & Geißdorf 2021: 156). When the application of the local law would be disadvantageous to the commercial interests of the metropole, it would not be applied. Since the usual rules governing transfers of movable property operate along a property paradigm today, expedient classifications of stolen or illicitly transferred collection items as property that defer to the market are highly likely to frustrate the restitution claim. The operation of choice-of-law rules that have not been adjusted to fit their colonial context will be stunted and classificatory complexities will befuddle the claim.

Western property norms may govern restitution claims brought before European or American courts, but they do not protect property from state control. In addition, they leave postcolonial constellations of international law unaccounted for. Colonial subjectivities can be expected to colour decisions about the definition, status, and protection of identifiable human remains encased in cultural property and the classifications of cultural relics, human remains, and natural or legal person among legal systems. Racialised ideas attach to them.

PrIL's capacity for moral outrage may end up being smothered by its dogmatism. Kollewijn opposed the indiscriminate application of ordinary choice-of-law rules in 'inter-regional' cases because these rules might have been formed by mummified thinking that does not heed the requirements of international co-existence. He maintained that PrIL's connecting factors could guide, but not indiscriminately assign, legal relationships to legal systems in a pre-determined manner. This insight was borne from his realisation that PrIL rules presuppose a certain equality between potentially applicable laws from the East and the West that was absent from colonial law which referred to 'inter-racial conflict of laws' as 'quasi-international private law' (Kollewijn 1951: 313). He registered outrage over German and French colonial theory that maintained the superiority of the law of the colonising state while refusing to grant the rules of the colonies the status of law . He argued that, even when courts and legislatures apply the unilateral method which prioritises their own public policy, they still needed to consider the views, values, and principles of foreign communities (Banu 2018: 131-132; 134).

So much of the scholarly discourse on colonialism and decolonisation omits the inter-spatial conflicts dimension. An important reason for this is the prominence enjoyed by human rights argument. The challenges raised by a plurality of legal systems and normative orders in colonial space are easily overlooked. Whether dogma should be allowed to block PrIL's transposition into the constructive action needed to solve the challenges posed by space time and ontology in complex restitution claims is a question adjudicators, policymakers, and scholars cannot sidestep.

2.7.2 Internal conflicts and human rights argument

Heritage fulfils human rights functions at jurisdictional pressure points that include access and participation rights for Indigenous peoples (Tünsmeyer 2020: 341). This explains why the narrative of individual rights is so prominent in areas of international heritage action. Human rights frameworks have a decisive role to play in questions of access to justice and *locus standi*. Human rights argument also features in the case studies and deserves analysis for this reason alone. However, it is also necessary to determine if human rights doctrine and practice can remedy the removal of sacred cultural material during the colonial era. Could PrIL refine the human rights argument or will the methods, tools, and techniques it offers for internal and external conflict of laws be absorbed by human rights law?

Human rights frameworks have been roped in with regards to normative conflicts between western law and Indigenous customary law in restitution claims. Jiménez proposes using interpersonal conflicts rules to identify the law to be applied when Indigenous peoples and other minorities lodge claims to cultural property located within the territory of the state in which they live. The scope of her proposal appears to include claims from those who produced or received sacred cultural property, as the sacred is not exempt from the operation of the system she proposes. She submits that Latin American legal systems are obligated to consider cultural diversity and legal pluralism and to recognise Indigenous peoples' human rights at national levels. As an ethical imperative resembling a constitutional imperative, cultural diversity cannot be separated from respect for human dignity. She highlights the need for external conflict rules that apply in an international context to be fully aligned with fundamental human rights and argues that the same applies to internal or interpersonal conflicts rules that designate Indigenous law for application (Jiménez 2019: 446).

The system proposed by Jiménez focuses on the application of connecting factors in internal conflict of laws to accommodate pluralism. She argues in favour of a choice-of-law rule to settle tensions between states and cultural communities in internal conflicts over cultural property:

> If an object of cultural value for an indigenous people (community) is (to be) returned to the national territory (of the state it inhabits), the final destination of such object is governed by the law of that indigenous people (community), unless that indigenous people (community) decide that it be governed by the national law of the state. (Jiménez 2019: 450)

Jiménez proposes that, in claims for the return of Indigenous peoples' cultural property, the bases of their group identity should determine the governing law. Personal connecting factors such as an individual's association with a cultural group and the laws of that group are to be used to identify the normative systems and dispute resolution mechanisms governing their cultural property (Jiménez 2019: 442). She maintains that interpersonal law rules can secure 'material justice' in the realm of human rights if a 'result-oriented' approach is followed, while formal justice can be achieved through conflict of laws (Jiménez 2019: 439, 444, 447). Favouring the integration of ethnic or religious law into the legal systems of Latin American states based on a human rights model, Jiménez calls for the formulation of new choice-of-law rules that would be justifiable on cultural diversity or legal pluralism grounds and would permit the application of ethnic or religious law based on ethnic and religious affiliation as connecting factors.

Colonial law facilitated the dominant position of certain forms of western legal authority by making use of the doctrine of interpersonal law. Could this strategy work in combination with a fundamental rights test? The human rights model uses all-encompassing and emancipatory language, but can it alleviate the tensions in the structure of the state and its domestic law that can complicate the issue of who defines cultural property? Depending on the tier of government involved the value ascribed to cultural material may differ A convincing determination of whose legal system should decide the issue of possessory rights will need to consider the implications of translating group claims into individual rights for the realisation of self-governance (Lixinski 2019b: 606). Ultimately, the question is whether cultural autonomy can be achieved through party autonomy as part of a human rights model.

Jiménez argues for freedom of choice based on the principle of party autonomy. She proposes that individual members of Indigenous groups should be permitted to choose or reject their own customs as the legal system that governs their affairs in litigated cases, since this idea supports notionally universal principles of human rights that align with individual autonomy. If claimants are free to choose between the application of state law or the law of the Indigenous group the claimant is affiliated with, the authority to decide to apply or refuse to apply Indigenous law is removed from the hands of a judiciary that has colonialist sympathies. A basic requirement of the proposal is that any interpersonal conflict rule conforms to relevant international human rights instruments so that it can be accommodated at the constitutional level once the necessary changes have been made (Jiménez 2019: 437–438).

Individual autonomy is the theoretical foundation for the conflicts system in the latest 'postmodern' perspective (Hatzimihail 2021: 196). The ability for parties to choose the court or law applicable to their dispute encapsulates a broad range of techniques or PrIL rules (Mills 2009: 291). The regulation of European PrIL features party autonomy in questions of jurisdiction and the law applicable to contract, family law, and succession. Party autonomy is also recognised and applied internationally in the 2005 Hague Convention on Choice of Court Agreements. In a provision addressing the application of Indigenous law and jurisdiction, the 2016 American Declaration on the Rights of Indigenous Peoples establishes the right of Indigenous peoples to make use of their own juridical systems and customs. Article XXII states:

> '1. Indigenous peoples have the right to promote, develop and maintain their institutional structures and their distinctive customs, spirituality, traditions, procedures, practices and, in the cases where they exist, juridical systems or customs, in accordance with international human rights standards.
> 2. Indigenous law and legal systems shall be recognised and respected by national, regional and international legal systems.
> 3. Matters concerning indigenous individuals or their rights or interests in the jurisdiction of each State shall be conducted in such a way as to afford indigenous individuals the right to full representation with dignity and equality before the law. Consequently, they are entitled, without discrimination, to equal protection and benefit of the law, including the use of linguistic and cultural interpreters.
> 4. States shall take effective measures in conjunction with indigenous peoples to ensure the implementation of this article.'

Notably, the Declaration does not offer members of Indigenous communities a choice in respect of the forum, or the applicable law.

Cultures overlap and change. In the complex conglomerates of modern society, people are part of multiple groups and communities and participate in multiple cultures at once (Ruiz Abou-Nigm 2019: 386). Permeable lines divide groups along members' place of residence, social background, genetic dispositions, and individual preferences and values (Holtorf 2020: 311). Importantly, individuals are not separate entities but persons-in-community who are conditioned by and dependent on their relationships with others, and their multiple cultural identities may conflict. The moment several cultural property regimes start operating separately, new clashes over the changing global public interests different types of property are designed to serve, will ensue.

In complex colonial contexts conflicts of law may occur in both directions simultaneously. Neither internal conflicts rules nor external conflicts rules are readily transferable to these contexts. A system of conflicts rules predicated on ascriptive markers of group identity such as ethnicity, or on non-ascriptive markers such as religion or choice, may rub against the hierarchy of application of international, national, and individual sources of normativity in the domestic sphere. A significant risk exists that these connecting factors will not fully align with the hierarchy of application of international, national, and individual sources of normativity in the national sphere (Mills 2009: 293).

An ordering by tribal, community or religious affiliation, rather than by national boundaries, challenges the notion of the universality of state structures and requires active reconciliation with international law as it is generally understood (Glenn 2011: 254–255, 270). The perceived preferential treatment of certain groups based on ascriptive criteria like ethnicity, tribal affinity, or race, could trigger political opposition in societies marked by ethno-nationalism. Policy objections surfacing in the wake of identity politics may potentially derail the realisation of fundamental rights. Categorising people in terms of their religion or origins can generate competition among religions, which will destabilise conceptions of the religious or cultural value of complex material. The recognition of cultural diversity in internal conflicts will not be a natural consequence of attempts to decant complex histories into tribal affinity, ethnicity, and religion when normative conflicts between the laws of various communities must be resolved. One of the problems with choice-of-law rules for external conflicts is that they tend to be generic and take no account of the special nature of cultural heritage. Similarly structured rules in internal conflicts about heritage objects seem unlikely to succeed for the same reason. If connecting factors invite cultural bias, cross-cultural conflict could ensue in the global governance debate, which would make a common understanding of the role and function of sacred cultural property harder to achieve. Special account needs to be taken of inter-state cultural diversity in internal conflicts without triggering ethnocentric conflicts or mummified notions of a 'clash of civilisations.' A strategy that singles out 'connecting factors' for choice of law based on cultural or tribal affinity, ethnicity, and religion is unlikely to stabilise multi-cultural societies. Attribution of human remains to specific ethnic groups does not guarantee repatriations. Societies in cultural transition can find support in the recognition of their autonomy in the constitutional rules of the state in question, but where constitutional mechanisms fail, one group's cultural autonomy may subordinate the group culture of another. While party autonomy may support Indigenous control over the care of their cultural heritage it will not guarantee cultural autonomy for groups; it will need the steadying force of public law and the public policy exception when internal conflicts arise in restitution claims to sacred cultural material.

Human rights norms can be expected to continue to surface in debates about restitution, but it would be too much to expect them to resolve ownership disputes. Human rights language re-inforces a distinction between public and private. This restricts the space in which communities and collectives may situate themselves and makes it harder for them to achieve their aspiration to govern their own resources (Lixinski 2019b: 601, 608). The fragmentation caused by the distinctly separate development of international cultural heritage law from human rights norms further diminishes the likelihood of successful restitution claims grounded in unrefined human rights doctrine. While there is broad agreement that protection must be extended to cultural diversity and the freedom of communities to protect the way of life they choose, the bigger challenge is to recognise that protection of the right to culture cannot protect against cultural intolerance and conflict. The market does not automatically ensure the security of human resources, and it needs rules and institutions to establish and promote it (Christodoulidis 2018: 15; Supiot 2007: 94).

Cultural rights tend to be weak and are unlikely to trump political and socio-economic rights when it comes to protecting the interests of future generations. Attempts to ground Indigenous peoples' control over their cultural heritage in 'group culture' deserve to be treated with caution. Unintended consequences may increase the risks they are exposed to (Lixinski 2019b: 567). The normative systems of Indigenous groups require recognition within a state's territory in ownership claims, which implies recognition of cultural diversity. Yet to engage directly with the question of 'property' the dissociation between 'cultural property' and 'heritage' must be bridged so that conceptions of cultural property can contribute fully to the integration between the community and the heritage they need for their integration and survival (Lixinski 2019b: 563, 581). To conceive of challenges in terms of either 'property' or 'heritage' may significantly impact how communities 'can (or cannot) control their own heritage on the ground' (Lixinski 2019a: 50).

Heritage debates are typically focused on ethics and may not align with property debates focused on law. The contribution of human rights is clearer when they function in the service of intergenerational justice as a moral claim and a catalyst for communities that prioritise duties over entitlements (Bailey 2013: 125–126). Even when rights are lacking, rectificatory duties, obligations, and responsibilities may arise or be assumed. IFormer colonial powers, or the organisations they have membership of, may consider it important to assume responsibility for their colonial pasts. France, Belgium, Germany, and others have demonstrated a certain responsiveness to source countries and representatives of diaspora communities who are speaking up.

2.7.3 *Assumptions regarding the effect of the passage of time on primary legal rules*

Using the passage of time to dilute the restitution claim has long been part of the UK government's strategy in respect of the Parthenon Sculptures. It resorted to a predictable line of argument: That the Marbles have resided in London for longer than the modern state of Greece has existed (UK Government Select Committee on Culture, Media and Sport, Minutes of Evidence, Annex IV, March 2000: The Parthenon Sculptures 10.4). The thrust of the argument is that acquisitions of ownership under colonial-era law remain valid as a matter of principle notwithstanding changes to the law and incompatibility with today's views of justice. In a German museum context, it has been suggested that it is not just a matter of consulting old legal texts when analysing the legal position under old law, but also observing the legal practices of that time, which may not align with contemporary legal standards. Thielecke and Geißdorf concede that restitution claims for colonial-era objects may succeed under contemporary law in rare instances. They use the example of collectors' diary entries or other historical documents that sufficiently detail the circumstances of a removal so that ostensible links can be drawn between the legal basis of an invalid acquisition under historical law and theft under contemporary German law. While restitution would be indicated, they add that the right to restitution may not be enforceable given that claims of ownership must be filed within a certain timeframe in the statute of limitations or be deemed waived (Thielecke & Geißdorf 2021: 159). An international civil case concerning private rights must be filed timeously to proceed. The need for legal certainty of commercial transactions decrees that legal reality adapts itself to the prevailing factual situation, which favours new possessors of looted art (Campfens 2024: 148).

In civil law systems, the lapse of time tends to affect the substantive rights of the person to whom an obligation is owed. In common law systems, misappropriation, theft, or looting may interrupt the running of the limitation period or trigger it afresh. The obligee's inactivity over a certain period may also have legal implications. On this point neither the Sarr and Savoy report nor the Arts Council England (ACE) guidelines contain the same level of granular detail as the Deutscher Museumsbund (DMB) *Guidelines on Care of Collections.*

It is frequently assumed that the decision about the effect of the passage of time on a restitution claim is to be made by the limitations imposed by legal systems in Europe and that a single system must apply. However, an English PrIL ruling followed ethical reasoning to prevent statutes of limitations from barring, suspending, or extinguishing claims on public policy grounds. In *City of Gotha and Federal Republic of Germany v Sotheby's and Cobert Finance SA.* ([1998] QBD no 1997/G/185) the court had to rule which legal system would govern the time limitation for a claim brought by the Federal Republic of Germany (FRG) and the City of Gotha before an English court to win back a tiny medieval painting (*The Holy Family with Saints and Angels* (1603) in the Dutch Mannerist style, by Joachim Wtewael (1566–1638) that had been looted and smuggled. A Russian trophy brigade looted the painting from the Friedenstein Castle collection in the City of Gotha, Thuringia, shortly after the end of the Second World War. A smuggling ring took the painting to West Berlin where things did not go according to plan with the delivery. Cobert, a Panamanian corporation, bought it at a London auction in 1988 and put it up for sale through Sotheby's barely three years later (Roodt 2019: 344, 346).

The religious motif of the painting is indisputable, but the 'religious' and the 'sacred' are not synonyms. This claim was not connected to the colonial-era but highlights the mimesis that played out between Germany and Russia during and after the Second World War. Wtewael's painting was taken forcibly as unilateral 'compensation' for Russia's losses in the war. Trophy brigades started preparations for removals in 1943, before the fate of the war was decided. A bureau of experts was tasked with composing lists of so-called 'eventual equivalents'—i.e., what Soviet officials wanted to receive after the war as 'restitution in kind' to compensate Russia for the cultural losses sustained during the Second World War. Projected provisions included art works from museums and private collections in the Axis countries. Few 'trophies' were inventoried or labelled (Akinsha & Kozlov 1995: 50). The Allies never approved this policy to remove trophy art. The loss of

The Holy Family only became apparent in 1965 when Germany compiled an inventory of losses incurred at the hands of trophy brigades.

Required to interpret German law on the limitation of proprietary actions when a third party acquires possession of a work of art in England, Moses J. focused on the question of whether Germany's claim was time-barred under German law and Cobert could successfully invoke the lapse of time as a defence. *The Holy Family* was looted more than 50 years before action was taken for its recovery, which is longer than most legal systems would permit. Moses J. did not follow the time limits imposed in uniform law and refused to interpret time limitations in a mechanical manner. Instead, when the classification of limitations raised an issue, he supplied a PrIL response that relied on the juridical framework of exception (Roodt 2019: 348–350). The laws of both Germany and England were held to govern title and issues as to the protection of the rights which flow from that title (*City of Gotha*: sub 'Is the German Limitation Period Relevant?'). German law allows a good faith purchaser to acquire title after ten years if the purchaser remains unaware of any defect throughout that time. Negative prescription applies after 30 years regardless of good faith, so that a bad faith possessor gains a possessory right while the deprived owner's ownership right disintegrates over time. No 'new owner' may sell or bequeath clear title. The success of the restitution claim depended upon whether the 30-year limitation period for claims for return of stolen objects under German law had expired. The court held that the 30-year limitation period under German law ran irrespective of whether claimant was aware of the existence of the claim or identity of defendant, and that it had run out (*City of Gotha*: sub 'Limitation under German Law'). English law favours the dispossessed owner, however long the period since the original theft. Moses J. adopted a broad view of the general rule in the English Foreign Limitation Periods Act of 1984 that brought the treatment of foreign law into focus. He held that a new claim for recovery arises against a possessor who changes the nature of their possession; consequently, the time limitation had not run out and no time-bar applied in the case. Under the Limitation Act of 1980, over time, certain purchasers of stolen goods can be recognised legally as the owner when there is a purchase unconnected to the theft, made in good faith, and more than six years following that purchase. Moses J. highlighted the potential to identify from the Limitation Act of 1980 an English public policy against criminal gain by a thief or a transferee who lacked good faith. He intimated that he would have invoked this public policy exception if the application of German law resulted in a ruling that favoured a possessor who was not in good faith, because this would run against the English court's standards of justice expressed in the Limitation Act.

The *City of Gotha* ruling exemplifies an important choice for justice that does not rely on just one legal system. Rather, a 'common rule of adjudication' was extracted to control the obstacle of time in the restitution proceedings which prevents embezzlers and robbers from counting any period of possession by preceding holders to their own advantage as part of the limitation period. The rule was not formulated for a narrow category of cultural material that depicted religious subject matter, such as the *Holy Family,* so it is fair to say that the ruling encourages a critical appraisal of the effect of the passage of time on restitution claims for cultural property. It demonstrates that it is appropriate to confine 'acquisition' to the circumstances of an extended period of continuous innocent, open possession. If conversion, theft, looting, forced sale, conflict, and genocidal conflict occurred in a custody chain, the juridical framework of exception deserves to be invoked and the argument that the passage of time legitimises the position of the possessor in these circumstances challenged.

Non-retrospectivity cannot be assumed in the context of the application of primary legal rules. As indicated in Chapter 1, legislation is typically given prospective application only for the sake of due process or to guard against impairment of contracts. Both the National Stolen Property Act (NSPA) of 1948 and Archaeological Resources Protection Act (ARPA) of 1979 apply retrospectively in the US despite stating, at the time of ratification, that the 1970 UNESCO Convention is understood not to be retrospective (Titi 2023: 253). A critical view of the assumed effect of the time factor on restitution claims to sacred imperial artefacts is called for.

2.7.4 Disconnect between status of complex material, complex colonial histories, and the category in a conflicts rule

The ease with which the special status of cultural heritage can become disconnected from the category in a PrIL 'choice-of-law rule' poses issues for cultural heritage litigation. The object may not have been recognised or designated as cultural heritage and the PrIL rule may be applied regardless of when removal took place. The 'common rules of adjudication' proposed by Chechi are intended to prepare the ground for legal uniformity across cultural heritage decision-making and to assist adjudicators to surmount the troublesome aspects of classification, standing, prescription, statutes of limitation, and the non-application of foreign laws in PrIL (Chechi 2014: 84–98). More specifically, the proposed 'common rules of adjudication' are designed to counter the legal diversity which PrIL rules foster or to circumvent the application of PrIL rules. Chechi's idea of extrapolating 'common rules of adjudication' has potential to bridge the cavernous divide between Anglo-American and Continental traditions. This *lex culturalis* was conceived to support states in adjusting their statutory or constitutional norms in response to adjudication, and to inspire elaboration of more rules for judicial as well as non-judicial contexts (Chechi 2014: 244–249, 292, 296ff). Significant blind spots manifest when objects removed from the contexts with which they retain intimate relationships, such as sculptures extracted from temples, are put into circulation and the validity of the transfer is governed by the *lex situs* rule. This rule does not prioritise the legal system of the community for whom cultural material is sacred, nor does it grant special status and policy protection to this legal system. The risk is that the meaning or significance of the cultural material at stake may not be fully understood or accepted under either the potentially applicable law (the *lex causae*) or under the law of the court that is hearing the case (the *lex fori*). Even when a special choice-of-law rule for cultural heritage exists (the *lex originis*, for instance), there is no guarantee that an adjudicator will prevent an object from being subsumed under the ordinary-goods-to-be-owned category in the juridical framework of circulation. Repatriation claims relating to histories of colonial violence, in which objects were appropriated in the wake of genocide, cannot be adjudicated as ordinary claims in respect of things. The same must be said for conversion, theft, forced sale, and conflict. If such circumstances are present in the custody chain, the question of whether certain cultural objects should be returned to a deprived state or community cannot be fairly settled with reference to the law of the place where the object ended up.

In places where the recognition of foreign concepts and public law, and the enforcement of foreign judgments form part of PrIL's remit the public policy exception provides balance and neutralises choice-of-law rules that do not promote international policy. The reach of the juridical framework of exception exceeds that of proposed 'common rules of adjudication,' which introduces the question of whether the proposed *lex culturalis* can help or hinder PrIL in its task.

2.7.5 Challenges posed by new technologies

New technologies that render the physical location of objects obsolete, harbour intriguing potential to radically change the Savignian modes of thinking about PrIL. The technological revolution challenges our most solid fundamental premises about 'how to draw the best connection between cases and polities' (Hatzimihail 2021: 3–4). Digital technologies support digital information-sharing that strengthens coordination in ways that transcend geographical limitations (Preamble of the Qingdao Recommendations for the Protection and Return of Cultural Objects Removed from Colonial Contexts or Acquired by Other Unjustifiable Means, 2024).

Technological advancement confers numerous benefits on society, yet problems such as migration, ecological destruction, and environmental devastation undermine them. Normative uncertainty further undermines the benefits of the technological revolution. The lack of clarity in rules, procedures, and authority regarding maintenance and access to new models and technologies renders inappropriate use of the technology for cultural appropriation more likely (Magnani et al. 2018: 168; Kreps 2015: 4, 5).

The Joint Declaration on the Return of Benin Bronzes and Bilateral Museum Cooperation signed by the governments of Germany and Nigeria on 1 July 2022 aims for a new understanding of cultural cooperation. It encourages German public museums and institutions to continue to display Benin Bronzes on loan. The declaration supports the notion of 'unconditional' return, but clauses 10 and 12 expect Nigeria to commit to several undertakings. It must contribute to 'the universal role' of the Benin Bronzes by 'cooperating in the field of exhibitions and research and by ensuring their display is accessible to the general public and to research'; facilitate 'the circulation of … the Benin Bronzes, by collaborating on international travelling and joint exhibitions' while clause 11 portends arrangements on digitalisation and copyright in the transfer agreements. Aside from over-insisting on public access much value is being ascribed to technocratic governance. Lack of clarity regarding the legal status of digital images and uncertainties regarding the public domain make for unpredictable outcomes. Further use of information pertaining to the material in question, such as image rights and use of photo material, should be regulated by joint agreement to promote clarity (DMB *Guidelines on Care of Collections* 2021: 90). 'Technocratic nihilism' leads nowhere.

The British Museum refused to collaborate with a proposal which the Institute of Digital Archaeology (IDA), one of the UK's top organisations for heritage preservation, made in 2022, to make a full-scale reproduction and near-exact replica of two Parthenon Sculptures, namely the Selene Horse and scenes from Peirithoos's marriage feast. In March 2022, the IDA proceeded to make high-quality scans despite not having access to the top and back edges of the stonework. However, it is unrealistic to expect robots carving full-scale reproductions and near-exact replicas to settle disputes concerning the ownership and belonging of collection items that evoke relationships, knowledge, and sacrifice. Technology could perpetuate the colonial perspective that the best place for originals is in museum collections in the West instead of with the communities who produced them. This risk arises, for example, when the repatriation of facsimiles of important stolen materials and the recreation of digital copies of artefacts in digital repatriations are promoted as a form of access for source communities (Krupa & Grimm 2021: 52, 55). How digitisation of sacred items affects their intangible qualities is one of the acutely under-researched areas (Dawson 2016: 8).

Some technological applications could encourage erstwhile colonial powers to face historical injustice or defuse the repatriation claims they face (Roodt 2022). One example is blockchain technology, which is claimed to allow objects with contested ownerships to be 'displayed by one museum while having the ownership rights with the source communities' (Whittaker et al. 2021: 312–313). Blockchain technology has a database structure that allows a piece of data about the creator, owner, and possessor of the object to be accumulated in a chain. The dataset is decentralised and, once added, the information in the chain cannot be altered. The sequence of multiple blocks creates a unique chain. Peer-to-peer control over the data, combined with a tamper-evident ledger, renders the chain secure (Ruan et al. 2019: 975). This technology has potential to register artefactual provenience. In theory, an increase in the number of such registrations would result in a decrease in market transactions involving looted objects, since items on the register would become unsellable without registered provenance and provenience information (Whittaker et al. 2021: 321). Differentiation between ownership, exhibition, reproduction, moral and ethical rights, etc., in blockchain may one day give scope to negotiate along novel pathways. However, for now the amount of computing power and energy required to create and maintain this solution raises a host of concerns about the plunder of natural resources. The drive for growth advances growth as an end in and of itself, and comes at the expense of future generations.

The frequency with which the digital is layered onto the world of things gives rise to tensions in the digital space. Blending the physical and the digital renders ontological clashes and confrontations inevitable because they impact structural and socio-cultural values differently. Physical forms of cultural heritage include material or corporeal artefacts and even digital artefacts, whereas intangible heritage is embodied in people and the generations they give life to (Roodt 2022). Intangible cultural heritage is a safeguarding process in which stakeholders at the national and local levels deserve to participate, yet the very institutions in possession of sacred cultural material may pose as saviours without full and meaningful participation and consultation of deprived communities. The safeguarding of intangible cultural heritage must be checked by the safeguarding of the Free, Prior, and Informed Consent requirement as well as provisions on the rights to equality, non-discrimination, self-determination, freedom of religion, cultural rights, land and resources, and languages (Human Rights Council Report 2020: para 28; Recommendations no 86 and no 87). Many museums have stopped displaying human remains based on their link to personhood and dignity despite contention (Stahn 2023: 283).

Balanced decisions about the use of technology in the dissemination of archival and artefactual information are more crucial than ever before, but the studies undertaken to support the restoration of the law in respect of restitution and repatriation do not address the implications sufficiently. Girard cautioned that technology widens divisions between rich and poor while rendering them undifferentiated through scientific technique. Overtaking politics and seducing institutions, technology accelerates fragmentation, which promotes societal collapse and accelerates war (Girard 2010: 39–40, 64; Little ed. tr. 2003: 67).

2.7.6 Tort/delict

Depending on the approach and feasibility under potentially applicable laws, a restitution dispute may be categorised as an action for compensation for delict or tort. The conflict rule is the *lex loci delicti*—the law of the place (jurisdiction) where the injury had materialised or where the alleged negligent act or omission occurred. It matters greatly where injuries were incurred or where transnational corporations' delictual actions occurred, whether at the place of their headquarters or the corporation's local subsidiary (Banu 2022: 386–388).

The law of delict was virtually absent from Savigny's *System.* Savigny maintained that delictual liability was closely related to the public policy of the forum and that all measures concerning delicts were local measures aiming to promote a specific moral or public interest—a 'coercitive, strictly positive statute' that operates as an overriding local statute (von Savigny & Guthrie 1869: para 374). CLT hardly engaged with the category of tort/delict (Kennedy 2010: 813, 827). Prior to the 19th century, references were made to criminal cases alongside other PrIL categories, but tort/delict was approached through the remedies that were being sought within the *lex fori.* A reconceptualisation took place in the 19th century, when the concept of obligation underwent further development (Hatzimihail 2021: 182). In many former colonies however, including in South Africa, the issue of choice-of-law in respect of the law of delict remained *res nova* for an inordinately long time. The Eastern Cape High Court entered a ruling in a cross-border defamation claim as late as 2010 (*Burchell v Anglin* 2010 (3) SA 48 (ECG)). A glacial pace in the evolution of the applicable law of delict holds back the scrutiny that is needed in respect of the implications in complex colonial contexts.

PrIL scholars are intimately acquainted with the rule of double actionability in English law, namely that to be allowed to bring a suit in England for an alleged wrong committed abroad, two conditions must be met: The wrong must be actionable according to English law, and it must not be justifiable according to the law where it occurred (*Phillips v Eyre* (1870) L.R. 6 QB 1). It is a lesser known fact that British colonial rulers were absolved from responsibility during the many rebellions against colonial rule, including in this instance. Edward Eyre, the then governor of Jamaica, approved the use of martial law to suppress the Morant Bay rebellion against British colonial rule. An Indemnity Act was promulgated in 1865 to absolve colonial rulers of responsibility for atrocities committed against the inhabitants of Jamaica during the violent suppression of the rebellion. Two British subjects resident in Jamaica, a landowner and a coroner, joined Baptist missionaries to agitate for political reform. Having sustained injuries during the rebellion, they instituted proceedings against Eyre for compensation for assault, battery, and false imprisonment (Kostal 2005: 432–434). The court in England ruled that this tort would have been actionable according to English law, but the law of the place of injury, Jamaica, made the tort 'justifiable.' The double actionability rule and its reformulations exonerated Eyre from responsibility and ensured that he was protected against being tried on the merits of the case. No compensation was held to be payable. Every subsequent attempt at holding Eyre responsible failed because the claimants were unable to demonstrate that the foreign law contravened the forum's fundamental values (Banu 2022: 386). The ruling makes a 'liberal jurisprudence of power' seem unattainable (Kostal 2005: 454; Banu 2022: 386).

In functional terms, the double actionability rule operates as a rule of public policy which excludes the application of any foreign rule that imposes tort liability unless there is a corresponding rule of English law. The double actionability rule was prospectively abolished in the Private International Law (Miscellaneous Provisions) Act 1995 for all torts except defamation and with the exemption of 'acts or omissions giving rise to a claim which occurred before the commencement' of the relevant Part of the Act (s 14(1)). The 1995 Act has been largely superseded by the Rome II Regulation in the EU, which also applies only to events occurring after its entry into force. However, the old common law rule of double actionability persists in many jurisdictions following the common law. Cyprus only repealed the rule after its accession to the EU. The rule of double actionability (Article 2(b)(2)(b) of the Law on Civil Wrongs) is repealed by Law No. 129(I)/2006 Act to Amend the Law on Civil Wrongs (Cap. 148). A claim against a person or property may be filed regardless of whether the country where an act or omission has taken place permits this (new Article 3(2)(b)). The double actionability rule was brought up once more in 2018 in *Athanasios Sophocleous & Ors v Secretary of State for the Foreign and Commonwealth Office & Secretary of State for Defence* [2018] EWHC 19 (Q.B.). This was a claim for damages instituted by 34 claimants for personal injuries sustained during an uprising against English colonial rule between 1956 and 1958. It related to alleged assaults and other acts of violence perpetrated by members of the UK armed forces, seconded British police officers, and agents of the colonial administration in Cyprus. Emergency powers shielded English colonial officers from liability in Cyprus. Some 60 years after the injurious actions took place, it fell to an English court to determine the law governing the limitation of the causes of action. The court at first instance was asked to allow an exception to be made to the double actionability rule and to allow English law to apply, even if the acts had been justifiable under the local Cypriot law at the time. Because the Crown bore responsibility for justice in Cyprus, the court recognised that the tort could be 'localised' in England rather than Cyprus. It held that English law alone (rather than both English and Cypriot law) governed the personal injury proceedings, even if the defendants were officials of the state which made the law that could absolve them from liability by rendering the claims not actionable under Cypriot law (at para 187). It noted that:

> where a state stands to be held to account for acts of violence against its citizens, it should be held to account, in its own courts, by its own law and should not escape liability by reference to a colonial law it has itself made. (para 197)

This ruling demonstrates how the juridical framework of exception could weigh in on the case outcome. Cyprus is an independent state that would have welcomed the application of English law to redress an injustice done to its citizens.

The defendant Secretaries of State lodged an appeal, and the Civil Division of the Court of Appeal reversed the ruling. It adopted the view that it would be incorrect to impose liability on the Secretaries of State if there would be no such liability if they were sued in Cyprus (para 52). It held that, whenever the double actionability rule still applies 'it must remain the general rule.' It reasoned that 'it would [not] be right to ignore the law of Cyprus' (para 51). Both the law of Cyprus and the law of England and Wales applied to determine the limitation period of the action. The CA confirmed that English colonial officers were shielded against liability in Cyprus for state power abuses against English subjects based on the reasoning that the defendants 'should be entitled to rely on the law of Cyprus at the time when liability arose' (para 51). The contemporary position of the law had to be set aside. It was irrelevant whether the territory in question is a colony whose laws are made by the Queen in Council or a dominion with its own legislature (*Athanasios Sophocleous & Ors v. Secretary of State for the Foreign and Commonwealth Office & Secretary of State for Defence* [2018] EWCA Civ 2167 para 40). The CA also connected the rationale of the double actionability rule (that persons conducting themselves in a particular country should not be liable if by the law of that country there is no liability for their acts or they are released from liability for such acts) to the principle of the comity of nations (that a person who is protected by the law of one country in respect of acts done in that country is also protected against legal proceedings in other countries regarding those acts if they cause damage in that country) (para 52). Interestingly, the court at first instance noted the disingenuity of invoking the doctrine of comity in this instance (para 197).

Banu criticises the ruling on appeal (Banu 2022: 389). She argues that torts occurring when no colonisation has been perpetrated must be distinguished from torts inflicted during uprisings against colonial rule in a colony whose laws were made by the Queen in Council. The criticism is warranted. The legacy of colonial histories poses weighty questions about the broader responsibility in respect of human fellowship. Mimesis may achieve normative effect in the formation, interpretation, and implementation of domestic and international law. The CA's approach to PrIL could have considered the policy implications of applying the Cypriot law and the principle of comity; instead, it confers normative effects on mimetic competition by blocking claimants from holding colonial officers to account for tortious harms committed during rebellions against colonial rule. PrIL techniques do so much more than identify an applicable law. They are remarkable tools for the accurate description of the facts and law in a case but require sharpening for complex colonial contexts which should not be overlooked.

2.7.7 Legal standards in uniform limitations law

The 1995 UNIDROIT Convention creates a framework for the restitution and return of stolen and illegally exported cultural objects. Its reach extends to undiscovered objects which the States Parties have not specifically designated or registered as cultural property and items that have been clandestinely excavated. Article 3 defines public collections and incorporates sacred or communally important cultural objects used by tribes or Indigenous communities in a Contracting State. Article 3(8) is the only provision that refers to 'sacred or communally important objects' used as part of ritual by an Indigenous community in a Contracting State. Its purpose is to render more generous time limitations applicable not only to public collections but also to sacred and secret material belonging to an Indigenous community (Jagielska-Burduk & Fincham 2024: 555). Under Article 3(4), the time limitations that apply to a cultural object forming an integral part of an identified monument are not for all intents and purposes treated the same as the time limitation that applies in respect of 'a sacred or communally important cultural object belonging to and used by a tribal or indigenous community as part of its community's traditional or ritual use' (the time limitation applicable to public collections under Article 3(8)). The statute of limitations for cultural objects forming an integral part of an identified monument or archaeological site, or belonging to a public collection, is three years from the time the claimant knew the location of the cultural object and the identity of the possessor. A longer time may be set in the domestic legal framework of a signatory state.

Colonial takings cases may take a long time to surface and would not be covered by the time limit suggested in Article 3 (75 years) in their domestic law (Campfens 2021: 189). States with laws and policies based on the absolute inalienability of this material may make declarations to render applicable longer time limitations in their domestic law. The period available for bringing claims in respect of collection items used by tribal or Indigenous communities may be extended under Article

3(5). Thus far, China, Ecuador, Guatemala, Myanmar, and the Netherlands have made declarations (Jagielska-Burduk & Fincham 2024: 552, 560).

The 1995 UNIDROIT Convention's time limitations apply insofar as the loss of the artefact occurred after ratification and implementation by states on the national level (Article 10(1)). The ritual use by a tribal or Indigenous community is impaired by illegal exportation of an object and an order for return may be issued (Article 5(3)(d)). Provision is also made for the scenario when an Indigenous community has made an object for its ritual use (Article 7). These provisions hardly go far enough, considering that the meaning of the sacred goes beyond ritual. Protected reserves and sites of burial, pilgrimage, religious, or spiritual significance deserve special consideration as present manifestations of the human past (e.g., 2003 Asian Development Bank Environmental Assessment Guidelines Table 22: 93). The ethics of spiritual property are not confined to ritualistic uses by practicing communities.

States whose cultural heritage was damaged and depleted during the colonial era are supportive of the idea that the removal of cultural heritage cannot be subject to time limitations and that restitution claims deserve to be heard on their merits (Chechi 2014: 285–292). If the limitation periods set in the conventions were removed, the ratification of cultural property and heritage conventions by African states can be expected to increase.

2.8 Conclusion

A nuanced understanding of the nature and function of law in the context of complex colonial histories considers how cultural material was removed but widens the aperture of the lens beyond just this question. It makes room for questions of normativity in claims for restitution in relation to the hurdles presented by time and space. It also takes account of the challenges which normative uncertainty introduces. Normative uncertainty undermines many of the assumed benefits of the technological revolution. This complicates the achievement of justice in internal and external conflicts in colonial settings.

Positive international law is necessarily embedded in the law and ethics that preceded it. Moral norms once underpinned the ethic of international law. Some would argue that they persist notwithstanding interruptions during the colonial era (Glenn 2011: 250). PrIL is a valuable discipline for making it necessary for states to adopt a policy in relation to the outside world, whether implicit or explicit. PrIL adjudication might reveal the propensity of a court to default to its own law, to justify cultural imperialism, or to halt the smuggling and title laundering of certain cultural material and secure their return to source communities. The responses of states reveal the innate political character of PrIL. It makes sense to widen the lens to include PrIL in the consideration of the broader inequalities of the international legal order, and to check if it can alleviate the indeterminacy of the law and cast light on conceptions of time that provide excuses to avoid ruling on the merits of claims.

Chapter 2 pieced together how the obligations engendered by the sacred fit within the juridical framework of exception. Having considered the internal and external dimensions of conflicts of laws during the colonial era, it is evident that colonial overlays and undercurrents of law accommodated avoidance tactics in the external and internal conflicts that occurred between legal systems and rules. It was suggested that PrIL stands to benefit significantly from the theory of the sacred in claims for restitution. Among other things, the sacred is open to multi-normativity that dissolves the time distance behind which cultural and educational institutions hide.

Chapter 3 starts from an understanding that cultural property and heritage indicates who belongs to the society that produced or 'received' it. This understanding confers priority on the application of the juridical framework of exception.

Bibliography

Akinsha, Konstantin & Gregorii Kozlov, with Sylvia Hochfield. 1995. *Beautiful Loot: The Soviet Plunder of Europe's Art Treasures* New York City: Random House.

Al Attar, Mohsen, Nicole Aylwin & Rosemary J. Coombe. 2009. 'Indigenous Cultural Heritage Rights in International Human Rights Law' in Catharine Bell & Robert K. Paterson (eds.), *Protection of First Nations Cultural Heritage: Laws, Policy, and Reform* Vancouver: UBC Press 311–342.

Asian Development Bank. 2003. *Environmental Assessment Guidelines* <https://www.adb.org/sites/default/files/institutional-document/32635/files/environmental-assessment-guidelines.pdf>

Bailey, Saki. 2013. 'The Architecture of Commons Legal Institutions for Future Generations' in Saki Bailey, Gilda Farrell & Ugo Mattei (eds.), *Protecting Future Generations Through Commons–Trends in Social Cohesion, No 26*, Strasbourg: Council of Europe Publishing 107–139.

Banu, Roxana. 2018. *Nineteenth Century Perspectives on Private International Law* Oxford: OUP.

Banu, Roxana. 2022. 'Teaching by Historicising Private International Law' *International Journal of Law in Context* 18(4): 383–392.

Batiffol, Henri. 1956. *Aspects Philosophiques du Droit International Privé* Paris: Librairie Dalloz.

Bennett, Thomas W. 1980. 'The Interpersonal Conflict of Laws: A Technique for Adapting to Social Change in Africa' *The Journal of Modern African Studies* 18(1): 127–134.

Bollée, Sylvain. 2019. 'Thoughts on the Dallah Case: The Hypothesis of the Indeterminacy of the Legal System' in Horatia Muir Watt, Lucia Bíziková, Agatha Brandão de Oliveira & Diego P. Fernández Arroyo (eds.) *Global Private International Law: Adjudication without Frontiers* Cheltenham: Edward Elgar Publishing 342–349.

Byrne, James G. 2015. *Factors Determining the Repatriation of Cultural Heritage from Museums; the Place of Cultural Rights in British Museums Practice* Master Thesis, SOAS University of London.

Campfens, Evelien. 2021. *Cross-Border Title Claims to Cultural Objects: Property or Heritage?* PhD Thesis, Leiden University (Meijers-reeks Eleven).

Campfens, Evelien. 2024. 'Private International Law and Cultural Heritage' in Lixinski, Lucas & Lucie K. Morisset (eds.) *The Routledge Handbook of Heritage and the Law* London: Routledge 145–156.

Canales, Jimena. 2015. *The Physicist & the Philosopher: Einstein, Bergson, and the Debate that Changed our Understanding of Time* Princeton, NJ: Princeton University Press.

Chechi, Alessandro. 2014. *The Settlement of International Heritage Disputes* Oxford: OUP.

Chen, Zhen. 2022. 'Is a Mummy a Person or a Property: The Classification and Choice of Law of Cultural Objects in Private International Law' *The Chinese Journal of Comparative Law* 10(2): 274–296.

Christodoulidis, Emilios. 2018. 'Dogma, or the Deep Rootedness of Obligation' in Daniel Matthews & Scott Veitch (eds.) *Law, Obligation, Community* London: Routledge 3–17.

Cook, Walter W. 1941. '"Characterization" in the Conflict of Laws' *Yale Law Journal* 51(2): 191–212.

Council of Europe, European Court of Human Rights, *Guide on Article 7 of the European Convention on Human Rights* updated on 31 December 2019.

Council of Europe, *Explanatory Report to the Council of Europe Convention on Offences relating to Cultural Property* Nicosia, 19 May 2017, CETS No. 221.

D'Avout, Louis. 2017. 'Property and Proprietary Rights' in Jürgen Basedow, Giesela Rühl, Franco Ferrari & Pedro De Miguel Asensio (eds.) *Encyclopedia of Private International Law* Cheltenham: Edward Elgar Publishing 1429–1436.

David, Valeska. 2020. *Cultural Difference and Economic Disadvantage in Regional Human Rights Courts: An Integrated View* Cambridge, United Kingdom: Intersentia.

Dawson, Peter. 2016. *The Design and Development of Digital Return Platforms for Northern Indigenous Heritage; Knowledge Synthesis* Final Report for the Social Sciences and Humanities Research Council of Canada.

Effiboley, Emery Patrick. 2020. 'Reflections on the Issue of Repatriation of Looted and Illegally Acquired African Cultural Objects in Western Museums' *Contemporary Journal of African Studies* 7(1): 67–83.

European Commission DG Home Affairs. 2011. *Study on Preventing and Fighting Illicit Trafficking in Cultural Goods in the European Union*, October 2011.

Forrest, Craig. 2010. *International Law and the Protection of Cultural Heritage* London: Routledge.

Gallagher, Steven. 2017. '"Purchased in Hong Kong": Is Hong Kong the Best Place to Buy Stolen or Looted Antiquities?' *International Journal of Cultural Property* 24(4): 479–496.

Garnett, Richard. 2012. *Substance and Procedure in Private International Law* Oxford: OUP.

German Museums Association (DMB). 2021. *Guidelines for German Museums: Care of Collections from Colonial Contexts* 3rd ed., April 2021 <https://www.museumsbund.de/wp-content/uploads/2021/03/mb-leitfaden-en-web.pdf>

Gillies, Lorna. 2015. 'The Contribution of Jurisdiction as a Technique of Demand Side Regulation in Claims for the Recovery of Cultural Objects' *Journal of Private International Law* 11(2): 295–316.

Giorgallis, Andreas. 2023. 'The Return of the Holy Doors of St Anastasios from the Kanazawa College of Art' *Art Antiquity and Law* 28(2): 161–169.

Girard, René. 2010. *Battling to the End: Conversations with Benoit Chantre (Studies in Violence, Mimesis, and Culture)* (tr Mary Baker 2007) East Lansing: Michigan State University Press.

Glenn, H. Patrick. 2011. 'The Ethic of International Law' in Donald E. Childress III (ed.) *The Role of Ethics in International Law* Cambridge: CUP 246–270.

Grenfell, Laura. 2013. *Promoting the Rule of Law in Post-Conflict States* Cambridge, UK: CUP.

Grodecki, Jan K. 1959. 'Conflicts of Laws in Time' *British Yearbook of International Law* 35: 58–82.

Guedj, Thomas G. 1991. 'The Theory of the Lois de Police, A Functional Trend in Continental Private International Law-A Comparative Analysis with Modern American Theories' *The American Journal of Comparative Law* 39(4): 661–697.

Habermas, Jürgen. 1996. *Norms and Facts* Cambridge, MA: The MIT Press.

Hatzimihail, Nikitas E. 2021. *Preclassical Conflict of Laws* CUP online.

Hawkins, Amy. 2024. 'Remaining British Judges Face Pressure to Resign from Hong Kong's Top Court' *The Guardian*, 12 June.

Holtorf, Cornelius. 2020. '"Cultural Heritage is Concerned with the Future": A Critical Epilogue' in Veysel Apaydin (ed.) *Critical Perspectives on Cultural Memory and Heritage: Construction, Transformation and Destruction* London: UCL Press 309–311.

Huber, Ulrik. 1686. *Heedensdaegse Rechtsgeleertheyt,* soo Elders, als in Frieslandt Gebruikelijk (ed.) Amsterdam: Zacharias Huber (tr Percival Gane *The Jurisprudence of My Time* Durban: Butterworth & Co. Africa Ltd 1939).

Human Rights Council Report. 2020. *Repatriation of Ceremonial Objects and Human Remains under the UN Declaration on the Rights of Indigenous Peoples*, A/HRC/45/35 21 July 2020.

International Law Commission Study Group. 2006. *Report on the Fragmentation of International Law: Difficulties Arising from the Diversification and Expansion of International Law*, 13 April 2006, report finalised by Mr Martti Koskenniemi.

Jagielska-Burduk, Alicja & Derek Fincham. 2024. 'Article 3 of the 1995 UNIDROIT Convention: Claims for Restitution of Stolen Cultural Objects' in Ana Filipa Vrdoljak, Andrzej Jakubowski & Alessandro Chechi (eds.) *The 1970 UNESCO and 1995 UNIDROIT Conventions on Stolen or Illegally Transferred Cultural Property: A Commentary* Oxford: OUP 545–560.

Jakubowski, Andrzej. 2015. *State Succession in Cultural Property* Oxford: OUP.

Jiménez, María Julia Ochoa. 2019. 'Conflict of Laws and the Return of Indigenous Peoples' Cultural Property: A Latin American Perspective' *International Journal of Cultural Property* 26(4): 437–456.

Joint Declaration on the Return of Benin Bronzes and Bilateral Museum Cooperation between the Federal Republic of Germany and the Federal Republic of Nigeria, 1 July 2022 <https://www.auswaertiges-amt.de/blob/2540404/8a42afe8f5d79683391f8188ee9ee016/220701-benin-bronzen-polerkl-data.pdf>

Kennedy, Duncan. 2010. 'Savigny's Family/Patrimony Distinction and Its Place in the Global Genealogy of Classical Legal Thought' *The American Journal of Comparative Law* 58(4): 811–841.

Kollewijn, Roeland Duco. 1951. 'Conflicts of Western and Non-Western Law' *The International Law Quarterly* 4(3): 307–325.

Koppenol-Laforce, Marielle, Paul Sluijter & Eva Milou Moison. 2017. 'Conditions for Recognition and Enforcement of Foreign Judgments in the Netherlands' <https://www.houthoff.com/-/media/Houthoff/Publications/mkoppenol/Lexology>

Koskenniemi, Martti. 2011. 'Empire and International Law: The Real Spanish Contribution' *University of Toronto Law Journal* 61(1): 1–36.

Kostal, Rande W. 2005. *A Jurisprudence of Power: Victorian Empire and the Rule of Law* Oxford: OUP.

Kreps, Christina. 2015. 'Appropriate Museology and the "New Museum Ethics": Honoring Diversity' *Nordisk Museologi* 2: 4–16.

Krupa, Krystiana L. & Kelsey T. Grimm. 2021. 'Digital Repatriation as a Decolonizing Practice in the Archaeological Archive' *Across the Disciplines* 18(1/2): 47–58.

Labadie, Camille. 2021. 'Decolonizing Collections: A Legal Perspective on the Restitution of Cultural Artifacts' *ICOFOM Study Series* 49(2): 132–146.

Last, Kathryn V. 2007. 'Cultural Pluralism and the Return of Cultural Heritage' in Stephen Tierney (ed.) *Accommodating Cultural Diversity*, Burlington: Ashgate 123–143.

Leslie, R.D. 1977. 'The Repugnancy Rule in African Law and the Public Policy Rule in Conflict of Laws' *Acta Juridica* 117–127.

Little, Janet P. (ed and tr). 2003. *Simone Weil on Colonialism: An Ethic of the Other* Lanham, Maryland: Rowman & Littlefield Inc.

Liu, Zuozhen. 2016. *The Case for Repatriating China's Cultural Objects* Singapore: Springer.

Liu, Zuozhen. 2017. 'Will the God Win?: The Case of the Buddhist Mummy' *International Journal of Cultural Property* 24(2): 221–238.

Lixinski, Lucas. 2018. 'Across Public/Private International Legal Divide in the Governance of Global Public Goods' *Denver Journal of International Law & Policy* 47(1): 1–28.

Lixinski, Lucas. 2019a. *International Heritage Law for Communities: Exclusion and Re-Imagination*, Oxford Scholarship Online.

Lixinski, Lucas. 2019b. 'A Third Way of Thinking About Cultural Property' *Brooklyn Journal of International Law* 4(2): 563–612.

Lubina, Katja. 2009. *Contested Cultural Property: The Return of Nazi Spoliated Art and Human Remains from Public Collections* PhD Thesis, University of Maastricht.

Magnani, Matthew, Anni Guttorm & Natalia Magnani. 2018. 'Three-Dimensional, Community-Based Heritage Management of Indigenous Museum Collections: Archaeological Ethnography, Revitalization and Repatriation at the Sami Museum Siida' *Journal of Cultural Heritage* 31: 162–169.

Manacorda, Stefano. 2011. 'Criminal Law Protection of Cultural Heritage: An International Perspective' in Stefano Manacorda & Duncan Chappell (eds.) *Crime in the Art and Antiquities World: Illegal Trafficking in Cultural Property* Springer 17–48.

McLachlan, Campbell. 2009. *Lis Pendens in International Litigation* Leiden: Martinus Nijhoff Publishers.

Mills, Alex. 2009. *The Confluence of Public and Private International Law* Cambridge: CUP.

Moran, Mayo. 2019. 'The Problem of the Past: How Historic Wrongs Became Legal Problems' *University of Toronto Law Journal* 69(4): 421–472.

Morris, John H. C. 1966. 'The Time Factor in the Conflict of Laws' *International and Comparative Law Quarterly* 15(2–3): 422–435.

Muir Watt, Horatia. 2014. 'Future Directions?' in Horatia Muir Watt & Diego P. Fernández Arroyo (eds.) *Private International Law and Global Governance* Oxford: OUP 343–382.

Muir Watt, Horatia. 2016a. 'Jurisprudence Without Confines: Private International Law as Global Legal Pluralism' *Cambridge Journal of International and Comparative Law* 5(3): 388–403.

Muir Watt, Horatia. 2016b. 'Conflicts of Laws Unbounded: The Case for a Legal-Pluralist Revival' *Transnational Legal Theory* 7(3): 313–353.

Neidhardt, Alberto Horst. 2018. *The Transformation of European Private International Law A Genealogy of the Family Anomaly* PhD Thesis, European University Institute.

Nicoletopoulos, George P. 1948–1949. 'Private International Law in the New Greek Civil Code' *Tulane Law Review* 23: 452–477.

Oh, Si-Jin. 2018. 'Historical Injustice in East Asia: A Case for Interspatial Law' *Pacific Focus* 33(3): 414-433.

Okoli, Chukwuma S.A. & Richard F. Oppong. 2020. *Private International Law in Nigeria* Oxford: Hart Publishing.

Oppong, Richard. 2007. 'Private International Law in Africa: Past, Present and Future' *The American Journal of Comparative Law* 55(4): 677–719.

Paterson, Robert K. 1996. 'The "Curse of the London Nataraja"' *International Journal of Cultural Property* 5(2): 330–338.

Prott, Lyndel V. 2009. 'Ten Years in Force The Unidroit Convention on Stolen or Illegally Exported Cultural Objects' *Art Antiquity and Law* 14(3): 195–218.

'Qingdao Recommendations for the Protection and Return of Cultural Objects Removed from Colonial Contexts or Acquired by Other Unjustifiable Means', adopted at the International Conference on the Protection and Return of Cultural Objects Removed in Colonial Contexts, hosted by the Alliance for Cultural Heritage in Asia in Qingdao, China, on 20 June 2024.

Riles, Annelise. 2005. 'Taking on the Technicalities. A New Agenda for the Cultural Study of Law' *Buffalo Law Review* 53(3): 973–1034.

Roodt, Christa. 2007a. 'Reflections of Theory, Doctrine and Method in Choice of Law' *Comparative and International Law Journal of Southern Africa* 40(1): 76–102.

Roodt, Christa. 2007b. 'A Wider Vision in Choice of Prescription Law' *Yearbook of Private International Law* 9: 357–373.

Roodt, Christa & David Carey Miller. 2013. 'Stolen Cultural Property: Implications of Vitium Reale in Private Law and Private International Law' *Transnational Dispute Management* 10(5): 1–10.

Roodt, Christa. 2015. *Private International Law, Art and Cultural Heritage* Cheltenham: Edward Elgar Publishing.

Roodt, Christa. 2019. 'The Holy Family on an Unholy Odyssey: Legal Ownership of Stolen Trophy Art' in Jane Milosch & Nick Pearce (eds.) *Collecting and Provenance: A Multi-Disciplinary Approach* Lanham, Maryland: Rowman & Littlefield 343–358.

Roodt, Christa. 2022. 'The Role of Digital Technology in the Restitution of Cultural Artifacts' *Georgetown Journal of International Affairs* Online (18 July).

Roodt, Christa. 2024. 'Article 4 of the 1995 UNIDROIT Convention: Possessor's Rights and Claims for Restitution of Cultural Objects' in Ana Filipa Vrdoljak, Andrzej Jakubowski & Alessandro Chechi (eds.) *The 1970 UNESCO and 1995 UNIDROIT Conventions on Stolen or Illegally Transferred Cultural Property: A Commentary* Oxford: OUP 561–578.

Ruan, Pingcheng, Gang Chen, Tien Tuan Anh Dinh, Qian Lin, Beng Chin Ooi & Meihui Zhang. 2019. 'Fine-Grained, Secure and Efficient Data Provenance on Blockchain Systems' *PVLDB* 12(9): 975–988.

Ruiz Abou-Nigm, Verónica. 2019. 'Bridging and Balancing: Diversity and Integration in Private International Law' in Verónica Ruiz Abou-Nigm & Maria Blanca Noodt Taquela (eds.) *Diversity and Integration in Private International Law* Edinburgh: Edinburgh University Press 362–388.

Salomon, Charles. 1889. *L'occupation de Territoires sans maître: Étude de Droit International* Paris: Giard.

Sarr, Felwine & Bénédicte Savoy. 2018 November. *The Restitution of African Cultural Heritage: Toward a New Relational Ethics* <https://www.about-africa.de/images/sonstiges/2018/sarr_savoy_en.pdf>

Szászy, István. 1974. *Conflict of Laws in the Western, Socialist and Developing Countries* Leiden: A.W. Sijthoff.

Schneider, Marina. 2016. 'The 1995 UNIDROIT Convention: An Indispensable Complement to the 1970 UNESCO Convention and an Inspiration for the 2014/60/EU Directive' *Santander Art and Culture Law Review* 2(2): 149–164.

Schoeman, Elsabe, Christa Roodt & Marlene Wethmar-Lemmer. 2013. 'South Africa' in B. Verschraegen (ed.) *International Encyclopaedia of Laws: Private International Law* Alphen aan den Rijn, The Netherlands: Wolters Kluwer Law and Business.

Singer, Joseph W. 2000. *Entitlement: The Paradoxes of Property* New Haven: Yale University Press.

South African Law Commission, Issue Paper 4, Project 90, 1996.

Stahn, Carsten. 2023. *Confronting Colonial Objects: Histories, Legalities, and Access to Culture* Oxford: OUP.

Struycken, Antoon Victor Marie. 2009. 'Co-ordination and Co-operation in Respectful Disagreement: General Course on Private International Law' *Collected Courses of the Hague Academy of International Law* 311(2004): 8–551.

Salmond, Sir John William & Patrick John Fitzgerald. 1966. *Salmond on Jurisprudence* 12th ed., London: Sweet & Maxwell.

Siehr, Kurt. 1994. 'International Art Trade and the Law' *Collected Courses of the Hague Academy of International Law* 243(1993): 25–288.

Staker, Christopher. 1987. 'Public International Law and the Lex Situs Rule in Property Conflicts and Foreign Expropriations' *British Yearbook of International Law* 58(1): 151–252.

Supiot, Alain. 2007. *Homo Juridicus: On the Anthropological Function of the Law* London: Verso.

Taubenschlag, Raphael. 1972. *The Law of Greco-Roman Egypt in the light of the Papyri, 332 B.C.-640 A.D* (2. ed., revised and enlarged) Milan: Cisalpino-Goliardica.

Thielecke, Carola & Michael Geißdorf. 2021. 'Collections from Colonial Contexts: Legal Aspects' DMB *Guidelines for German Museums: Care of Collections* Berlin: German Museums Association 153–164.

Titi, Catherine. 2023. *The Parthenon Marbles and International Law* Switzerland: Springer.

Tünsmeyer, Vanessa. 2020. 'Bridging the Gap Between International Human Rights and International Cultural Heritage Law Instruments: A Functions Approach' in Anne-Marie Carstens & Elizabeth Varner (eds.) *Intersections in International Cultural Heritage Law* Oxford: OUP 320–342.

UK Government Select Committee on Culture, Media and Sport, Minutes of Evidence, Annex IV, March 2000: The Parthenon Sculptures.

Von Savigny, Friedrich Carl. 1840–1849, 1851. *System des heutigen römischen Rechts* (*System of the Modern Roman Law*) Berlin: Veit und Comp.

Von Savigny, Friedrich Carl & William Guthrie. 1869. *A Treatise on the Conflict of Laws, and the Limits of their Operation in Respect of Time and Place, tr. with notes by William Guthrie; with an appendix containing the treatises of Bartolus, Molinaeus, Paul Voet, & Huber* 2nd ed., revised, Edinburgh: T & T Clark.

Vrdoljak, Ana F. 2008. *International Law, Museums and the Return of Cultural Objects* Cambridge: CUP.

Wheaton, Henry. 1866. *Elements of International Law* (Eighth edition, edited, with notes by Richard Henry Dana, Jr.) London: Sampson Low, Son & Co.

Whittaker, Amy, Anne Bracegirdle, Susan de Menil, Michelle Ann Gitlitz & Lena Saltos. 2021. 'Art, Antiquities and Blockchain: New Approaches to the Restitution of Cultural Heritage' *International Journal of Cultural Policy* 27(3): 312–329.

Wadsworth, Tanner J. 2023. 'The Advantages of Giving Up: Greece and the Futile Quest to Force the Parthenon Marbles Home by Judgment' *Columbia Journal of European Law* 29(1): 129–151.

Wolff, Martin. 1944. *Private International Law* Oxford: OUP.

Yap, Ji Lian. 2008. 'Appraising the Market Overt Exception' *Journal of International Commercial Law and Technology* 3(4): 254–258.

Yntema, Hessel E. 1953. 'The Historic Bases of Private International Law' *The American Journal of Comparative Law* 2(3): 297–317.

Zeidler, Kamil. 2016. *Restitution of Cultural Property: Hard Case, Theory of Argumentation, Philosophy of Law* Gdańsk: Gdańsk University Press.

3 Restoring the law for the restitution of 'sacred' cultural heritage

3.1 Introduction

PrIL delimits legislative powers in the field of private law. It keeps an eye on international private law relationships and on the administrative powers of justice associated with such relationships (i.e., foreign policy). The traditional private law model based on title is not considered the best model to guide adjudicators to a 'just' outcome in claims for historical losses, and the role of the law has been taken over by the 'ethical' model. In terms of access to justice, however, a lack of transparent neutral procedures to implement and clarify soft-law norms has proven problematic (Campfens 2021: 219). Alternative dispute resolution (ADR) procedures remove the need for choice-of-law analyses and technical defences but consent to 'clear' the title of tainted objects by means of ADR is likely to be withheld in paradigmatic cases (in general, Roodt 2015: 54, 149).

The grounds for claims for the return of sacred heritage looted or trafficked during the colonial era are traceable in treaty-making, bilateral negotiations, and policy guidelines regarding the unethical removal of cultural material from former colonies. However, gaps, ambiguities, and inequalities lurk within the interlocking network of domestic, provincial, national, regional, international, and transnational norms. The primary legal norms that apply in those normative spaces cannot, on their own, ensure justice or equity in the face of human greed. While a more complete, stable legal concept of *res extra commercium* would be ideal, further work would be needed to resolve the classificatory complexities of sacred cultural material in international civil litigation. A common understanding of the sacred may promote global justice, but a degree of simplification is required to better define it.

In tactical argument, assumptions, obscure language, artificial distinctions, and disciplinary bifurcations enlarge the normative potential of mimesis. The artificial analytical distinctions, conceptual fragmentations, and dichotomies that fuel mimetics made it possible for the British Parliament to effectively state-sanction the improper acquisition of the Parthenon Sculptures in 1816 without seeking advice on the correct application of legal rules and principles or engaging with questions of conflicts of law.

Courts in the territories of the former colonial masters are on the demand-side of the trade. They are expected to arrive at doctrinal solutions when confronted with concrete problems of jurisdiction, the nature and function of the material in

DOI: 10.4324/9781003583967-3

question, and having to decide whether title claims raise procedural or substantive questions. Adjudicators and policymakers may actualise the normative effect of mimetics if the critical distinction between the juridical framework of circulation of goods and the framework of exception is overlooked. Some of the most significant interactions between the juridical framework of circulation and that of exception to circulation occur where restitutory claims involve cultural property and heritage stolen or looted during the colonial era and trafficked since. Too often the exceptions to ordinary commercial or property law regimes go unidentified.

Overlooking external and internal conflicts of law in the intense rivalries between the European empires propagates the 'radically underdetermined' nature of the law of restitution and repatriation of cultural property and heritage. Any attempt to redesign the normative framework and environment that takes account of the sacred must account for location. For the Parthenon Sculptures, ultimately neither the giver (the Ottomans in occupation of Greek heritage) nor taker (Lord Elgin and his men) was competent to make new rules or decisions concerning the cultural inheritance of the Athenians. Because the meaning of the Parthenon Sculptures is embedded in the location of the temple, a claim in respect of them cannot be evaluated against any standard other than the integrity of the immovable temple located where the Athenians erected it. PrIL is also attuned to the boundaries and limits of legal systems that affect the nature of rights and autonomy across borders, one's belonging to a community or allegiance to a law, and the legitimate bases of legal and political authority. Chapter 2 suggested that a deeper understanding of 'normativity' and its breadth and scope may help to curb the normative pressure which mimetic competition can generate for sacred material removed in the colonial era. This chapter focuses on the scope for PrIL theory and techniques to reflect the ontology of complex cultural material removed from colonial contexts when the colonial 'overlays' is acquired are removed. Viewing PrIL as a subject of problems and solutions rather than a set of substantive norms it suggests that the normative framework for restitutionary proprietary claims in respect of sacred material could be improved by seeing the hard edges of decisions and policies in the light of the philosophical foundations of PrIL. Operating at one step removed from the actual controversy in questions about *locus standi* or choice of law, PrIL engages with prior questions that invite meta-reflection on the methods of decided cases. Its philosophical foundations may cast fresh light on the fragmented conception of international law and the hurdles which the time factor raises to restitution in Public International Law (PublIL) and international cultural heritage law.

Having established the significance of PrIL for access to justice and dispute resolution regarding contested cultural heritage, the question is whether conflicts rules and the general principles and methods of PrIL can meet the challenges that the intangible cultural heritage poses. Overlooking the intangible dimension—oral tradition, ceremonial culture, religious devotion, etc.,—may enable deterioration, disappearance, and destruction of the material in addition to loss of the traditions and knowledge associated with the object. Seeing the interrelation between the intangible cultural heritage and tangible heritage in temple adornments and the location and the culture in which they were created evokes the social, religious, and oral traditions that gave them meaning and context. It brings the ground of the claim into view.

The criteria for ethical PrIL judgments remain largely invisible in transnational cases, making it necessary to define the circumstances in which ethical reasoning ought to change the outcome of the case (Childress III 2011: 7). The most obvious point at which ethical reasoning can be expected to emerge is when claims for restitution and reparation overlap. This starting point is useful for raising critical questions regarding PrIL's core function in cases that implicate colonial competition and the sacred.

3.2 Overlapping claims for restitution and reparation

Efforts to seek reparative justice or compensation for the violence incurred during European rule and the losses suffered on account of historical wrongs may also highlight the potential to raise restitutionary claims in the same case. Consecutive versions of the *Guidelines on Care of Collections* issued by the German Museum Association (DMB) provide international and non-European perspectives on interrelated types of cases differentiated by the colonial context, which encompass what was procured not only during a period of formal colonial rule but also during struggles against conquest (e.g., DMB *Guidelines on Care of Collections* 2019: 25–33; DMB *Guidelines on Care of Collections* 2021: 30). Heritage can be used to accomplish goals that do not concern the heritage itself and it may not always be possible to maintain a sharp distinction between restitution and reparation in claims based on private or civil law. Repatriation of human remains could potentially be claimed under both heads of argument. Where the subjugation and exploitation occurred in a territory other than the coloniser state PrIL methods are potentially relevant both in civil claims for restitution and repatriation of human remains and in claims for sacred cultural material.

The Nama and Herero litigation illustrates the potential for restitution or repatriation claims overlapping with claims for reparative justice in transnational cases. In the 2019 *Rukoro* ruling, however, because the claimants failed to prove that the human remains were involved in a commercial activity and that Germany's acts of expropriation caused a direct effect in the US, the jurisdiction hurdle was not cleared. The choice-of-law question could not arise for consideration as part of the merits of the case.

Free circulation of the remains of genocide victims is morally repugnant. When claimants can formally show that they suffered injuries at the hands of a particular defendant and a clear relationship exists between the benefit and the wrong, their claims for reparative justice provide a certain normative leverage. Even when reparations litigation does not result in success, some objectives on the reparations agenda in transitional and non-transitional contexts may be achieved because of the pressure it helps to generate.

The time and cost required for international civil proceedings would suggest that civil trials spur mimetic competition. Court prosecutions may conceivably fuel hatred, but Girard theorised that a public penal system and judicial decisions discourage reprisals and prevent the self-perpetuation of vengeance (Girard 1972: 16ff, 22). Klabbers argues that court proceedings and tribunal hearings relieve inter-state tensions as 'sublimated forms' of sacrifice (Klabbers 2016: 249, 260–261). Klabbers questions the palatability of the idea of sacrifice enabling normative evolution, but his argument does not focus on sacred cultural heritage and is not premised on Girard's theory of mimetics and the sacred in express terms. While one cannot assume that the application of PrIL to claims deriving from colonial excesses will generate the pressure needed to achieve settlement of some objectives, the ritual and choreography of the proceedings may prompt the start of settlement discussions. Institutions may be moved in the direction of accountability for historical wrongs even when legal consequences for non-compliance are no longer possible (Moran 2019: 452, 455–456, 460–461).

3.3 Revisiting PrIL's core function in cases that implicate the colonial competition and the 'sacred'

Different visions of the function of PrIL highlight 'policy' approaches that detract from its autonomy and self-reliance (Hatzimihail 2021: 176). There is an acute need for flexible PrIL techniques that promote the integration of societal diversity and coordinate legal diversity in substantive laws and in choice-of-law rules (Fresnedo de Aguirre 2019: 341).

In Savigny's framework, the law of the court in question may be favoured over foreign law for reasons of politics, the mandatory nature of a rule, or political economy. Savigny cites the example of laws that recognise slavery as a legal institution, while the laws that apply in the territory of the court do not recognise slavery, considering it 'totally immoral to treat a man as a thing.' The court hearing the case would not recognise slavery as a legal institution if the state in which it is located does not recognise it as such; the enslaved person cannot be treated as the property of his master 'under general legal incapacity' (von Savigny & Guthrie 1869: para 349, 37). Savigny was 'brutally clear' in his acknowledgement that rights could be exercised immorally. Strikingly, he did not think 'reasons of public interest' created exceptions that applied to Jews (e.g., von Savigny & Guthrie 1869: para 349, 36). Enlightenment philosophers of Kant's ilk were undecided as to whether rights could be exercised immorally (Kennedy 2010: 833–834).

PrIL's function plays out at different levels as well as inter-spatially, in the horizontal coordination of a plurality of legal frameworks, rules, norms, principles and choices. A fine balance is needed to coordinate legal diversity and pluralism on the one hand and maintain social order on the other. Comity and the public policy exception deserve special attention in this regard.

Fitting legal subject matter into legal categories—obligations, things and persons, delicts, etc.—is an intermediate step between abstract legal ideas and material circumstances that precede the creation of doctrinal systems. This step serves to communicate or alter legal ideas that can impact the material world (Hatzimihail 2021: 179). When assigning a set of facts to a legal category, it is understandable that forum law may direct the assignment, but when assessing an issue or foreign rule, international judicial comity is fulfilled by application of the rule in the setting from which it emanates (Garnett 2012: para 3.06). Comity justifies deference to foreign cultural property and heritage law of foreign judgments and their definitions of cultural heritage. Comity may be defined as international duty and convenience with limits expressed through the public policy exception. As will be explained more fully, the precise point at which the limit of tolerance arises will always remain unclear (Michaels 2019: 17).

The public policy exception in PrIL enables a court to apply its own law if the foreign applicable law is manifestly contrary or incompatible with a public policy of the forum, e.g., when the foreign law identified for application violates a fundamental principle of justice or is repugnant to good morals. The public policy doctrine defines the outer limits of the 'tolerance of difference' implicit in choice-of-law rules and rules governing the recognition and enforcement of foreign judgments and arbitral awards. This function is of cardinal importance in multicultural societies in a globalising world (Struycken 2009: 395; Michaels 2019: 17). 'Recognition' can achieve what another pillar of PrIL, choice-of-law rules, may not be able to achieve. The decision of whether to allow the application of a foreign legal rule requires adjudicators to consider if, in light of current societal values, they will accommodate or deny 'foreignness.' If they decided to deny it, the public policy exception is invoked to escape from the rule (Muir Watt 2017: 111). The 'negative effect' of this traditional mechanism of the general PrIL theory is to exclude the foreign law, judgment, or concept. Its 'positive effect' is the application of another law, which is most often that of the forum (Fresnedo de Aguirre 2019: 342–343).

The leading example of the public policy exception in UK courts is the racially discriminatory and confiscatory 1941 Nazi decree depriving Jewish emigres of their German nationality and leading to the confiscation of their property (e.g. *Oppenheimer v Cattermole* [1976] AC 249). In the *Kuwait Airways Corp* case, the court disregarded a provision in the foreign law that constitutes so grave an infringement of human rights that English courts ought to refuse to recognise it; 'to do otherwise would affront basic principles of justice and fairness' which the courts seek to apply in the administration of justice (*Kuwait Airways Corp v Iraqi Airways Co & Anor* [2002] UKHL 19 para 18). English courts have also considered it arguable that the corruption of foreign public officials is contrary to English public policy or that such a policy is developing (see e.g., *Crane Bank Ltd v DFCU Bank Ltd* [2023] EWCA Civ 886, paras 61–63 on the recognition of the public policy exception based on a policy of combatting corruption). When the threshold for tolerance has been crossed in the applicable law or its application introduces issues with public policy or moral values, the choice-of-law process will be interrupted, and the law of the court directed to apply.

The flexibility of the public policy exception makes its operation hard to pin down, but it can function to guard against the application of commercial rules that would be morally repugnant in the context of violence, force, and duress. Both comity and the public policy exception are 'safety nets' that have the potential to coordinate primary and secondary legal rules across statutory enactments and conventions on the protection of cultural property and heritage. This coordination can be performed in both the juridical framework for circulation and exception. Without PrIL fulfilling its crucial co-ordinating function in the framework of exception in colonial contexts, more pressure can be expected to accumulate to improve judicial responsiveness in areas such as access to justice, social responsibility, and moral standards.

A disciplinary identity crisis obfuscates PrIL's broad co-ordinating framework of global conflict of laws systems and its co-ordinating function. Normative conflicts in a legal pluralist framework push the legal relationship to the centre of the stage. PrIL is both private and international, standing within and outside domestic legal systems. Either dimension could determine the conceptual framework for an international dispute (Graveson 1974a: 42; Graveson 1974b: 216). An internal vantage point may be assumed because, as an institutional part of a particular domestic legal system, PrIL's capacity for resolving normative conflict depends on its capacity to manage diversity internally while subject to the peculiarities of state power. An 'external' vantage point may be assumed as a strategic view of the challenges faced by contemporary legal theory that does not negate the need for international intercourse and to 'live in the world' (Graveson 1974b: 198). Outside of any domestic legal system, PrIL can ensure accountability in the relationship between global law and justice (Muir Watt 2016a). In the relationship between 'Self and Other' and 'the forum and the foreign', new ways may be found to negotiate the increasing complexity of a multi-plural world in 'respect for alterity' and 'reception of the foreign' (Muir Watt 2014: 374; 2017: 125). Normative conflicts change what the law 'is' because the setup on the stage changes.

No method should become isolated from its theoretical foundations and from the policy implications of broader political, social, and legal processes (Hatzimihail 2021: 7). As a method or a technique, splendid isolation renders PrIL incapable of meeting the challenges of our age (Neidhardt 2018: 29). According to the Archimedean metaphor, two things are needed to change the world: A lever and a firm place to stand. PrIL helps to stabilise the theoretical ground so that its method and technique can be better aligned.

If the theoretical ground is firm and stable, the 'lever of the law' can be used to shift some of the load of the past. Deploying PrIL's ethic of responsiveness to the Other as a lever can curb the pressures of capitalism and ethnographic difference in normative spaces within the interlocking network of domestic, provincial, national, regional, international and transnational norms. This will improve the visibility of criteria for ethical judgments in transnational cases. Not only will the public policy exception be deployed as needed, but more of the juridical framework of exception will be available to alleviate the pressure which accumulates through continued circulation of sacred cultural material. PrIL's core function and purview must be clarified, starting with its depth potential, putting comity and the public policy exception to work, and establishing how best to communicate its potential and the tools to achieve it.

3.4 Acknowledging PrIL's depth potential

Cost/benefit analyses indicate that, in disputes involving cultural property, uniform law fares better than PrIL rules and approaches because the cost of application of uniform law is lower, the number of cases is smaller than other civil and commercial cases, and the risk of national courts under-estimating the global welfare needs of the international community and its members, is lower (Kono 2020). If the source state has adopted the 1995 UNIDROIT Convention on Stolen or Illicitly Exported Cultural Objects, the uniform law embodied in the convention's provisions will apply. For example, having signed the 1995 UNIDROIT Convention, France and the Netherlands cannot legislate against it. However, neither Germany nor Britain signed up to the Convention, and their position would be different because in these jurisdictions property law and heritage treaties interact differently in international civil claims. Whereas some (secondary) legal norms and rules have been harmonised in the 1995 UNDROIT Convention, neither the 1995 UNDROIT nor the 1970 UNESCO Convention on the Means of Prohibiting and Preventing the Illicit Import, Export and Transfer of Ownership of Cultural Property regulates the basic questions regulated by secondary legal norms. For instance, the conventions do not venture to propose rules on the competency of the court to hear the case, stipulating which court assumes jurisdiction; neither do they stipulate which law is supposed to govern a dispute over cultural objects that were stolen or transferred illegally. They do not determine the scope and reach of application of differing national laws, and do not indicate when additional steps need to be taken to have judgments reached in the courts of country X, recognised and enforced in the courts of country Y. These conventions do not contain mechanisms to ensure the consistent application of treaty norms in dispute-settlement. Importantly, they do not embody the full PrIL system replete with escape clauses and core techniques that control the application of choice-of-law rules. While international instruments contain special rules regarding protections and returns of cultural heritage, these are not always applicable. Harmonised or uniform law does not fully support restitution of sacred material and resort may need to be had to residual conflict rules that could fill the gap.

Seeing PrIL's function merely as solving international disputes through recourse to the most appropriate legal system sells the discipline short. A more adequate explanation of the drivers and consequences of socio-political developments in PrIL is urgently needed, for PrIL's tools may be expected to disappear when they cease to be useful to those who can use them (Riles 2005: 1016). As a field of law regulating private relationships with a relevant link to at least one foreign system in a private law approach, PrIL does not enable the application of foreign law as a concession or a favour to a foreign state. Rather, its application is obligated under PublIL, which the statutory rationale for the application of foreign law does not reveal. The primary legal norms may simply indicate application 'because our system ordains it' (e.g., Private International Law (Miscellaneous Provisions) Act 1995; Private International Law (Implementation of Agreements) Act 2020)).

PrIL's dimensions are not confined to time and space. The differences in culture, concept, and the governance in relation to diversity give rise to 'three-dimensional problems of space, time and depth' (Graveson 1974b: 229). The public policy exception and comity principle condition the relationship between international and domestic law to 'overcome differences of legal systems.' On the other hand, as the *Rukoro* litigation indicated, deference to the market may prevent the establishment of jurisdiction in a claim arising from genocide. This deference could conceivably preclude the recognition and enforcement of a foreign judgment. Attention must turn to PrIL's depth potential in its relationship to time, i.e. historical injustice. Its common rules of adjudication and the structure of arguments about principles that coordinate primary and secondary legal rules may activate the ethic of PrIL, even if the interpretation of conflicts rules and techniques such as classification can also shut it down.

Hessel Yntema (1891–1966), a US legal scholar, located the purpose of the conflict of laws in defining the exceptions necessary in the substantive rules of local law. He found it obvious that 'the reasons for these exceptions, and not the formal doctrine, present the real issues' (Yntema 1953: 316–317). Yntema conceived of practical and equitable considerations by which conflicts cases could be adjudicated, without assuming that domestic or local law is supreme when a conflict of laws arises. In writings that adopted a critical stance in respect of 'a shallow and even a brutal philosophy … that law is power' he foreshadowed the need to undertake restorative work in relation to public policy. He was wary of an 'exaggerated local policy' that permits the sovereign and its agents 'to do as they please.' His approach demonstrates the political relevance of PrIL doctrine and practice and shares common ground with Krygier's definition of the rule of law (Krygier 2024).

3.4.1 The public policy exception

Of all the branches of law, PublIL and PrIL articulate international public policy most clearly. Public policy differs in its 'national' and 'international' character. In international matters it would not necessarily include everything embraced by the term 'public policy' as it is applied to a purely internal matter (e.g., insurance, war risks, or the compensation payable by those who committed torts). Because the public policy exception offers an escape from the ordinary conflicts of laws method and is not concerned with domestic substantive rules which parties may not set aside (so-called mandatory rules), the scope of 'international (or external) public policy' is 'narrower' than that of 'national public policy.' The highest test of domestic or national public policy may be found in a country's constitution, but the public policy exception in PrIL may also be constitutionally constrained (e.g., the PrIL of prescription and limitation). This is because the evolution of the fundamental principle of a certain state is reflected in domestic rules and may be relevant when determining the scope of international public policy (Fresnedo de Aguirre 2019: 343).

The operation of the international public policy exception can be seen beyond fundamental principles enshrined in human rights conventions and PrIL conventions (Fresnedo de Aguirre 2019: 341). Its operation is also discernible in relation to peace treaties, international humanitarian law, investment treaties, and treaties for the protection of cultural property. PrIL's public policy exception operates in relation to national and international law, but PrIL is more than just a part of private or civil law. As stated at the outset of Chapter 3, PrIL also has its eye on foreign policy. The assumption that the framework of exception encompasses only criminal law joins forces with the inaccurate idea that PrIL is a dimension of private law Together they create a conceptual hurdle to restitution claims as the framework of exception is underused.

The 'architecture' and operation of contemporary cultural heritage law depend on norms, rules, and principles that belong to frameworks of criminal or civil law and case law. The interface between local, domestic, and PrIL conceptions of property in the juridical framework of exception is constituted partly by criminal law and criminal procedure, but the outcomes of civil restitution claims also depend on this framework because criminal law principles and proceedings have implications for civil actions and limits that affect de-accessioning decisions (Zeidler 2016: 40). In other words, while the tenets, procedures, and remedies available in civil and commercial law differ fundamentally from those in criminal cases, the policy implications of criminal deeds, crimes against humanity, and the crime of aggression have ramifications for civil actions concerning the protection of cultural heritage that may invoke the tenets of PrIL. It is not the precise elements of crimes or genocide that concern PrIL nor the exact nature of the criminal liability when the elements are proven to co-exist, but the policy implications. For instance, the non-application of the statute of limitations defence when crimes against humanity including the looting and destruction of cultural property occurred would be justifiable on public policy frounds. Arguably, this is a constructive interpretation of national law in light of the current state of international law (Chechi 2017/2018: 286).

Inadequate definition of the juridical framework of exception will necessarily muddy the waters around the obligation to return sacred cultural heritage. The relationship between national and international law, moral merit, and ethics is decidedly complex, but realistic legal discourses on restitution must take an active interest in the relationship between PublIL and domestic laws. To resist the normative effect of mimetism in regulatory and ethics frameworks several branches of law need to work together. For instance, colonial reparations claims originate outside PrIL's ambit yet may affect the development and application of conflict principles for ownership and title of cultural objects collected through colonial-era looting and theft.

PrIL's public policy exception can render inapplicable ordinary property and commercial law rules in civil courts. When courts identify policy issues in the cultural sphere and sufficient normative leverage justifies the suspension of the rules that support commerce, they may suspend the commercial thrust of art market transactions, including the rules of contract. Where a criminal offense has been committed, the public policy exception requires transplanting the question of whether the defendants acted with the 'purpose' of facilitating a criminal act from international criminal law to PrIL (Ferrando 2019: 236, 241). Making this purpose fit within the material scope of PrIL legislation such as the US Alien Tort Statute (28 US Code 1350) can obscure the juridical framework of exception because of the shadow case by the juridical framework of circulation.

3.4.2 Comity

The Roman-Dutch law scholar Ulrik Huber (1635-1694) compiled the introductory lectures *Praelectionis ad Pandectas* while appointed to the University of Franeker and the Court of Friesland. His tract 'On the Conflict of Different Laws in Different States' (*De Conflictu Legum Diversarum in Diversis Imperiis,* lib.1 tit 4) appeared in 1689 as part of the *Praelectionis. De Conflictu Legum* marks his contributions to the Dutch school of Early Modern conflict of laws. Huber's propositions made a lasting contribution to the field as the basis of the English doctrine regarding the conflict of laws.

The notion of comity encapsulated the constraints dictated by reason on the authority of statesmen in interactions among legal equals with no 'common superior' aside from the 'collectivity of themselves' respectfully interacting with other members of the community of states. Huber's work was held in high esteem by British jurists of the 18th century, the North American British colonies that retained English common law after independence, as well as South African universities. Joseph Story (1779–1845), the influential American lawyer, was also schooled in Huber's propositions. Story attributed the obligation to apply foreign law to comity but downplayed it as a mere 'courtesy'. The decision to apply or not to apply foreign law to best meet the public policies of their own domestic order was up to the discretion of responsible officials in each state (Rubin 1997: 132-133). Huber invoked comity as one of the three foundational axioms of his system in *De Conflictu Legum* (para 2, tr Davies 1937: 64):

> Those who exercise sovereign authority so act from comity, that the laws of every nation having been applied within its own boundaries should retain their effect everywhere so far as they do not prejudice the powers or rights of another state, or its subjects.

While the doctrine of comity provides a theoretical foundation upon which a conflicts system can be constructed, the rules and principles that make up the doctrinal solutions for concrete problems are the backbone of the system Huber put forward (tr Davies 1937: 58; Hatzimihail 2021: 425). His method moves from theoretical foundations to legal norms that make up a doctrinal system for jurisdiction, applicable law, and foreign judgments.

Huber associated the *comitas gentium* and the notion of PrIL as *jus gentium*. Granting recognition to foreign law and judgments was not a matter of courtesy for Huber. He considered the operation of the comity principle a matter of international duty and convenience. He acknowledged that the forum could refuse the effects produced by legal acts—judicial decisions—in its territory if recognition would give rise to prejudice. This exception to his comity doctrine is open to interpretation either as an escape clause, or as a defence of domestic policy (Hatzimihail 2021: 478). Huber's desire to ensure the other provinces observed Frisian law, and his main concern was with conflicts between Friesland and the United Provinces of the Netherlands explains why his comity doctrine was uniquely associated with legal duty. Holland could afford to take unilateral action in respect of the eastern provinces and their dealings with the rest of the world (Hatzimihail 2021: 383–384, 430).

Evidence of Huber's influence in the classical conflicts doctrine that emerged in the second half of the 19th century on the European continent is harder to trace compared to the British colonies (Hatzimihail 2021: 354–356). Between 1870 and 1946 the understanding that PrIL was mandated by PublIL dominated continental jurisprudence. Savigny, using the law-of-nations doctrine in conflicts law, postulated that international law requires states to apply foreign law in appropriate cases. While highly convincing, Savigny's formulation is incomplete as it does not take account of national laws mandating PrIL. The American understanding became evident during the high point of classical conflicts, when the US Supreme Court defined comity as 'neither a matter of absolute obligation … nor of mere courtesy and goodwill' and derived a reciprocity requirement for the enforcement of foreign judgments (*Hilton v Guyot* 159 US 113, 163–164 (1895)).

Adjudicators may rely on comity to reject the application of the foreign law indicated in choice-of-law rules and to refuse recognition and enforcement of foreign judgments that contravene fundamental principles and values or overriding mandatory rules—i.e., rules which cannot be set aside by any foreign law that may claim application by virtue of PrIL rules—in the court's legal system. Because internal as well as external conflicts prevailed in the colonies, Huber's comity doctrine is instructive. Comity theory does not determine the actual rule of law but operates more as a policy-oriented enabling principle. Noting the structural and doctrinal similarity of transnational recognition and enforcement approaches, Stamboulakis observes that a broad conception of comity supports a presumption that reinforces a free acceptance of foreign decisions without review of the merits of the original decision, and limits grounds of refusal that are usually strictly enumerated. These grounds act as 'safety valves' that safeguard the policies of the forum. The source of the underlying legal instrumentation—be it general law, statutory regimes, or domestic enactments of treaties to harmonise recognition and enforcement—is less important (Stamboulakis 2023: 260). The activation of a broad conception of comity promises to be of benefit to restitution claims for sacred cultural heritage.

When assessing a foreign rule, international judicial comity is fulfilled by application of the rule in the setting from which it emanates. The assessment will be more compelling if the colonial context were fully acknowledged. An adjudicator's point of view is bound to be shaped by the laws and customs of their own state. However, applying the PrIL of their own state does not mean they are compelled to apply their own substantive law (Banu 2018: 133, 135).

Comity calls for mutual respect and understanding between nations, recognition of foreign concepts, and recognition and enforcement of judgements which disincentivise parallel litigation in courts in different states. Reciprocal accommodation is particularly beneficial in relation to standing. Sacred stones believed to embody ancestral spirits are accorded legal standing in jurisdictions such as India, where the courts recognise the legal personhood of Hindu deities. Nothing prevents western courts about to rule on *locus standi* from following suit by virtue of comity. This is the appropriate legal mechanism by which the sacred can be acknowledged. Legal personhood may be more readily granted to many different role occupants: groups of humans and bodies corporate whose behaviours the law seeks to regulate despite restrictive tendencies towards religion in law, non-humans, and more-than-humans. Since English law was known to restrict legal personality to corporations, personified groups, or series of individuals with animate content, it posed a 'formidable' conceptual difficulty when English courts were asked to recognise 'a pile of stones' as a party entitled to sue. Asked to assess the personhood of an inanimate temple that had lain in ruins for centuries against the principles of legal personality, the English court turned to Sir John Salmond, who noted that 'legal persons, being the arbitrary creations of the law, may be of as many kinds as the law pleases' (Salmond 1966: 306; *Bumper Development Corporation v Commissioner of Police for the Metropolis* [1991] 1 WLR 1364, 1371–1372). Although the Hindu temple was unrecognisable as a juristic entity under English law, imposition of 'any fetter of an artificial procedural nature imported from the *lex fori*' which might otherwise prevent recognition of an enforceable right under the *lex causae* is not the preferred course of action, according to Salmond (at 1373). Salmond uses English law to explain that a court may attribute personality to a group of persons as corporate entities, institutions such as churches or hospitals, or the body of persons administering an estate or property of the dead. An English court would not refuse to recognise the legal personality accorded to a foreign Roman Catholic Cathedral under the law of the country where it is situated (by virtue of enabling legislation that confers on an officer the right to sue for the protection and recovery of its contents), simply on the ground that English law would not recognise a similarly constituted entity as a legal person (*National Bank of Greece & Athens S. A. v Metliss* [1958] AC 509, 525). Recognition can be facilitated by clear instructions regarding next friend representation or guardianship, but guardianship is no prerequisite for recognition (Cacot 2021: 59–61).

The *Bumper* cases demonstrate how return claims involving sacred cultural heritage can be settled when personhood is attributed domestically and recognised internationally. The English precedent underlines the value of the comity of nations as the touchstone in cases relating to material alienated during the colonial era, when determining whether legal personality attributed by legal system X ought to be recognised by the forum when its recognition is required for the case to proceed to the merits.

Value judgments played a significant part in the rulings on the Zhanggong Zushi mummy and the question of the claimants' *locus standi*. Whereas the Chinese courts confirmed the obligations implicit in cultural material that communally belong to groups who possess traditional knowledge about sacred traditions, the Dutch court remained passive in the face of the mummy's need for protection and did not concede standing to its custodians. The Dutch court applied domestic law and jurisprudence to require the claimants to show that they were natural or legal persons qualified to bring civil proceedings. The court reasoned that any uncertainty about the identity of the claimants would cause inevitable procedural problems, including uncertainty over who would be bound by the ruling or against whom to seek execution of an order for costs. It took the view that the claimants did not make a convincing case that they qualified to bring proceedings or that an exception should apply (*Amsterdam District Court, Village Committee of Yangchun and Dongpu v Oscar van Overeem* 2018, para 4.2).

The International Law Association (ILA) Committee on Participation in Global Cultural Heritage Governance made normative suggestions for changes in institutional practice to help remove obstacles to standing for collective claimants and non-state actors such as cultural heritage non-governmental organisations (NGOs) (Resolution 01/2022). However, the scope for judicial findings on *locus standi* to coincide will remain limited without a more convergent conception of the nature and value of sacred material—both tangible and intangible. Divergent conceptions make it harder to identify rules of law supporting return, and comity's role in surmounting conflicting determinations on standing and outcomes in parallel litigation is easily obscured.

3.4.3 Common structure of recognition and enforcement argument

With regards to the recognition and enforcement of foreign judgments, categories of allowable or objectionable foreign decisions differ across legal systems. In some systems, these categories (which may include exorbitant or excessive types or measures of damages, for instance) serve to prohibit enforcement (Stamboulakis 2023: 164). Others remain silent in this respect. European Union (EU) Member States' courts follow the Brussels Model which includes the Brussels I Regulation and adopts a closed system that is also exhaustive (Regulation (EU) No 1215/2012 of the European Parliament and of the Council of 12 December 2012 on jurisdiction and the recognition and enforcement of judgments in civil and commercial matters (recast) OJ L 351, 20.12.2012). Closed approaches aim to exclusively set out all acceptable bases for recognition and enforcement, as well as any allowable grounds for refusal. Matters or jurisdictional bases that are not enumerated in this approach, or that fall foul of a ground of refusal, are excluded so that the foreign decision cannot be recognised and enforced in that jurisdiction at all. If the judgment coming for recognition and enforcement is from another Brussels Model participant, the Brussels Model's provisions fully regulate this process (Stamboulakis 2023: 145–146).

Outside of the Brussels Model, transnational recognition and enforcement approaches are largely doctrinally similar and functionally equivalent. They share common concepts of reciprocity, limitations, or exclusions, as well as instrumental features facilitating transnational consensus and adoption of the underlying instruments. In practice, diverse judgments emanate from disparate legal systems. Contemporary critics of the comity doctrine have pointed out that it struggles to meet the greater need for predictable and harmonised recognition and enforcement necessitated by the increasing internationalisation of cross-border dealings (Stamboulakis 2023: 260). To have the final ruling of the Chinese court in the Zhanggong Zushi mummy case recognised and enforced in the Netherlands, legal action is required. If informed by a broad conception of comity it may succeed. Chapter 2 highlighted the procedure for recognition and enforcement of judicial orders in the Netherlands issued by a foreign court. However, in this instance even successful recognition will not result in the return of the Zhanggong Zushi mummy because its current whereabouts are unknown.

3.4.4 Human remains: Primary legal norms and classificatory challenges in secondary legal norms

In relation to legal claims to human remains primary legal norms create a measure of legal certainty. For instance, under the Native American Graves Protection and Repatriation Act (NAGPRA), museums are required to inventory their collections and assess the items for shared group identity that may be traced back 'historically or prehistorically' to an identifiable earlier group (para 3001). Evidence may be based on ten different categories. Kinship, folkloric, oral tradition, historical information, or expert opinion are included among those, with determinations based on a preponderance of evidence. Disputes may be settled upon identification of the ethnic group most closely affiliated with a dead person, or the 'homeland' of the deceased. The updated Final Rule to improve implementation of the NAGPRA (43 CFR Part 10 of 13 December 2023) limits the inventory requirement only to human remains and associated funerary objects rather than all Native American collections. Federally recognised tribes used to bear the full burden of proving affiliation for claims to objects designated as culturally unidentifiable to succeed but the definition of cultural affiliation has been clarified and the category 'culturally unidentifiable human remains' eliminated.

To prove that the Stone Being T'xwelátse belonged to their cultural patrimony, the Nooksack community was asked how they would rate its importance in terms of its cultural, historical, and traditional significance to the Nooksack and the Stó:lō people as a whole (Schaepe 2005: 30). The T'xwelátse was handed to the Nooksack in 2006, and the Nooksack community returned it to the Stó:lō in Canada. It now resides at the Reach Gallery Museum in Abbotsford, British Columbia. One of the abiding lessons of the Stone Being's story is that the distinction between history and prehistory is ethically irrelevant. Distinctions between human fossils and human remains for ethical purposes are unwarranted (Stahn 2023: 285).

While Indigenous perspectives of ancestry consider human remains affiliated by their relationship within the cultural group, the European conception of cultural affiliation contemplates a blood relationship (Woodhead 2002: 340). Indigenous groups' conceptions of time also differs from European conceptions. Considering the scales of space time and depth, one might say that a geological sense of time goes with an astronomical sense of space. Acknowledgement of the agency of the non-human makes way for a more unlimited perception of time than humans are capable of, possibly transcending the outdated subject-object dualism of traditional archaeological theory (in general, Barad 2003: 828). Space time perspectives will provide vital clues for identifying local knowledge and culturally specific information about cultural material, traditions, and customs that can fill in the identity subtext of objects and the intangible dimension of knowledge they embody. Widening the spatial perspective may reveal the integrated relations that connect the material object and the community's relational dimension. This could permit the juridical framework of exception to steer such claims. Normative change will benefit further from widening temporal perspectives and from scaling the depth dimension of the law.

Occasionally disputes involving human remains make it to the courts and adjudicators are faced with deciding costly lawsuits with indeterminable facts and uncertain applicable law. The nature of the material object may need to be determined first to select which rules to apply and yet smuggling operations and the cross-border transfer of a tangible cultural object could undermine the special status of an object that would make its transfer null and void (*Tribunal civil de la Seine, Duc de Frias v Baron Pichon*, 17 April 1885, Clunet 1886, 593). The nature of the cultural material in question has implications for adjudicators' use of the PrIL toolbox in international disputes. Called upon to ascertain the type of cultural heritage in issue under their respective legal systems (assuming they categorise a material object as 'cultural property' or 'cultural heritage'), national courts are unlikely to concur. The classification of sacred cultural heritage such as human remains and their encasements will require special attention. Whereas Chinese law does not distinguish human remains from other kinds of cultural relics, common law legal systems have a no-property rule in corpses or any part thereof unless specifically enabled by Parliament or Congress. Although human remains are not 'cultural property' in any general sense, Honoré's theory and normative framework allows for situations in which a corpse would feature among the incidents of ownership and be considered property. The legal argument which the village committees advanced in the Amsterdam District Court was that the Dutch Burial and Cremation Act (*Wet op de Lijkbezorging*) applies and precludes property rights in human remains (*Village Committee of Yangchun and Dongpu v Oscar van Overeem,* Amsterdam District Court 2018). Ownership could not vest in corpses, and the right of disposal belonged to none other but themselves as trustees (para 3.1). The Dutch collector's counterargument that 'corpses' have internal organs overturned their argument. Indeed, the mummified monk's remains are artefactual and not awaiting burial. The Amsterdam District Court circumvented the issue raised by the argument that the mummy was a corpse by finding that the village committees lacked standing to sue.

The classification of legal rules or facts or causes of action forms part of the choice-of-law method to determine the 'applicable law' in international civil proceedings. Classificatory challenges relating to the rules, facts, and causes of action may arise. To identify which rules and which legal system's rules are invoked by the facts of the dispute in question, courts prefer to employ a single, predominant category to determine a single applicable law. If this is inconclusive, the court will not formulate or apply special conflicts rules. Choice-of-law rules are general in scope and not tailored to cultural property (Chechi 2017/2018: 274). For instance, the choice-of-law rule governing the validity of transfer of property rights, the *lex situs* rule, is designed as a conflicts rule for proprietary rights in commercial trade. It applies to all manner of moveable property in an acontextual way and does not take account of the special nature or needs of cultural property. Chechi cautions that choice-of-law rules lead to unpredictable outcomes and detrimental effects for the resolution of disputes (Chechi 2017/2018: 293).

The success of restitution claims for cultural heritage in western courts frequently turns on proprietary rights. Property rights are protected not only in property law (rights *in rem*), but also in the law of tort. Claims for the restitution of stolen property based on tortious acts are typically governed by the law of the place of the tortious act. In Chinese law, the liability for tort can be discharged by returning the property in question (Tort Law of the People's Republic of China, No. 21, 2009). Claims for material damages could compensate cultural communities for harms of cultural appropriation if intellectual property or tort law were relied on to rectify civil wrongs in heritage protection (Brown 2005: 44).

Competitive elements of self-sacrifice notwithstanding, the monks who dedicated years of their lives to self-mummification did not do so to encourage heritage tourism, confer research benefits, or cater to touristic voyeurism. Still, whether human remains and mummies constitute 'property' is of considerable importance to those with purchasing power on the art market. Should mummies be classified as property because human activity produces them, and it is assumed that property rights vest in them? Had the mummified monk's case reached the merits stage in Amsterdam, the 'potentially applicable law' would have had to be determined if the choice of law method had been invoked. The potentially applicable legal systems could be the law at the time of the claim (Dutch law), the time of the acquisition (Hong Kong law), or the time of the theft (Chinese law). Regarding the category of 'property,' domestic property law may enable characterisations such as 'material,' 'immaterial', 'tangible,' and 'intangible,' but the exact divisions among the categories vary considerably across different legal traditions and systems. Consequently, under the law of X a mummified monk of known identity may be considered a person who owns their body (or a deceased person who owns their body after death) and is autonomous and free to determine how their body is to be disposed of (or not) , but the law of Y may recognise property rights in it. The applicable law may recognise property rights over human remains; consider mummies as property on account of the human activity needed to produce them, permit autonomous persons to own and dispose of their bodies as they choose, recognise that a deceased person owns their body after death, or recognise possessory rights of surviving relatives while making funeral arrangements (van Vliet 2006: 109–123). The 'applicable law' would govern the validity of the creation, content, exercise, and transfer of property rights.

In the civil law tradition, legal systems generally do not recognise property rights in human remains (Paterson 2017: 71, 81). In Dutch law, mummies tend to be classified as property rather than dead persons by virtue of being archaeological finds, which 'overshadow(s) the fact that these are dead persons' (Van Vliet

2006: 112). Moreover, objects made from human remains, such as the ashes of a cremated corpse, are more easily recognised as property than the human remains themselves (Van Vliet 2006: 3). Ordinary human remains would not be recognised as property, but the position is likely different for, e.g., ḍamaru handdrums made of the skulls of a male and female child for Tibetan Buddhist ritual use. A beaker made from a skull is also likely to be recognised as property.

Chinese law does not distinguish human remains from other cultural relics protected under the 1982 Law on the Protection of Cultural Relics of the People's Republic of China, No. 76, as amended on 29 June 2013 (Liu 2017: 229). Chinese law extends protection to historic human remains enshrined in religious sites and temples as cultural relics. The encased mummified monk qualifies for legal protection as a 'cultural relic' (Liu 2017: 225). Dead bodies may not be disposed of as commodities under Chinese law. Human remains could also constitute part of the inheritance of heirs (Yuen 2018: 63–64).

The legal definitions of human remains and 'cultural property' that inform the process of classification are not objective. They reflect the institutional power structures that control the heritage narrative; the process of determining what is recognised as heritage and who may develop a collective sense of identity and memory form part of this narrative (Linn-Tynen 2020: 262).

The obvious—that sacred cultural material engender obligations which deserve the respect of the judicial system—may be glossed over precisely because it is so self-evident. The substantive and procedural questions raised with respect to removal of sacred material from complex colonial contexts could miss the bodies of knowledge that hold this insight because of the assumptions hiding underneath the classification of the legal rules, factual problems, or cause of action in the PrIL toolbox. If due attention is paid to the nature of the sacred and the common structure of arguments, it is more likely that the ethic of PrIL will be activated. A closer look at PrIL's potential in the ethical domain is warranted because activating the ethic of PrIL in its relationship to historical injustice brings into view new pathways to restitution.

3.5 Activating the ethic of PrIL

The link between the generation and global circulation of value on the one hand and the destruction of cultural forms of life on the other hand calls for greater scrutiny of the role of law in the construction and maintenance of global value chains (Mills 2019: 118). The tentacles of colonialism run deep in the private sphere where PrIL struggles to relieve the jurisdictional pressures of access to justice and social responsibility. Private actors exercise power beyond the state in global supply chains in which the interests of small constituencies are catered to by co-opted regulators. PrIL techniques may simply replicate broader structures of law and historical power relations, permitting perverse results. Given PrIL's role in the modern imperial enterprise, sceptics doubt that it has the empowering epistemology or appropriate methods to drive multistate justice or change the perspective from which questions of legal theory emanate (Muir Watt 2016a: 390, 394–397).

Daring examples of conflicting claims, values, interests, ideals, and norms 'beyond the remit of state law' are multiplying (e.g., in torts committed by transnational corporations), but theory has not yet caught up with practice (Muir Watt 2016a: 401). The formal doctrines of the conflict of laws have the capacity to harbour an obsession with rights, which discourages theorisation (Muir Watt 2016b: 341).

The ethical dimension in society aspires to co-operation and mutuality (Wilde 2013: 105, 117, 119–120, 191ff). 'Solidarity' expresses what binds members of society. It may also give expression to the essence of our obligation to society (Bergson 1935: 6, 67). Global solidarity depends on connections between various levels and degrees of interhuman solidarity in different social contexts. It is built on a normative ideal with a moral aim located in the cultural sphere. It will be easier to increase PrIL's capacity in cross-border private law relations at the micro-level of interhuman interaction in a framework of global solidarity if the analytical and conceptual elements of the global justice debates connected to PrIL can emerge from the shadows. The links between well-founded perspectives in the global justice literature and 'normative approaches excavated from PrIL's own arsenal' deserve to be made apparent (Banu 2018: 304).

3.5.1 PrIL's technical arsenal

Dialogue about restitution is becoming more common in our day, but a dialogue between fundamentally different world views will not always reorganise those world views into broader perspectives on, for example, what an object is and what obligations it engenders (Silverman 2015: 291). If dialogue fails and court proceedings follow, the position of one party will be confirmed and that of the other(s) negated. To apply a single rule of judgment to both positions 'as though it were merely a litigation' would 'wrong (at least) one of them' (Lyotard 1988: xi). There is much to discover about the cultural and political processes at work by examining PrIL's technicalities, however. The way in which the PrIL arsenal is used, foregrounds the relationship between legal thought and substantive values in PrIL outcomes. PrIL's technical arsenal may be analysed through the doctrinal canon, but also through ethnography, which makes accessible as theory what is considered commonplace. PrIL devices such as characterisation, the public policy exception, and comity are also highly constructive analytical aids for the legal pluridiversity that marks restitution claims arising from colonial contexts. Ultimately their neglect is a neglect of the core of legal thought. A willingness to excavate PrIL's technical arsenal assumes considerable importance, therefore. Michaels 2019: 26) intimates that PrIL's technique and method in relation to foreign law is subtle yet powerful, as it 'takes the Other more seriously than mere deference would.' Although he did not share this insight in relation to the removal of sacred cultural heritage during the colonial era, it provides a helpful perspective on the relation between the foreign law and the forum's law.

'Tolerance', 'recognition' and 'hospitality' have been used as lenses through which PrIL scholars consider the basic ethics of PrIL (e.g. Muir Watt 2017: 111ff). The degree of deference to the foreign may be so low as to evoke an attitude of 'wilful ignorance.' Any potentially applicable foreign law may have to 'beg' to be acknowledged. With recognition, the foreign is at times deferred in accordance with a hierarchical relation. The 'recognition' of identity is insufficient both in ethics and in PrIL (Michaels 2019: 19). The reason is not hard to see, for non-recognition is inescapable if the structural relations established during the early years of European modernity define the wider context. The disciplinary divisions transmitted by modernity express value judgments implicit in binaries of public/private, civil/criminal, forum/foreign, domestic/international. PrIL may be tempted to intrude too far, cementing one identity to the exclusion of all others (Michaels 2019: 19–20). Foreign law may request or demand recognition by the forum because of its 'need'. Because the relationship is predicated on need, it is 'ethical' before it is 'ontological' (Michaels 2019: 16–23). However, recognising ourselves in the claims, generosity can be extended. With hospitality, acceptance is unlimited and unconditional. Striking parallels emerge between the PrIL relation between the foreign law and the forum's law, and Lévinas's conception of the 'face' of the Other whose needs already place them in a certain relation to me (Michaels 2019: 21).

Neither unlimited hospitality nor mere survival offers a satisfactory explanation of the foreign law/forum law relation. The question is what that relation might entail (Michaels 2019: 23). Michaels employs the parallels with Lévinas's conception to argue that an ethical approach to PrIL must recognise the other as 'both similar and different,' but also as 'both independent and related.' The recognition by a European court of the limitations imposed by Chinese law in respect of cultural relics is essentially a question which the court that hears the request for recognition must answer.

The technical dimension of legal form is an important antecedent for the cultural study of PrIL. PrIL was purported to be purely instrumental. It was designed to answer formalistic and doctrinal questions about jurisdictional scope and thereby achieved the appearance of neutrality (Muir Watt 2014: 377). The technical legal knowledge that is required for the optimisation of the tools of conflicts jurisprudence lodges in theories, models, arguments, techniques, and methodologies whose application requires technical expertise (Riles 2005: 982–984). Riles maintains that the tools play such an important role in the production of legal knowledge that they need to be viewed as 'politics by other means' (Riles 2005: 986).

PrIL cannot be isolated from the political processes around it without risking disciplinary demise. The technical legal knowledge embedded in the structure and tools employed by PrIL jurisprudence is connected to moral philosophy; in combination, it becomes more possible for 'substance' to resist 'form.' When drawing the line between movables/immovables, procedure/substance, etc., adjudicators must apply legal precepts, methods, and arguments to guide them in the direction of corrective justice for a liberal jurisprudence. Excavation of the methodological arsenal of PrIL leads Michaels to submit that PrIL is an 'ethic of responsivity' and that we 'operate in ethical theory and practice' when applying PrIL doctrines (Michaels 2019: 27).

The tools in the PrIL toolbox need sharpening to be fully operational in relation to complex colonial contexts. The legal nature of complex cultural material will require classification, and it may be useful to start with the question as to the moveable or immovable nature of fragments prised off temples and monuments in the example of the Parthenon Sculptures. This will be followed by closer scrutiny of the classification that steered the restitution claim for the Zhanggong Zushi mummy. The classification of the cross-border dispute about ownership of cultural objects for choice-of-law purposes is part of how courts determine the governing law. They use this method to identify a connecting factor, but the way in which they approach this method does not always honour the depth dimension of PrIL.

3.5.2 Classificatory choices regarding the Parthenon's sculptural decorations

When parts of a monument designed for a particular site are taken to a new location, rights, entitlements, and duties may be similarly transposed. The common law tradition classifies most interests in land and permanent buildings as real-property interests, whereas tangible movables, intangibles, and rights of action are chattels personal. The fundamental PrIL principle is that the law of the place where real property is situated governs exclusively as to tenure, title, and descent of such property (Huber *De Conflictu Legum* 1.8.15). Generally speaking, the internationally employed distinction between movable and immovable categories is favoured over distinctions between personalty/realty and moveable/heritable property.

Determining the movable or immovable status of frescoes, friezes, and sculptures detached from the original immovable structures raises challenges for PrIL (Prott 1992: 389ff). Monuments and architectural marvels have a clear geographical connection, and the 'habitat' for which they are constructed carries greater significance than the place of production for other works of art. This characteristic qualifies them as immovable, even if there is no universally accepted coherent justification. If the physical criterion, as opposed to the rights attached to the property, is the most important touchstone for the characterisation of tangible property in an international context, a sculpture's physical attributes will determine whether it will be treated as an ornament, a fixture, a fitting, or an integral part of the architectural structure (in general, Carruthers 2005: 12–14). Yet, the decision on the same facts may go in two directions. In a famous case about jurisdiction, a French court had to make a ruling in respect of 11th-century frescoes removed from an abandoned chapel in France and put up for auction in Switzerland. The court at first instance held that the frescoes were immovable by nature, whereas the Court of Appeal considered their cultural character and held that they were immovables by intention. The Court of Appeal noted that immovables were better protected by law than movables, and that this protection was necessary for ensembles of artistic, historical, or archaeological interest which are exposed to spoliation (*Cour d'Appel de Montpellier, Ville de Genève et Fondation Abegg v Consorts Margail* D.1985.208). The highest court held them to be moveable, however (*Court de Cassation, Fondation Abegg v Ville de Genève* D.1988.325; Prott 1992: 389).

Neither the British Museum nor Greece has questioned which law governs the validity of the transfer of the Parthenon Sculptures. Only one scholarly treatise analyses this dimension of the dispute (Carruthers 2005). The Ottoman legal code applied in the territory of Athens at the time of their removal. Based as it is on the Code Napoléon, movables and immovables are given distinctive treatment. Among the immovables listed in the code are things immovable by nature, things immovable on account of the purpose for which they are employed, and things immovable because the thing in relation to which they are utilised is immovable. To characterise the Parthenon Sculptures as 'moveables' and to use this characterisation to rely on the law of Britain for the proprietary questions in the dispute, is an expedient that introduces hurdles for the restitution claim. It is not a standard that was espoused in the Ottoman code. Competing European Empires made decisions that affected the Parthenon Marbles in occupied Athens, and yet the only law deemed fit to determine whether tangible property should be treated as movable or immovable was the law of the country with effective control over the property. In a recent significant development, the Republic of Türkiye denied that it had given authorisation for the removal of the Parthenon's sculptural decorations from the Acropolis (Twenty-Fourth Session of the ICPRCP, UNESCO Headquarters, 29–31 May 2024, 4:33:01).

Successive directors at the British Museum and ministers for culture have held fast to an understanding of cultural ownership that does not foreground the Sculptures as part of the Parthenon. Hiding behind the individual aesthetic of each sculpture and the spectacular cultural production and artistic inspiration the Sculptures carry fosters a fragmented narrative that rules out the possibility of restoring the unity of the monument. There is no indication in the 1816 House of Commons Report that the Parliamentary Committee considered the question of applicable law in its evaluation of the evidence before the purchase of the Parthenon Sculptures from Elgin. The Parliamentary Committee did agree, however, that the sculptures, pediments, and frieze form a 'whole' that ought to be 'kept entire as a School of Art, and a Study for the formation of Artists' (*HC Report* 1816: 11). If this logic is applied, the law governing the validity of unauthorised removals of sculptural works that are intrinsically part of buildings, churches, chapels, temples, or monuments must be determined by the law of the place where those sculptures were located before they entered a public or private collection after their removal. The requirements of the governing law in respect of export permits and the legal effect of this omission did not elicit further interest from the Parliamentary Committee. It proceeded on the flawed premise that British law and standards are the only standards that matter.

The wide publicity of the Parthenon Marbles case in the Intergovernmental Committee for Promoting the Return of Cultural Property to its Countries of Origin or its Restitution in Case of Illicit Appropriation (ICPRCP) has prompted the restitution of fragments that carry symbolic weight (Machado Haertel 2021: 501). I

Physical and de facto considerations are important determinants of the characterisation of intangible property. The Parthenon Sculptures and frieze have tangible qualities intrinsically part of the design, but it is their intangible sacred knowledge that cannot permit the classification to shift to 'movable' every time a fragment is prised off and illegally exported. They were not created as free-standing sculptures, and they need the whole to be understood. The legal system governing a PrIL dispute about ownership of dispersed fragments will be challenged to approach the whole as an embodiment of 'sacred knowledge.'

The natural and historical environment of the frieze fragments in the inner chamber, the metopes on the exterior wall, and the pedimental sculptures cannot be moved to new locations without inviting narratives that may colonise their original meaning. Poseidon and Athena competing for the patronage of Athens on the West Pediment and the Great Panathenaic procession on the frieze would be better understood if placed in the direct vicinity of the monument they were created for. By the same token, PrIL rules governing fragments severed, chipped off, and decontextualised from the intricately unified Parthenon cannot be applied without reference to the intertwined tenets of several different legal disciplines and the ethical frameworks that form part of legal discourses. The law of their place of origin must have the opportunity to determine the question of title. The law of the place they were taken from cannot be ruled out in the classification. Since tules that are devised or interpreted without regard for the significance of sacred cultural heritage for the source community will encourage the dismemberment of important cultural ensembles, value-based *de jure* considerations must be accommodated to help shape the interpretation of the rules that govern sacred cultural heritage.

3.5.3 Scrutinising characterisation in the Zhanggong Zushi mummy case

The claimants' arguments before the Amsterdam court did not capture the sacred quality of the mummified monk and the duties imparted by it. In ownership disputes that implicate the tangible and intangible dimensions of sacred 'cultural property/heritage,' the sacred uncovers obligations. Separating out, for analytical purposes, the mummified human remains and the sculpted encasement of Zhanggong Zushi fragments the material and the spiritual. To its community of origin, its status as a sacred object is as important as its physical integrity. The restitution claim involves the whole object, and neither reasoning nor philosophical argument can justify a differentiation between human remains and other sacred cultural material for purposes of PrIL classification. To effectively resist the forces of fragmentation which litigation sets in motion, a judicial willingness to draw from both extra-legal social expectations and the law is needed.

The sacred casts into sharper relief the procedural and substantive questions plaguing international disputes that straddle jurisdictions and legal systems in the external conflicts dimension. It stakes a claim to substantive normativity and lays bare the formalism that refuses to accommodate traditions concerning the dissemination of knowledge and authority that aspire to. This situation gave the court scope to dwell on standing and to circumvent substantive argument. The Dutch ruling demonstrates the typical hindrance that standing poses to restitutionary civil claims. The legal opinions of Chinese lawyers presented to the Amsterdam court were not accepted. Withholding recognition of the Chinese village committees' legal standing made them unqualified to litigate under Dutch law. This interpretation gave the adjudicators the opportunity to circumvent the question of ownership and the responsibility of caring for the remains. The relationship between legal title and the provenance of an object or collection was not directly brought into play and none of the arguments featured the international legal framework for the protection of cultural property or the 'normative pluralism' evoked by the case. Because the case did not proceed to the merits, there was no opportunity for the court to classify the facts, dispute, or cause of action by means of the choice-of-law method of PrIL or to dismantle obstacles in the way of its restitution. Even if the claimants had based their standing on the argument that village committees enjoy legal capacity as special legal persons based on Article 96 of the General Rules of the Civil Law of the Peoples' Republic of China, the court could still find reason to refuse to recognise their right to sue. Recognition of a claimant's standing in their home state does not automatically infer that adjudicators in the forum state will do the same.

Since no ruling could be made about which law should govern the dispute, no consideration was given to the status of the Zhanggong Zushi mummy as cultural property in Chinese law. Moreover, when proceedings were launched in Amsterdam, no scope existed to request recognition of a Chinese judgment. No decision on ownership could be made and the 1995 UNIDROIT Convention was not invoked. To the extent that human remains are considered part of the customary beliefs and practices of a social group, they can be thought of as 'cultural' (Hubert 1992: 106; Woodhead 2002: 321). There are mandatory rules in Dutch law that express its public law interests and their impact; these rules could circumvent the application of PrILs' choice-of-law rules. An example of a mandatory rule that integrates the criteria and procedures for restitution claims into domestic legislation is the Dutch Cultural Property Originating from Occupied Territory (Return) Act of 2007, which prohibits the importation of cultural property from an occupied territory. Since Hong Kong was not an occupied territory between 1994–1997, the 2007 Act cannot find application. If the remains of a sacred ancestor classed as a cultural treasure with religious, cultural, and sociological significance, were classified as human remains, burial could be compelled under the Dutch Burial and Cremation Act. However, the burial of a treasure could inflict damage or be tantamount to an expropriation. Had the court reached the stage of ruling on ownership, its acknowledgement that the monk's spiritual community was involved and invested in his decision to undergo self-mummification would not necessarily mean that notions of communal ownership were being recognised. Nonetheless, treating the material in question as human remains may have drawn attention to the respect individuals owe to one another and the communities in which they operate. The popular humanist view of remains as a dead person who used to be, and who still is, entitled to their human rights is an ethical argument that acknowledges that identified human remains need to be treated with dignity and respect.

The strongest justification for applying foreign law in adjudicatory processes is found in the level of embeddedness of a private law relationship in a community. The sacred is part and parcel of this 'embeddedness.' A restitution claim cannot succeed when courts ignore the complex nature of sacred material or fail to identify the significance of human remains embedded in cultural property and heritage. The characterisation of the legal nature of the Zhanggong Zushi mummy is a question which each potentially applicable legal system may answer to a different level of satisfaction. The question is worth pursuing because the method's logic may help develop more systematic thinking to prevent classificatory ineptitude.

In choice-of-law, the category determines the relevant 'connecting factor' between the legal relationship at the heart of the dispute and a particular jurisdiction. The characterisation will set in motion different sets of principles. Characterising the removal of cultural material as a tort, a matter of family law, or a crime such as theft may mean the difference between restoring property to families and communities and denying them return and restoration. The connecting factor determines the cross-border distribution of wealth, power, and resources. In examples involving compensation claims, for instance, localising the tort in the colony or the metropole—or both—lowers or raises the degree of responsibility for the injury resulting from the brutal implementation of colonial rule or the depletion of resources of developing states (Banu 2013: 198, 302; 2022: 386). The laws of the state where the tort occurred (*lex loci delicti*) may provide for a lower standard of care and/or lower compensation quantum than the home state laws.

The Higher People's Court considered the theft and smuggling as well as the transaction that preceded van Overeem's purchase. It demonstrated a willingness to take account of the problematic backdrop to the case, i.e., the steady westward flow of the illicit trade in antiquities and cultural trafficking, a side-effect of the globalisation of world trade and the role of free ports in the Asian antiquities trade. Cultural trafficking of Buddha statues continues notwithstanding export embargoes issued by the Ministry of Culture Standards for the export of cultural relics (*Oscar van Overeem, Design & Consultancy Oscar van Overeem B.V. v Yangchun Village and Dongpu Village Committees*, Fujian Province Higher People's Court, 2021 Min Min Final No. 302, 19 July 2022: sub 'Trial court's fact findings' para 12). To determine which law governed the claim for the stolen mummy, the Intermediate and Higher People's Courts of Fujian applied Article 37 of the 2010 Chinese Private International Law Act. If parties do not choose the law to be applied, the *lex situs* at the time the legal fact occurred applies (Min Min Final 2022: sub 'Reasons and facts' para 2). The Intermediate People's Court in Sanming interpreted Article 37 in light of the objectives of the 1970 UNESCO and 1995 UNIDROIT Conventions, observing that the place where the theft occurred points to the application of Chinese law, which makes the applicable law foreseeable and imposes a duty on buyers of stolen cultural property to ascertain the applicable law. The *lex furti* favours the protection of cultural property and the return of illicitly trafficked cultural property. A series of legal facts occurring in several places highlights the necessity to stipulate which place should determine the applicable law. Contrastingly, the law where the transaction took place favours the laundering of title to stolen cultural property and provides scope to select conflicting norms. Its application renders title uncertain and makes it more difficult to facilitate the return of cultural objects (Min Min Final 2022: sub 'On issues relating to the law applicable to the settlement of the dispute'). Since good title cannot be acquired in respect of stolen cultural property in China under the Property Rights Law of China, the court ruled that the village committees retained title to the Buddha statue.

The rulings of the Chinese courts demonstrate awareness that classifying the encased mummified monk as cultural property could invoke the juridical framework for the circulation of goods, which serves and facilitates global trade in art markets. The *lex situs* rule assumes that the location of commercial transfers in international art market sales is ascertainable even when the objects in question were removed during the colonial era and exported after the sale. It leads to focusing on the location of the thing after the most recent transfer in the transaction chain. Such a narrow focus improves the level of certainty regarding which body of law determines whether title or stewardship is defective, yet the rule cannot settle questions about 'just title' or interruptions in lengthy title chains. The routine application of the *lex situs* rule in proprietary claims to cultural material removed from places under formal colonial rule shuts down ethical reasoning in restitutionary claims. Without an ethical grounding, it will facilitate title laundering in cultural trafficking, and play havoc with restitution claims for cultural objects removed, looted, or stolen from colonies. Long ownership transfer chains introduce risks for dispossessed families and communities if their members have provided sacred heirlooms or ritual material to dealers or traders. There may also have been inter-dealer transfers before objects were transferred to traders, donors, or museums.

It would not be realistic to expect a court to balance the relationship between the rights of the cultural community and the rights of researchers when the very proceedings are predicated on property and ownership. Because rights seem less relevant than 'responsibility' in normative ethics in restitution and repatriation of human remains, it seems reasonable to foreground duty-oriented conceptions of communal responsibility.

The duty to protect national heritage is embedded in the Chinese Constitution and the 1982 Law on the Protection of Cultural Relics (s 2). The movement and removal of cultural relics are subject to the 1982 law (ss 50 and 51) and other administrative regulations. Goods deemed to be merchantable may circulate freely between different civil persons of equal standing subject to general civil law (including contract law and property law) unless specific legal requirements must be complied with. Limited merchantable goods cannot circulate freely. Limitations protect the public interest, state ownership, and the rights of weaker parties (Liu 2017: 232). For instance, property exclusively owned by the state, such as mineral deposits, is prohibited from being circulated (Article 81 General Rules of the Civil Law of the People's Republic of China). State-owned cultural relics are inalienable. They may not be bought or sold without state approval. Export prohibitions apply to state-owned cultural objects and valuable non-state-owned cultural objects, except in cases of state-authorised exhibitions or special circumstances authorised by the State Council (s 60 1982 Law on the Protection of Cultural Relics). The 1982 law declares state ownership of cultural relics in collections of state-owned institutions and temples. Transactions and donations involving material taken from them are prohibited. Cultural relics are not exclusively owned by the state. Citizens may own cultural relics subject to the administrative regulations that limit their circulation, through lawful inheritance or gifts; purchase from galleries or auction houses; mutual exchange; or legal transfer. Privately owned cultural relics may be traded and exported if customs authorities grant authorisation (Liu 2017: 232). With this regulatory framework as a backdrop, the lack of proof of authorisation given to export the Zhanggong Zushi mummy means that it had to have been smuggled into the Netherlands (Chen 2022: 285). If the ownership of the relic by the Yangshun and Dongpu village committees qualifies as privately owned, its movement and export are subject to Chinese export restrictions. If it qualifies as a form of state ownership, it is entitled to protection as an inalienable state-owned cultural relic that is prohibited from being exported.

It is reasonable to expect that courts will conduct provenance checks in these circumstances, to ensure that buyers and sellers have complied with these protections.

3.5.4 Alternative choice-of-law rules for validity of transfers of mummies?

The Sanming Court acknowledged that the mummified monk was a special kind of human remains with significant historical and religious importance but did not categorise it as a special cultural object; instead, it categorised the mummified monk as a cultural property in accordance with the Law on the Protection of Cultural Relics (San Min Chu Zi 2020). Although the court acknowledged that the villagers preserved Zhanggong Zushi's memory for thousands of years as an ancestor and spiritual guide, it did not pursue this line of thought.

Critics have argued that, to categorise mummies as properties is to objectify them and could encroach on their human dignity (Chen 2022: 284). Chen submits that cultural relics containing human remains qualify for special treatment to facilitate claims for their return (Chen 2022: 282, 284–285). Mummies and other encased remains contain biological information about a person, and they deserve to be distinguished from both ordinary and other cultural properties. Like frozen embryos, mummies appear on a 'continuum of life forms between a person and a property.' Strict dichotomisation of ancient Chinese artefactual human remains—either as a person or as property—could be considered inappropriate since stolen human remains would be missing persons from the perspective of religious or cultural communities (Chen 2022: 286). Chen suggests that a new category that acknowledges the personhood of mummies should be devised for an altogether new choice-of-law rule for mummies. She considers the *lex originis* the best connecting factor for a new rule unless it does not provide protection to the good faith purchaser, or the dispossessed owner chooses in favour of the application of the *lex situs* rule (Chen 2022: 296). Chen's emphasis on good faith is at odds with the standard set in the 1995 UNIDROIT Convention. Article 4 steers away from conceptions of good faith. The possessor must meet a clear due diligence test under the 1995 UNIDROIT Convention before the possessor of a stolen cultural object is obliged to return it to the dispossessed owner. China ratified it in 1997 and it entered into force in 1998.

The development of alternative conflict rules for cultural property and heritage disputes could be futile if they did not integrate the tangible and intangible dimensions of sacred belongings. Since the *lex situs* and *lex furti* rules already encompass the place from which a cultural object was stolen, an alternative choice-of-law rule would not add value. The place of the transfer or theft denotes 'where' violence was perpetrated against people and what limits could apply in respect of responsibility. Existing choice-of-law rules can take account of cultural trade and trafficking moving from east to west if the legal categories and connecting factors are interpreted with circumspection, to identify the footprints of colonialism. While this footprint may have faded in parts of Asia (e.g., antiquities looting in China has benefited cultural institutions in Japan), the direction of the illicit antiquities trade still follows the patterns created by western collectors and custodians competing and increasing demand for these items.

Choice-of-law rules cannot always diffuse the tensions at play in the art market, nor can they accommodate the level of complexity encountered in international cases involving sacred cultural property and heritage. Turning the focus to the common structure of PrIL arguments, the point at which mimetic violence reaches the public policy exception indicates the paradigm to be followed. In the case of the Parthenon Sculptures, the Ottoman law was the only applicable law in the place of the transfer at the time. To improve bureaucratic accountability, Mahmut II (1808–1839) established a regular salary system and set standards for legal liability for misconduct by officials and judges. Gifts may have been offered and expected in the Ottoman Empire to prompt officials to perform their duties, but that does not diminish Elgin's responsibility for succumbing to abuse of authority as the British ambassador (Rudenstine 2021: 453–455, 458–459; Kakaounaki 2024). The standard against which the removal of the Sculptures must be judged is the vesting law of the Ottoman Empire and its (mandatory) anti-corruption provisions.

Political corruption or international terrorism will always crowd out the enforcement of standards of trade in the art market in the priorities which states set for themselves. The point is that PrIL has the tools with which to control these behaviours, however. The public policy exception of PrIL has a clear role to play in bureaucratic misconduct and may help to combat egregious instances of corruption (e.g., *Crane Bank Ltd v DFCU Bank Ltd* [2023] EWCA Civ 886). The final ruling concerning the Zhanggong Zushi mummy sets out China's status in relation to the 1995 UNIDROIT Convention and demonstrates a high level of awareness of the importance of consistency between Chinese law and the objectives of the convention (Min Min Final 2022: sub 'On issues concerning the applicable law').

The common principles of PrIL have considerable potential to effect change in situations of parallel litigation that yields conflicting outcomes. They foster wider and more in-depth coordination across diverse legal systems and widen the scope for adjudicators to ascribe factual significance to foreign cultural property law (Jayme 2005: 943ff).

3.5.5 Verification of provenance in adjudicatory proceedings

It will be apparent by now that restitution processes that culminate in adversarial legal proceedings may assert property rights in the ownership claim. Knowledge about the chain of ownership, and whether the individual links in that chain are intact or disrupted by unlawful dealings, can be obtained or supplementedthrough provenance research. A critical provenance is one of the only avenues in adjudication towards distilling the 'truth' about diligence in trade dealings from the facts of a case. Without this ethical grounding, the *lex situs* rule may favour existing rights or invoke statutes of limitations which prevent claims from proceeding to the merits (*Winkworth v Christie Manson and Wood* [1980] Ch 496). Few legal instruments contain express requirements to undertake provenance research in the way Council Directive (EU) No 2014/60 of 15 May 2014 on the return of cultural objects unlawfully removed from the territory of a Member State and amending Regulation (EU) No 1024/2012 (Recast) does.

Knowledge about the context, including structural ambiguity and the ambivalence of legal concepts in the colonial era, is useful for any provenance researcher. When the facts concerning the mode and circumstances of acquisition can be determined only with great difficulty, provenance research may not yield results, and the risk of incorrect judicial decision arises (Bonell 2011: 719). Nonetheless, realising that the taint of historical injustice on the provenance of sacred cultural material is a substantive consideration that indicates that the 'juridical framework of exception' deserves to be invoked, can serve as a helpful anchor point for adjudicators.

Mental dispositions that enabled the collection and storage of others' cultural heritage continue to affect both former colonisers and the colonised (DMB *Guidelines on Care of Collections* 2021: 13, 25, 26). Consultation with Indigenous communities about proper treatment of 'ancestors' is strongly recommended (Human Rights Council Report 2020: para 66). Efforts to establish which cultural community has been deprived may ultimately uncover the approximate date of removal and information about when or how collectors came into possessionof the items. Claimants are frequently required to prove their right of ownership according to criteria and values set by the holding institution without external oversight (Byrne 2015: 4–5). Imposing this requirement for human remains and other sacred belongings could debase ancestors and be considered disrespectful to the dead and their descendants (Colwell 2017: 6). Provenance research must be handled sensitively to avoid distancing people from their culture.

The stolen and smuggled Zhanggong Zushi mummy evokes provenance questions that courts should confront. The Chinese villagers' claim was predicated on van Overeem's failure to undertake (provenance) checks prior to his purchase. He claimed that he had bought the statue in good faith, was the lawful owner under Dutch law, and that it was not common practice to ask for details about the ownership history of collection items at the time. He asserted he bought the mummy from an unnamed third party in 1996 without any proof (e.g., bank statements) because he paid in cash or via bank transfer and did not keep a receipt (Hooper & Plafker 2017). If van Overeem paid another collector, Benjamin Rustenburg, 40,000 Dutch guilders (US $20,500) for the Buddha statue in 1995 or 1996, the date of the transaction is impossible to prove. Absent an obligation to retain transaction records for longer than 7 years, there is scope to claimthat he is not compelled to back up his version of events (Min Min Final 2022: sub 'Trial court's fact findings' para 17). The confusing testimony prompts the question as to whether therewas a record that was destroyed or whether no records were kept. Cash payments for high value cultural objects always raise red flags. Buyers need verifiable records to establish due diligence.

Presiding officers are responsible for considering both the facts and the law in trials that are not jury-based. Correct interpretation of the law is not the only facet of legal decision-making. In this case, none of the facts were subject to verification. The court's assumptions about the provenance of the statue revealed what information it considered a priority. Since the court wasted no time on seeking a plausible provenance, the treatment of the evidence and the burden of proof leaves much to be desired. Accepting without question that van Overeem had bought the mummified monk from another art dealer in 1996 is a value judgment; this type of information typically requires verification (Amsterdam District Court, *Village Committee of Yangchun and Dongpu v Oscar van Overeem et al.*, ECLI:NL:RBAMS:2018:8919 12 December 2018, para 2.3). The prioritisation of privacy protection over theft and illicit trafficking in culture is a deathknell for efforts to verify provenance. Provenance research demands value choices. These choices may conceal or reveal problematic aspects of the international trade of cultural material. Unlawful dealings that disrupt the links in the chain of custody and ownership raise legal and ethical dilemmas. It is reasonable to expect that collectors and antiques dealers would be willing and able to produce bank records, invoices, and export permits.

The villagers' averred that the Zhanggong Zushi mummy disappeared from Yangchun at the end of 1995, while van Overeem claimed that the mummy he purchased had been shipped to Amsterdam months before Zhanggong was taken from the village. He insisted that no hard evidence existed that the two statues were one and the same. His statement that the statue had already been transferred twice by the time he acquired it went untested, and so did the question of an export licence. His assertions undermined the villagers' claim, but the provenance he supplied and the claim that he had bought the mummified monk from a collector and art dealer only in 1996, remained unverified (*Village Committee of Yangchun and Dongpu v Oscar van Overeem et al.*, 12 December 2018, para 2.3). Van Overeem stood on his argument that 'his' mummy was different from the one the villagers reported stolen, as theirs had damage to the hands which 'his' did not. The fact that the Meander Medical Centre's reports did not mention a hole in the left hand cannot constitute conclusive evidence of the factual position, for this type of observation may not have been relevant for the tests it completed. The claims advanced by van Overeem cannot be verified without consulting additional information and material that would enable identification and comparison. His line of argument instantly frustrated the claim in the court in Amsterdam. None of the facts as to how the Buddha mummy came into van Overeem's possession, or why there was no original sales agreement, receipts, or other evidential documents, were scrutinised. When the villagers demanded to know the identity of the new holder, van Overeem did not disclose this information and the court denied their request. A healthier perspective on the law and facts surrounding the improper acquisition of the Zhanggong Zushi mummy would have been to recognise that information about provenance, which still needed to be collected, processed, weighed, and ascertained, may inform decisions about rights and responsibilities in law. Instead, the Amsterdam District Court took it at face value that van Overeem no longer owned the statue (para 2.5). Genealogical evidence in the form of records or authentication reports could have confirmed the provenance and the proprietary claim of the village committees but was neither required nor presented. Occasion for the Amsterdam court to focus on provenance was limited by the court's position on lack of standing.

The authenticity of a cultural object and its composition renders the object a 'true and credible document of and from the past,' imparting both source value and emotional value (Zeidler 2016: 78–79). The authenticity of human remains encased in statuary encapsulates both historical information about the skills, techniques, and materials of the maker and the mummification process, as well as information gleaned by witnessing the event and the experience of the monk's completed work. Van Overeem's inability to provide proof of the facts he relied on raised the Chinese court's suspicions. The trial court in China considered aspects such as the historical documentation, image comparison, research on the text appearing on the cushion, verification of the artefact and its dating; testimonies of witnesses, expert opinions, police records, and van Overeem's statements as to provenance. It held that there were no grounds to dispute that the identity of the Ancestor Buddha stolen in Fujian was the same as the one which van Overeem had bought (Min Min Final 2022: sub 'Trial court ruling' paras 1–3).

As Good recommends (2018: 238), the Chinese adjudicators paid attention to the epistemological complexities involved in collecting, processing, and weighing information when they determined the facts of the case.

3.6 Aligning PrIL's core function and method with its theoretical depth

PrIL's disciplinary isolation from PublIL and from other legal disciplines compounds the daunting obstacles to restitution that inhere in the law itself. For instance, if restitution proceedings are brought in a court in a jurisdiction that recognises the acquisition of title to property in good faith, there is a real risk that the court will ascribe ownership to the current possessor if they are exercising a caregiver role over the sacred heritage. Adjudicators may not realise that such material might rotate between members of the source community or that transfer into institutional care or safekeeping is not permitted (Last 2007: 132–33). When in alignment with its method and technique, PrIL's theoretical depth provides a perspective on norms, responsibility and obligation. Its interdisciplinarity crosses private and public law so that it can map the steps for more realistic and lasting solutions that strengthen law's ability to counter mimetism.

The space time and depth dimensions of PrIL deserve systematic study. PrIL scholars have long grappled with the question of depth and what it means for PrIL. Ronald Graveson (1911–1991) conceived of 'evolutionary' depth as the 'juridical suitability' of a legal system (Graveson 1974a: 41; 1974b: 199, 229). PrIL's space time dimensions encompass the evolution and application of colonial law. The vantage and vanishing points of colonial European international law give precise indications as to when local law was supplanted. Struycken dismissed the relevance of differences in legal systems' development, sophistication, or reliability for PrIL purposes. His suggestion is convincing enough. However, his application of the 'civilised' test raises difficult questions for provenance researchers who strive to equalise the balance of power in restitution processes when he argues that only the laws of civilised countries can rank equally for choice of law purposes and that the principle of the equivalence of legal systems gives rise to the presumption that every foreign law deserves respect as a matter of principle, the only justifiable exception being the Nazi regime (Struycken 2009: 220–221). Conventional rules were applicable only when all parties were contracting parties, but to gain this status, a state had to meet the 'civilised' test. The 1907 Hague Convention was the first to invite an African state, Abyssinia (modern-day Ethiopia), but it was conspicuously absent from the negotiation table. In building their European collections and classification of cultures in the 19th and 20th centuries, colonial European cultural institutions assigned priorities. Anthropologists imposed a hierarchy of religions on collections that elevated Christianity above those practiced by Africans and other 'heathens.' Conventions started to include the Ottoman Empire from 1856 onwards, but the Christian populations of Africa never made it to the top of this hierarchy. In every domestic legal system, mummified elements that resist PrIL's coordination demand adjustment before PrIL rules and tenents can be effectively applied.

Critical contemporary PrIL voices have been asking what it would take for PrIL and PublIL to be reunified (Muir Watt 2014: 358; Neidhardt 2018: 29). What would the ideal relationship between PrIL and PublIL look like? PrIL rules and principles are applied under obligation of PublIL but do not operate among states in a PublIL approach. To defuse the conflicting norms and claims to authority that characterise the legal pluralism of the contemporary world order, Muir Watt suggest that PrIL method must be unshackled from state authority and its capacity for 'heterarchical' conflict resolution developed (Muir Watt 2016a: 401–403). The determination of cross-border effects with reference to the ideological uniformity of internationalism stands in an oppositional tension with domestic statutes and judgments to domestic constitutional law and foreign relations law (respectively Banu 2018: 12–18 and D'Aspremont 2019: 293). Questions about normativity in the law of restitution cannot always be settled in the interaction between domestic legal frameworks and the framework of international law at the conceptual and operational levels; many questions arise intra-state and between private individuals and business enterprises. Neverheless PrIL rules and principles do not apply exclusively to these contextand relationships. Convergence of PrIL and PublIL would suppress PrIL's heterarchical conflict resolution capabilities and re-uniting them could resurrect the troublesome dichotomy between the 'civilised' and 'uncivilised.' 'Uncivilised' nations were excluded from the codification of the rules of war and cultural heritage. Repressive laws controlled every aspect of Indigenous life and livelihood, from land to education and culture. Race legislation followed on the heels of the delineation of social categories that served as its justification (Haller 1971: 722).

Reflecting on the implications of PrIL scholarship and teaching continuing in splendid isolation from PublIL and its development, the scholar Joel Paul cautioned that isolation breeds perverse consequences (Paul 1988: 153, 161, 173). He ascribed PrIL's isolation to liberal capitalism and European economic expansion. To surmount this fragmentation, he encouraged PrIL scholars to re-focus their attention on the common structure of arguments and principles of comity and public policy while relinquishing their fixation on the development of common PrIL rules (Paul 1988: 149ff). His advice, imparted 40 years ago, fell on deaf ears. Leading European PrIL commentators devote their attention to the development of uniform PrIL rules, and while the operation of the public policy exception in the areas of marriage, surrogacy, and gender-based discrimination is a popular field of study, few PrIL researchers venture into pressing contemporary issues such as the unethical collection of cultural objects during the colonial era.

Artificial boundaries drawn between the public and private spheres in normative conflicts arising from colonial-era collecting practices must be actively dismantled to promote tolerance, mutual accommodation, and peace It is never too late to call PrIL from the shadows of its own isolation and integrate its common rules into the juridical framework of exception in relation to restitution claims.

Common historical developments and shared argumentative structures between PrIL and PublIL demonstrate how, together, the two disciplines moderate the values that underpin common principles. They can join forces to surmount obstacles to restitution stemming from historical gaps in legal frameworks, and the orientation of these frameworks, or the structure of the law. The interrelation of the legal basis of restitution claims and the barriers standing in the way of success requires further systematic investigation.

3.7 Changing adjudicatory outcomes of claims for 'sacred' material

Adjudicators are expected to get foreign law 'right' in transnational litigation, and yet their position does not permit them to make authoritative claims to its meaning. A 'moral imagination' and a willingness to incorporate PrIL's ethic may help to train their attention on the legal standards in the trade and trafficking of sacred cultural material and the circumstances in which ethical reasoning is needed to change the outcome of cases. For instance, it could be unethical to deny the difference of the other by failing to acknowledge that a claimant is foreign or that a theft occurred in a foreign country (Michaels 2019: 15–16). The 'facile unwillingness to understand the other' also manifests in denying the similarity of the other in a common conception and expression of the sacred.

The perceived complexity of PrIL's technical devices nurtures the belief that they are 'anathema to questions of ethics' (Michaels 2019: 24). Their technicality hypnotises analysts and can blind them to PrIL's potential to improve the normative framework for restitution. The metaphorical qualities of the techniques in the PrIL toolbox inspire ethical treatment to broaden access to justice and improve social responsibility and respect for moral standards. Normative phenomena such as reputational pressure and compliance with moral standards counter the pursuit of profit and short-term gain. Would it suffice to establish the ethical relevance of PrIL cases? Michaels's formulation suggests that it is possible to go further. He considers PrIL not only ethically relevant, but constitutive of an ethic of 'responsivity.' PrIL is 'itself an ethic'; not merely a theoretical position, but 'a legal theory' (Michaels 2019: 11, 24, 26). Like ethics, PrIL is concerned with practice that either defers to the foreign law or rejects it on justifiable grounds, but because the legal doctrine that underpins PrIL practice consists of a 'particular kind of technical argument', arbitrary responses are curbed (Michaels 2019: 26–27).

Recent changes in law and discourse are eroding the foundations of classical dogmas. Common historical developments and shared argumentative structures between PrIL and PublIL may go a long way towards firming up the basis of claims (Neidhardt 2018: 29).

3.7.1 Getting the basis of the claim right

Adjudicatory rules must provide for situations where possessors fail or refuse to submit evidence of 'acquisition' and sale of sacred material in transnational litigation. 'Acquisition' is an unfortunate descriptor of unethical colonial-era removals. Many museum press-officers continue to use terminology such as 'acquisition' which should be reserved for the gaining of legal title to a collection items, to refer to cultural material that had been bartered, stolen, looted, and under-paid for (Díaz-Andreu 2018: 14). Violent and forceful taking render what is taken sacred when mimetic struggles culminatein violent conflict, war and genocide. Grievous breaches of fundamental human rights and interests lend urgency to more evolved conceptions of what constitutes evidence of 'acquiring' cultural property. Even for ownership challenges relating to artefactual human remains, what constitutes evidence of ownership needs to be broadened out considerably.

Van Overeem's litigation strategy concerning the artefactual human remains of Zhanggong Zushi was a lethal combination of arguments which the claimants were unable to surmount: that the claimants were not natural or legal persons, could not act in legal proceedings, and that the statue in van Overeem's possession (before exchanging it) was not Zhanggong Zushi as it was already located in Amsterdam by mid-1995. The Amsterdam court failed to attend to the vexing question of provenance. The interaction between law and facts was not observed and the court never verified the provenance dished up by the collector. The Amsterdam court did not connect the facts to the local sphere of social life of the claimants. This precluded a holistic view of the evidence that could have brought attention to the fact that van Overeem supplied no proof of the time and place of the purchase and sale of the Buddha statue, the mode of the transaction, the name of the transferor, or any receipt. He refused to do so for the subsequent exchange agreement with an unidentified third party. The Sanming Court presumed that he still had the Buddha statue in his possession and had to bear the legal consequences of his failure to supply proof (Min Min Final 2022: sub 'Trial court ruling' (c)). The Higher People's Court in Fujian ruled as follows:

> Although Mr Oscar claimed that the long-term worship of the Buddha statue involved in the case by the villagers of Yangchun Village and Dongpu Village and the Yangchun Village Committee and Dongpu Village Committee did not automatically confer ownership of the Buddha statue involved in the case, he never submitted his evidence of purchase or evidence of lawful possession. In addition, he did not appeal against the trial court's finding about the non-applicability of the bona fide acquisition regime, and he did not submit evidence that the Zhanggong Zushi statue was owned by another party. Therefore, it is held that his appeal regarding the ownership of the statue was untenable. (Min Min Final 2022: sub 'On the issue of ownership' (tr. Zhao 2024)

The Zhanggong Zushi mummy now faces an uncertain future.

In Girard's theoretical framework, the sacred engenders obligations to protect. For instance, a common understanding of the sacred and the obligations engendered by it invalidates exchange agreements and schemes collectors conclude among themselves. Guided by this understanding, a transfer of sacred cultural heritage to a third party pending trial cannot be accepted as a reason to avoid responsibility in a civil suit because it introduces more hurdles on the way to obtaining relief. The exchange agreement implicating the Buddha statue which van Overeem concluded with an unknown third party would be instantly marked out as contrary to public order. Although this argument was central to the villagers' claim, it did not garner traction in the court in Amsterdam. A common understanding of the sacred highlights just howuntenable it is that the last known possessor, who knows the Zhanggong Zushi statue's current whereabouts, holds the bartering agreement up as a banner to justify his non-compliance with the court order to return the mummy. The Fujian court cited Article 95 of the Provisions of the Supreme People's Court of the People's Republic of China on Evidence in Civil Litigation of 2001, to the effect that, where a party who bears the burden of proof in regards to the facts of a case asserts that the evidence being withheld is unfavourable to the person in control of it, a finding that the assertion is substantiated would be in order (Min Min Final 2022: Court's finding sub 'On the question of whether it should be returned'). When a possessor fails or refuses to submit evidence of the acquisition and sale of sacred material in transnational litigation, courts ought to treat any transfer as legally relevant fact.

The practical basis for this finding is clearly articulated in Chinese law, but Girard's theory explains where the duty of litigants and their legal counsel to inform the judiciary of the sacred quality of cultural material stolen and trafficked during the colonial era originates from.

Fragmented thinking separates values from daily life. This drawback is evident in educational systems that rely on machine-based thinking. Meanwhile, the likelihood of capturing aspects of the immaterial heritage in museum collections via inventory data, photographs, movies, sound recordings, and digital archive documents is steadily expanding (Kalibani 2021: 43–53). Fragmenting knowledge and precluding holistic learning will always put Buddha mummies at the mercy of marketplace structures.

Successful digital reunification—defined as the digitised representation of scattered artefacts and archival records in physically dispersed heritage collections—provides a way to visualise and study a collection in a comprehensive manner (Dawson 2016). Possibilities for 'virtual restitution' include digital 3D models, objects scanned and printed in 3D, databases comprising educational tools on the object, or online communities that engage with information about the object (Oruç 2022: 1138ff). Unfortunately, if information about stolen cultural property and heritage, or images and representations of such heritage, is not handled with utmost care, digitisation will not provide adequate support and protection for sacred cultural heritage.

Surviving tangible expressions of heritage traditions have helped to preserve the value of social practices and processes. For instance, ceremonies must take place at a site which is the center of the world for the tribe in accordance with the Native American concept of creation. Repatriation claims brought by Indigenous communities encompass intangible heritage embodying their spiritual life. Inevitably, what museums consider to be 'real' affects their repatriation practices (Byrne 2015: 11, 23). If the digital is considered 'real,' the institutional agenda can be expected to include digital repatriation, but it is by no means clear that property claims will be settled either comprehensively or permanently. 'Open access' to websites and databases, web hosting, and providing data in accordance with western values of archiving and accessibility can undermine the cultural autonomy of communities and nations. When clear agreements about digitisation are omitted, the scope to objectify the intangible increases. Digitisation without consent risks being offensive. Only with proper agreements in place could open data be an important support for transparency in restitution initiatives. Digitised resources must include a list of the institutions where the objects are kept, their provenance details, an oral history of the looting, and repatriation initiatives from the collection at a minimum (e.g. Museum am Rothenbaum Kulturen und Kunst der Welt 'Digital Benin: Reconnecting Royal Art Treasures' digital-benin.org). Concerns were forthcoming over the blanket recommendation of free and open access for restituted digital heritage as part of the second phase of returns anticipated in the report on *The Restitution of African Cultural Heritage: Toward a New Relational Ethics*, by Sarr and Savoy (Sarr & Savoy 2018: 176). The recommendation invites conflict with the report's central arguments (Pavis & Wallace 2019: 121, 124). Inputs provided by representatives of source states on the use of images of sacred objects would be invaluable (see e.g., the Art Council England 2022 Guidelines (6) and 2021 DMB *Guidelines on Care of Collections* (53)). A lack of equality in relation to digitisation proposals will defeat a relational ethic (e.g. *Recommendations of the Advisory Committee for Guidelines for Collections in Austrian Federal Museums from Colonial Contexts* 2023: 22).

If there is any doubt about the publication of images in online publications and open-access inventories and databases, they are best omitted (DMB *Guidelines on Care of Collections* 2021:19–21, 72, 123ff). Furthermore, any digital repatriation project involving culturally-sensitive material would need to be password-protected at the very least. If both the physical thing and the digitally created scans, copies, and the right to distribute and display them remain under the legal control of the institution undertaking a 'digital repatriation,' the status quo and the power imbalance are merely carried into the present (Oruç 2022: 1143). Restitution is complete only once digitisation, control of access, and commercialisation are settled to the satisfaction of both sides of a dispute about restitution.

Full-scale reproductions and near-exact replicas of stolen and looted material can be produced with 3D-printing technology. Light Detection and Ranging (LIDAR) scanners and stone-carving robots can recreate ancient sculptures in 3D in the same stone as their originals. A robotically produced marble facsimile of the Parthenon's Selene Horsehead poses a subtle ethical dilemma. If the originals were to be returned to Greece, the 'Universal Museum' model would be realised, but the British Museum rejects the making of near-perfect replicas of the original set. Is the replication of original sacred material justifiable if it facilitates the repatriation of the originals to states and communities that advance claims in respect of their sacred materials? What are the obligations of those responsible for material culture in the digital age when social context identifies material as sacred? The dilemmas which CT scans (computed tomography imaging), endoscopies, and bone samples of sacred artefactual remains invite cannot always be resolved by conferring superior status on science. Some may consider the question to be one of ontological primacy and would suggest that permission to reproduce, transmit, display, or share visual material follow the status quo in the restitution of lost artwork.

Opinions remain mixed as to whether digital assets can be of equal value to physical objects (Valeonti et al. 2021: para 3.2). Control of the digital heritage and records is confronted head-on in the Charter for African Cultural Renaissance (Article 27). The NAGPRA envisages pro-active repatriation of human remains and cultural objects, but it does not impose the same standard for traditional manuscript archives (Krupa & Grimm 2021: 50). Rights to documents must be negotiated separately (Douglas & Hayes 2017: 164). Given the complex barriers to access of digital reproductions, the same recommendation would be appropriate for proprietary rights to and exceptions for digital images and film negatives.

'Shared stewardship' of collection items indicates joint responsibility assumed by parties negotiating on equal terms concerning conditions of storage, presentation, research access, and digitisation (DMB *Guidelines on Care of Collections* 2021: 91). 'Shared ownership' is also a legal construct. Reflective of pluralistic legal institutions and values, it permits several rights and interests to co-exist in one object that embodies the 'common good.' Shared ownership also poses a hard question. Who holds the decisive vote on the standards that will inform shared title status when cultural paradigms conflict? 'Equitable solutions' for title disputes include attempts to honour both the interests of former owners and new (innocent) possessors (e.g., Francioni 2012: 719). In a significant development in law and equity in the Australian Federal Court, the notion of 'equity' featured as a conceptual basis for allocating and sharing resources and distributing burdens in the 20th century. 'Bulun Bulun equity' reflects the importance of protecting the interests of an Indigenous community in artistic works embodying ritual knowledge (*John Bulun Bulun v R & T Textiles Pty Ltd* (1998) Federal Court, 2 September 1998 Unreported). Various types of equity—*infra legem praeter lege, contra lege, ex aequo et bono*—capture international equality, proportionality, and the search for purpose and human dignity.

The model developed in Belgium is the result of a new regulatory intervention (*Projet de Loi Reconnaissant le Caractère Alienable des Biens liés au passé Colonial de l'État Belge et Determinant un Cadre Juridique pour leur Restitution et leur Retour* 28 September 2022). Frigo considers it an 'inauguration' of a new category of the 'intangible restitution' of cultural property (Frigo 2023: 181). This model defines restitution as 'the transfer of legal ownership of the object to be restituted, decided in accordance with the present law' (Article 3.4). Return means 'the material transfer to the State of origin of the object to be restituted, the restitution of which has been decided in accordance with the present law' (Article 3.5). The ownership of cultural property and heritage assets and their material availability are split to distinguish between the transfer of title (*propriété juridique*) and the material transfer (*remise matérielle*) (Frigo 2023: 180). This distinction deviates from the principle laid down in the Belgian Civil Code Book 3 (Property Law) Article 3.50, according to which the right of ownership confers directly on the owner the right to use, enjoy, and dispose of what is the subject of his or her right. However, goods linked to the Belgian colonial past are designated 'alienable' exclusively with a view to restitution and return, free of charge, to the State of origin under the conditions provided.

It cannot be assumed that property rights are synonymous with ownership (Hodgson 2013: 224). A property right may be defined as one of several possible constitutive elements of ownership. If the scope of material transfer is understood as including digital material and objects, a full restitution is achievable, but if the digital technology is restituted without the corporeal, the full meaning of the sacrifice embodied in heritage cannot be unlocked. Because the physical restitution of tangible cultural heritage has ontological priority over the digital, the digital cannot automatically stand in for the physical. Furthermore, a digital version cannot fully compensate for the loss of cultural identity because aonline resources of archival material and databases about embodiment cannot stand in for bodily, mental, and sense perceptions. The form of digitisation and online exhibition of cultural material requires the participation and express consent of source communities and countries of origin. Digitisation as well as restitution practice must respect the significance and interpretation countries of origin attached to those cultural materials (cf Recommendation 4 of the Qingdao Recommendations for the Protection and Return of Cultural Objects Removed from Colonial Contexts or Acquired by Other Unjustifiable Means of 2024).

A common ground for claims to sacred cultural material looted or trafficked during the colonial era would improve the normative environment, provided adjustments can be made to support such claims. A broad spectrum of practices and ethics, including so-called 'narrative norms,' enrich the interpretation and construction of legal texts relevant to such claims (Jayme 2005: 943ff). Narrative feeds into the normative. The sloppy contemporary 'common heritage' discourse carves against the grain of the sacred. Agreements that promote the idea that all humanity, not just the producing culture, has an interest in the common heritage of mankind confirm that the universal importance of sacred material is more valuable, and ethical, than their local importance. It misses the original idea of cultural heritage as the common heritage of mankind that took root in the wake of the Second World War. The 1954 Hague Convention was never intended as a guide to determine where cultural heritage belongs, but rather to support every culture in the world. Stalemates may follow the tracks left by a manufactured narrative that 'the great treasures of ancient art belong to no nation but to all of us as heirs to a common heritage' (e.g., Cuno 2008: 49) because the narrative legitimises appropriation, power, and forms of piracy. The 'European monumentalist vision' and its descriptions of 'monuments,' 'groups of buildings,' and 'sites' recast the Parthenon as 'universal heritage of humanity' that makes 'a discrete contribution to the heritage of humankind.' First Nations have no concept that one's culture can be shared by everyone. Arguments that African ethnographic material is a resource for understanding 'common human heritage' rely on a similarly fractured understanding of the sacred. The intimate relationship between heritage and the identity of a specific community or people is just one of the reasons why a clear image of the 'heritage of mankind' cannot emerge in complex colonial contexts.

With two nations claiming the Parthenon Marbles as their heritage, western museums hold onto two conflicting tales about the Marbles' connection to present-day Athens to justify the continued holding and display of items taken unjustly by a colonial power. This enlarges the scope for a narrative that challenges the continuity of ancient and modern Greek culture and harps on the disconnect between the Greek perception of Greekness in the 19th century and the European perception of Greek national identity (Kynourgiopoulou 2011: 156; Loukaki 2008: 46). Like the removal of the Parthenon Sculptures, the removal of human remains and the 'dismemberment' of collections or monuments that formed an integral part of sacred sites or practices is about more than identity or classification based on the history of an aesthetic. Premised on a common understanding across disparate religious traditions, history, art history, applied philosophy, and legal norms, the sacred is an integrative force that dismantles artificial distinctions drawn at the level of the material and its associated knowledge systems, and between the domains of the public and the private in discourses about law and morals. Girard's conception of the sacred offers a common definition across the humanities and social sciences which is nothing less than a prerequisite for progress with transnational restitution and repatriation claims involving colonial-era takings. Leaving the scope of the category of 'cultural objects' open-ended will delay progress, for what constitutes a sacred cultural object to a claimant may be a commercial asset for a defendant with a business that trades in those types of objects.

A broad conception of comity holds further promise for the restitution of sacred material. Value rationality helps foster global solidarity (Roodt 2015: 312). Comity invites value rationality to weigh in on the decision-making process in restitution claims and enables internal contradictions and fragmentation caused by procedural considerations to be surmounted. Decision-making based on formal or instrumental rationality alone cannot unlock opportunities to build global solidarity.

3.7.2 Applying ethical reasoning to expired time limitations

The argument that a claim is stale is not based on any legal institution as such, but rather on the passing of a substantial period of time between the translocation of cultural property and the raising of a claim (Zeidler 2016: 190). When legislative hurdles block the way to restitution, the law is the appropriate tool to use to rectify the historical structural discriminations against non-European states and peoples (Spitra 2021: 143; Goldmann 2021).

The substantive questions involving historic redress require courts to engage with the past. The past poses a legal problem for courts, not least because conflated perceptions of time create a conflict of social and cultural values. A widening of ontological viewpoints on historical injustice would be beneficial, allowing conceptions of historical time to converge in ways that foster mutual understanding.

There is authority for the view that the acquisition of cultural material in a colonial context highlights the purpose of the limitation period in statutes of limitation for legal action or prescription, i.e., to establish a degree of legal certainty or 'legal peace' in relation to title (Bonell 2011: 715). Statutes of limitation safeguard the integrity of the proceedings by prioritising policy goals, such as the finality of proceedings and removing the risk associated with evidence that has gone stale after lengthy periods of time have lapsed or that has become unreliable. Provenance research may support institutional reform and legislative and policy changes, but if statutes of limitation prevent a claim from proceeding to the merits, mimetics marches interminably onward. When PrIL theory and method is brought into alignment, however, and the depth clues normativity imparts are heeded, new responses can be generated.

The passage of time affects decisions about changing secondary rules such as collective choice rules or constitutional rules that determine how collective choice-rules may be changed. This task differs from establishing what effects the passage of time has on operational day-to-day rules. In civil proceedings, a true owner's claim to stolen property may be time-barred if the period since the original theft is longer than what the law permits. States that have ratified the 1995 UNIDROIT Convention follow limitations that represent the approximate average of many different national legal systems, i.e., three years after a claimant has gained knowledge of the whereabouts of the work, with an absolute limitation of fifty years from the occurrence of a theft. The time available to institute civil proceedings will have run out if these or similar 'ordinary' statutes of limitations were applied in respect of legal claims involving sacred cultural heritage removed during the colonial era. Clauses in conventions are unlikely to be given retrospective effect, while statutory limitations in the governing law may prevent a restitution claim from being heard on the merits.

Limitations rules may be subject to ethical reasoning, as the *Gotha* case demonstrates. The Federal Republic of Germany (FRG) and the City of Gotha launched proceedings in an English court to recover a painting by Joachim Wtewael that was looted from the Friedenstein Castle collection in the City of Gotha (*City of Gotha and Federal Republic of Germany v Sotheby's and Cobert Finance SA.* ([1998] QBD no 1997/G/185). When faced with long chains of successive illegal transfers, which is also a common feature in the removal of complex sacred material removed during the colonial era, compliance with minimum standards of due diligence must be held up as a judicial standard where applicable. An important way to foster wider coordination across diverse legal systems is to make room for 'normative ensembles and accommodation' by avoiding the imposition of a certain hierarchy of sources (Ruiz Abou-Nigm 2019: 370 credits Jayme for this idea). By seeking to coordinate several normative sources, a court may combine and reconcile different traditions and interpretations of statutory limitations in light of public policy.

In egregious cases such as genocide, the protection which time limitations give against civil responsibility ought to be suspended on public policy grounds. Public policy and provenance need to work in a more coordinated manner in cases concerned with the theft and looting ofhuman remains, artefactual human remains, and other sacred cultural material. While the ethics that condition western property norms in restitution claims can be differentiated from PrIL ethics (or PrIL as an ethic), the tensions that develop between them in the art market due to defects in the chain of title caused by theft and looting may be eased by ethical reasoning and interpretation across property law, PrIL, PublIL, and uniform law. The *Winkworth* case cautions that the *lex situs* rule in PrIL will favour extant proprietary rights if provenance is not prioritised. Therefore, it is incumbent on PrIL scholars, practitioners, and adjudicators to check that, where the effect of defective provenance depends on a choice-of-law ruling, links in the title chain are secure. The *Gotha* ruling shows that courts find it easier to identify and counter the risks of title laundering present in legal relationships at the point of adjudication if they perform these checks. It is especially vital to permit the ethic of public policy to shed light on claims where the nature and character of the material in question speak to mimetism and sacrifice.

3.7.3 Resisting 'form' in the preliminary stage of the trial: Parties' standing

To date, much of the disciplinary focus in PrIL has fallen on the vagaries of state power and its jurisdictional and choice-of-law implications. Numerous restitution claims are dismissed in the preliminary stage of the proceedings because the claimant is not granted standing to sue, and the merits are never reached because the moral dimension of the repatriation of sacred material is relegated to the background. The court hearing the case is likely to follow its own law to determine the procedural requirements for international civil litigation, for it would not be practical, convenient, or efficient to adopt foreign procedures; based on where the adjudicator in the forum draws the line between procedural matters and matters of substance, courts decline to rule on the merits of a case. Because a concept used at the domestic law and international law levels necessarily carries different meanings, the line between substance and procedure in the domestic sphere of law could be drawn differently compared to the international or conflicts sphere.

PrIL engages with the line between substance and procedure to ensure that the result is 'just and convenient' (e.g., North & Fawcett 2004: 70). In restitution claims, 'justice' and 'convenience' will rarely lie on the same side of the line. What is 'just' to the claimant may be inconvenient for the possessor to give up. A more satisfactory approach is for courts to assess whether an entity should be entitled to be sued in the forum, with reference to the wider factors at work rather than to resort to blanket procedural characterisations (Garnett 2012: para 5.08). *Locus standi* is readily taken to be a procedural issue in transnational litigation. Given how convenient it has been for courts located on the demand-side of the trade, in erstwhile colonial master jurisdictions to rule out moving the proceedings to the merits, there are sound reasons for limiting the historically wide interpretation of procedure for *locus standi* in PrIL. A wide view of procedure correlates to forum control that does not give due recognition to international judicial comity (Garnett 2012: para 2.08). This approach favours exclusion rather than integration. Nonetheless .there is a subtle margin of interpretation available that could make a difference in practice. When Indigenous peoples or religious communities with a strong interest in community-centric resource governance seek *locus standi* it is possible to declare an issue one for forum law to decide without necessarily taking this to mean that domestic law categories, preconceptions, and biases are the only ones with a bearing on the case (Roodt 2007b: 371). To disregard communities' and peoples' standing in court is to discount their culture, their access to that culture, their voice. It weakens the structures that support cultural life. A group lacking standing domestically may find that it is also precluded from bringing a claim in a foreign forum, even if the attribution of standing in the claimant's home state is not a reason that the foreign forum recognises a party as a proper juristic entity. Furthermore, even when religious societies have the requisite authority to bring a lawsuit involving sacred property in their country of origin, courts in Western Europe may hold parties to different standards of evidence or may decide differently (Last 2007: 131). Identifying the appropriate community authority to represent the group was not as difficult as the Amsterdam court made it out to be. It is unclear why the court deemed it necessary to disregard the village committees' exercise of ownership rights to the land on which the Puzhao temple is located, in accordance with Article 61(1) of the Property Rights Law of the People's Republic of China of 2007. The Chinese rulings in the Buddha mummy case show that a different reasoning is possible. 'Substance' may resist 'form' if PrIL's ethical dimension is effectively deployed from within the juridical framework of exception to circulation.

Ensuring that restitution claims for sacred cultural heritage removed during the colonial era succeed requires a court to step back from grounding its ruling on formal rationality. Designation of a legal question about ownership as a matter of 'substance' does not guarantee that an order for restitution will follow. The court that is being asked to recognise the claimant's status, or the governing law that is applied to settle a restitution question, may itself be primed and conditioned by colonial law. To counter the normative effect of mimetism effectively, value-rationality must also guide the courts when assessing the merits.

3.7.4 Clarifying the interplay between tort and public policy

Whether responsibility and liability for violence perpetrated by the state can be legally excluded is a public policy issue. *Athanasios Sophocleous v Secretary of State for the Foreign and Commonwealth Office & Secretary of State for Defence* (2018) EWCA Civ 2167 was concerned with an historic human rights infringement which revived the common law conflicts history of the double actionability rule for tort. The reasoning of the court at first instance in *Athanasios* was directed towards achieving justice. It declared that justice, comity or public policy should not be used to exempt the British government from 'liability in tort under English law by reference to the law of Cyprus' (para 196). In an unfortunate choice of language that befuddled the ruling, the court referred to the 'superior law of the United Kingdom' and the 'inferior local law' (para 188). Referring to the 'superior law of the United Kingdom' and the 'inferior local law' to get its point across may evoke a 'might makes right' approach (*Athanasios Sophocleous & Ors v Secretary of State for the Foreign and Commonwealth Office & Secretary of State for Defence* [2018] EWHC 19 (Q.B.) para 188). The Civil Division of the Court of Appeal (CA) disapproved of the language and reversed the ruling. The Court of Appeal recognised that the intentional infliction of harm by the state on its own citizens is inherently repugnant but reasoned that such repugnancy does not justify holding the law of the place where the torts were committed (Cyprus) irrelevant (para 44). It held that the law of Cyprus cannot be completely disregarded or disapplied in its entirety (paras 32, 43). It acknowledged that permitting limitations that exclude responsibility and liability for violence perpetrated by the state posed an issue (para 50). However, the court did not wish to go so far as to remove the veil drawn over the flexible exception of s 14(2) of the Private International Law (Miscellaneous Provisions) Act 1995 and insisted that this flexible exception should not be available 'too readily' (para 33). Because each law had full force and effect in the country in respect of which the law was enacted, the law made by the Queen in Council in right of her position as sovereign of Cyprus is in no way 'inferior' to English law (para 39).

The public policy exception would have been a more appropriate route for the Court of Appeal to follow, since the facts of the case invite the application of the juridical framework of exception. This approach minimises the conflict between the duty to defer to foreign law and the duty to avoid applying a law that is incompatible with fundamental values. The ethics within the device make it possible to respond in a subtle manner (Michaels 2019: 25). The public policy exception is directed only against the result of its application in the forum state. It is therefore able to minimise the impact of the foreign law without being directed against the foreign law *per se*. Instead of grabbing hold of some supposedly universal set of values as its standard of review, it relies exclusively on the values within PrIL's own position and minimises its impact. The only values that are 'actioned' are the values of the forum state, and the exception is triggered only when there are sufficient connections to the forum state.

The disappointing outcome of the *Athanasios* case presents an important learning moment regarding the depth of the law, demonstrating that the alignment between theory and method matters. Language that supports or confirms legal hierarchies validates the normative effects of mimetis and drives a wedge between theory and method.

3.7.5 Improving PrIL's responsiveness to provenance

PrIL must be receptive and responsive to critical provenance findings (Roodt 2019: 352–353). In the *City of Gotha* case referred to earlier one of the questions the court in England faced was whether English, German, or Russian law would supply the rules that would determine ownership of the valuable cabinet painting that had been subjected to a long chain of successive illegal transfers after its removal from the Friedenstein Castle collection by a Russian trophy brigade shortly after the Second World War ended. The facts invoked multiple legal systems, conflicting time limitations rules in the same proceedings, and multiple sources of law and history. The chain of custody and the frequency with which the painting had changed hands created uncertainty and scope to interfere with direct possession, as well as to conceal facts relating to ownership. None of the conventions offered a ready solution, and relevant revisions of EU law were introduced after the fact. Notwithstanding the uncertainties in provenance, the court made a confident ruling that the title position was governed by German law as the *lex situs* based on the painting's provenance. Neither the statutory limitations of English law nor of German law precluded a hearing on the merits. The decision is particularly noteworthy given that there was no reported German decision on the interpretation of the limitation of proprietary actions in the event of a third party acquiring possession when the case reached the court. Commentators had conflicting views, and a full discussion of German academic writing was unavailable at the time and remains so.

The result achieved in the Chinese rulings on the Buddha mummy could have been improved had the village committees taken steps to preserve evidence and assets abroad (Roodt 2024). It would have been worth checking whether injunctive relief measures such as freezing orders against property located within the forum's territory and belonging to van Overeem, were available. Search orders against defendants in civil proceedings allow for searches to be conducted on the premises of a named person to obtain evidence to support the claimant's case (either ongoing or planned). *Ex parte* injunctions that restrain further activities under complaint are usually included (Hartley 2009: 442, 463–467). An interdict against the conclusion of exchange agreements with other collectors or an order for disclosure of the name of a party with whom a defendant concluded exchange agreements could have been useful in the circumstances of the case.

Provenance demands greater attention in restitutory claims involving imperial artefacts for it adds to the law's depth dimension and supports the historicisation of PrIL. Historical and archival research reconstructs provenance and provenience as evidence in legal processes. This research enriches the narratives built around claims to have sacred cultural material restored to where they belong. In turn, historicising PrIL helps with the contextualisation of restitution claims; when normative pluralism presents challenges, adjudicators and scholars are encouraged to delve deeper into PrIL's techniques and methodological arsenal.

A critical provenance research methodology is more than just a tool for the accurate description of the life of objects. Research into the provenience and provenance of collection items may not be viable in every case. Nonetheless, the element of 'truth' about diligence in trade may be distilled from the facts of a case; this element gives weight to attributions of ownership in restitution claims. Best practice in provenance research supports sharing with prospective buyers all known provenance information about a seller and red flags (e.g., the likelihood that objects were removed during a civil war, genocide, or in contravention of export controls). It may take a long time for the link between certain human remains and genocide to be recognised. The DMB *Guidelines on Dealing with Collections from Colonial Contexts* Ahrndt et al. 2018) recognised for the first time that objects collected between 1904 and 1908 in central and southern Namibia were acquired or appropriated during the German Empire's genocidal colonial war against the Herero and Nama peoples, rendering it possible that such objects came from victims of this genocide. The pace of the enquiry must allow for the value of the sacred to emerge. The gaps and ambiguities in the provenance of sacred material taken during a genocide will inevitably challenge proof of ownership or rightful custodianship. The 'new problems of responsibility' and the disruptive and challenging problem of especially grievous historic wrongs require analytical tools that can identify and mediate artificial distinctions between legal disciplines and the effects of the 'law versus morality' positions in public and private law. A meaningful provenance may emerge only if once the role of sacred cultural material in the survival and integration of society is more fully understood.

The 2021 DMB *Guidelines on Care of Collections* caution that communities of origin sometimes deem it disrespectful when items are perceived solely in the context of colonial events. The *Guidelines* criticise the 2018 Sarr and Savoy Report's approach of presuming that 'acquisition' was unlawful unless the museum can prove the opposite as unsatisfactory (at 82). The reasoning is that the approach 'focuses on overcoming past injustices,' which is a German/European concern, and loses sight of aspects such as the significance of the collection items to the communities of origin.

Grounded in social criticism, provenance research can provide moral support to deprived communities that have been objectified for so long, because their knowledge is incorporated into the information about the object's itinerary. The need to bring the objects home weighs more heavily than the interests of buyers, scholars, or conservators. These ethics make the case for repatriation. Critical provenance information could signal the need to suspend the juridical framework of circulation from coordinating the primary and secondary legal norms designed for the protection of property, and invoke the framework of exception (Manacorda 2011: 41). For instance, a convention that invites criminal law to take centre stage instead of a residual role relies on criminal responsibility to inform policy in international civil proceedings instead of performing the accessory function it has done to date. The 2017 Council of Europe Convention on Offences relating to Cultural Property, signed 19 May 2017, is an example in point. The Council of Europe is the human rights body of Europe. The Council of Europe Convention facilitates the application of the standard of due care and attention in international criminal contexts and supports criminal or administrative penalties for the circulation of cultural property that was removed illicitly from archaeological sites.

3.7.6 At the intersection between provenance and public policy

How adjudicators approach the intersection of provenance and public policy is outcome-determinative. Real change will become possible only if policymakers and adjudicators cease to be blinded to the obvious because it is so obvious. For instance, the non-enforcement of foreign law could go against public policy where a foreign provision concerning cultural heritage protection claims application as applicable law and there is no impediment in forum public policy (Jakubowski 2009: 137, 145).

Theoretical depth enables the technical tools to be used with a steady hand claims for recovery based on public law should not be excluded from civil litigation against private business. In a welcome departure from the long-established case law originating with *Attorney-General of New Zealand v Ortiz* ([1982] 3 All ER 432 (QBD and CA); [1983] 2 All ER 93 (HL)), the English Court of Appeal recognised the foreign public law rules of Iran when assessing the due diligence of Barakat Galleries Ltd, in respect of carved chlorite jars, bowls, and cups excavated from a cemetery in the Jiroft region in Iran. They were broadly conceived of as 'antiquities' and 'cultural heritage' (*Government of the Islamic Republic of Iran v The Barakat Galleries Ltd* [2007] EWHC 705 (QBD); [2009] 1 QB 22 (CA)). Only one of the parties has ratified the 1970 UNESCO Convention but the public policy of promoting the return of stolen and illegally exported grave goods to their country of origin was aptly considered a part of the juridical framework of exception. The CA confirmed this by stating that '[t]here is international recognition that States should assist one another to prevent the unlawful removal of cultural objects …' (*Government of the Islamic Republic of Iran v The Barakat Galleries Ltd* [2009] 1 QB 22 (CA) para 155).

Conflicts, war, and duress make normative perfection impossible to achieve but interdisciplinarity confers greater awareness of PrIL's potential to re-balance aspects of historical injustice. Modern forms of the choice-of-law rules for tort reveal the postcolonial side of PrIL jurisprudence, but a colonial history lens quickly focuses attention on the difference that connecting factors can make to outcomes in cross-border disputes (Banu 2022: 386ff).

Historical evidence is gaining more relevance in legal proceedings. Bringing academic historians into the core of the legal inquiry and onto the stand in PrIL cases adds another layer to an already complex relationship between law and history (Moran 2019: 435, 438). Legal scholars may focus on normative conflicts, the claims they make on authority, the clues authority provides about the conceptual structure of legal consciousness, and the shifts that take place over time (Kennedy 2006). Making room for historians in civil proceedings for historic redress will provide more scope to analyse the consequences of plunder and war crimes of centuries past by identifying the origin of an idea and tracing it forward to the present.

3.7.7 PrIL and EU secondary law

In the context of relations between EU Member States and third states, there remains considerable scope for re-litigation of claims. EU secondary law prioritises harmonisation of the recognition and enforcement of foreign judgments in the EU and not beyond. As a result, the potential of comity theory to mitigate a strict reliance on territoriality and accommodate bilateralism and reciprocal (mutually acceptable) undertakings between governments is not utilised to the full. A fragmented system persists on a global scale in relation to third states.

Brexit demonstrated the declining potential of the EU normative space. Pan-European and global perspectives that offer different or complementary vantage points have been garnering more attention since. During the Brexit transition period—which started when the UK left the EU on 31 January 2020 and ended on 31 December 2020—the legal status quo was maintained while negotiations about the future relationship between the EU and the UK were ongoing. Greece put illicit trafficking of cultural objects and the return and restitution of stolen high-profile treasures on the agenda. This initiative lacked support at the time. Post-Brexit, the normative divide between London and Athens looms larger. Athens remains highly accessible to the populations of other EU Member States and is more welcoming to a larger part of the world than post-Brexit London may hope to be.

The tension between the cultural interest in cultural property and the principle of the free circulation of goods may be resolved either by the juridical framework of circulation of goods that affirms appropriation, removal and sale, or by restitution policies that are aligned with the judicial framework of exception. In the European Union, this tension is alleviated by the rules of private law, managed by secondary legislation. Cultural property is deserving of protection not as an interest of the market or the buyer in the EU, but of the community. It is worthy of preservation as part of national heritage (Articles 34, 35, and 36 of the consolidated version of the Treaty on the Functioning of the European Union; Magri 2017: 240–241).

In EU policy documents that ascribe value to heritage resources held in common and independently from their owner, reference is made to 'a shared resource and a common good' (Communication from the Commission to the European Parliament, the Council, the European Economic and Social Committee and the Committee of the Regions, *Towards an Integrated Approach to Cultural Heritage for Europe* COM/2014/0477 final/: 2). They require 'an evolved framework for collective governance' that can, and must, 'derogate ordinary provisions of private law' (Magri 2017: 242). A clear derogation at EU level is found in the restitution model addressed specifically to stolen and illegally exported cultural objects (Council Directive EU 2014/60 of 15 May 2014 on the return of cultural objects unlawfully removed from the territory of a Member State and amending Regulation (EU) No 1024/2012 (Recast) [2014] OJ L159). Council Directive EU 2014/60 devises a system of administrative cooperation between EU Member States which ensures the return of cultural objects unlawfully removed from their territories irrespective of property rights (Preamble 8). Post-return, the ownership of an object is determined by the law of the requesting state (Article 13). Another EU single market instrument designed to prevent illicit trafficking of cultural objects, enabling the return of those that have been unlawfully removed, is Regulation (EU) 2019/880 of the European Parliament and of the Council of 17 April 2019 on the introduction and the import of cultural goods OJ L 151, 7.6.201 (Preamble: para 6; Article 2(3)).

The action plan for 2020–2025 was the first EU Commission initiative to recognise that colonialism is embedded in European history and continues to affect society deeply (*A Union of Equality: EU Anti-racism Action Plan 2020–2025* COM(2020) 565 final 18.9.2020). The EU started paying more attention to the structural legacies and adverse effects of European colonialism on people of African descent the year before, when the European Parliament called on the EU and its Member States to take responsibility and adopt a holistic perspective on colonialism and slavery. The European Parliament Resolution on Fundamental Rights of People of African Descent in Europe (2018/2899(RSP) 26.3.2019), which expresses support for Indigenous peoples' repatriation requests and the establishment of an international mechanism to fight the sale of illegally taken Indigenous artefacts, was preceded by a pledge of financial assistance (Regulation (EU) No235/2014 of the European Parliament and of the Council establishing a financing instrument for democracy and human rights worldwide (adopted for the period 2014–2020): paras 8 and 9). EU institutions and Member States are called upon to offer public apologies and restitute stolen artefacts to their countries of origin, and Member States are requested to declassify their colonial archives.

Since heritage belonging to Indigenous peoples and other communities may not be included in the designations which the EU Member States provide, the tensions between the two juridical frameworks may be exacerbated. Indigenous communities are highly likely to require state support to raise a claim.

Conflict rules and principles have not kept track of the 'big picture' social and institutional effects. Compared to the level of scholarly attention given to common PrIL rules for contractual and non-contractual obligations in European and global market contexts, the political questions of imperialism and colonialism remain decidedly under-researched. In particular, delimitations in the application of ordinary commercial law rules and the involvement of private individuals and entities in transnational restitution claims implicating cultural material removed during the colonial era have proved less popular. Meanwhile, globalisation is co-evolving with. Constructed within the state, globalisation continues to draw the trade in ethnographic material within the purview of the juridical framework of circulation.

3.8 Conclusion

The social question of restitution is urgent. Generally, colonial histories are 'far more complex than African states' claims ...' disclose (Effiboley 2020: 81). Society must act in solidarity to repatriate artefacts that are simply not theirs. To avoid being incomplete, the geographical reach of initiatives should extend to regions and ethics frameworks and guidelines on the restitution and repatriation of human remains that have been traded on the art market must extend to human remains encased in or otherwise combined with cultural property. It is time for scholars to focus on the structural weaknesses and uneven applications that caused the lapses of legality during the colonial era. The conflicts of legal norms that occurred during the colonial era were internal (national or within the bounds of Empire) as well as external (international). These conflicts deserve to be studied with reference to the full spectrum of PrIL's potential in the secondary legal norms that condition the depth dimensions of law's application. In particular, the relationship between norms that are contrary to national public policy and international public order must be placed at the forefront to actualise fundamental norms and common precepts.

The Amsterdam hearing in the Buddha mummy case could have been a decisive victory for liberal jurisprudence, but mummified thinking enveloped this ancient relic when it reached Amsterdam. The Dutch court remained passive in the face of its need for protection. When van Overeem unjustifiably withheld evidence of the new owner's identity, the Dutch court sanctioned this evasive behaviour. The Chinese rulings in the Buddha mummy cases confirm a paradigm for value-rationality that changes adjudicatory outcomes about standing and classification. The rulings signal when the provenance record of cultural material invokes the public policy of promoting the return of stolen and illegally exported artefacts to their country of origin, and bring the juridical framework of exception into clearer view. The juridical framework of exception opens the frontiers of PrIL to global justice. PrIL techniques make it possible to eject a foreign legal rule that would legitimise violent looting and theft during the colonial era or render void ab initio any transfer that launders title. The potential of the public policy exception to constrain the commercial imperative of the art trade make it possible to counter the worst negative effects of commercial competition. This potential can be realised if criteria for assessing ethical judgment in cross-border restitution claims are better defined. PrIL's public policy exception is neither static nor immutable. The acceptability of a provision of foreign law must be judged by contemporary standards, and conceptions of public policy should move with the time. Legal uncertainty is therefore unavoidable but the overarching juridical framework of exception lends stability and enables greater consistency in the application of the law.

Courts within and outwith the EU would be well-advised to direct their attention to common PrIL principles to give more definition to fundamental human rights norms. Ossified scholarly understandings hold back advancement in the humanities and social sciences in the field of restitution but primary and secondary legal rules in frameworks for circulation and exception can be better coordinated. PrIL's common principles can support provenance research on human remains and other sacred material, and a broad-based definition of the sacred enables greater flexibility in questions about legal standing. In addition, any of the historical approaches to the pedigree of PrIL tenets may reframe the characterisation of a dispute. In restitution questions deriving from a colonial context, the legal system that counters mimetics most effectively, or the combination of rules from different legal systems that could counter mimetic competition, would be recommended.

Restitution and repatriation claims highlight many types of conflict between potentially applicable rules that display ambiguous or clashing definitions. All manner of normative gaps arise. Considering the effect choice-of-law rules may have on one's reading of the dispute about the Parthenon Marbles, the conundrum that arises is plain to see. If an English court were to apply its own law as forum law based on the public policy exception, it would encounter the question mark hanging over the British Museum's title. If a Greek court were to apply Greek law—whether based on a proprietary conflicts rule or a public policy exception—the historical timeline of the principle of state ownership to antiquities may indicate a gap. To effectively rein in the behaviour of private actors that exercise informal power beyond the state, neither a new tailored choice-of-law rule, nor harmonised residual conflict rules will resolve the ill effects of the trade in sacred cultural heritage on their own. A special conflicts rule may not necessarily be more effective than the *lex originis* and *lex furti* rules. PrIL's evolution towards global justice must occur at the epicentre of the 'juridical framework of exception' where the public policy exception can fulfil its function. This is confirmed in the cross-over of tort choice-of-law and public policy in the juridical framework of exception, where it could become evident that the designated applicable law should not govern the question at hand in complex colonial contexts. There is considerable scope to develop the limited vocabulary in PrIL for identifying and describing any potential risks brought by restitution claims. The most appropriate legal system is the one setting the standard of diligence or the compensation quantum for the tortious activity, and the entire PrIL system, including its escape mechanisms, need to be utilised to achieve this outcome.

The unique proportions and locations of every stone of the Parthenon reveal a perspective. All the architectural elements of the temple of Athena are subtly curved. Each metope and pediment figure of the 70,000 pieces of the giant three-dimensional jigsaw is unique and fits in only one place. There are imperceptible differences even among pieces that appear to have identical proportions, but none are interchangeable. The Parthenon Marbles are synonymous with restitution in a symbolic and emblematic sense, but they also stand for themselves as material objects. The dispute is a clear example of a hard case. The disputants have deployed the same argumentative tools and language in perpetuity. As a method for studying the role of law in the restitution claims for their return to Athens, the theory of perspective highlights the complex argumentative loops that have formed between hierarchically equal principles in the dispute, which need untying. Factors external to the system of law—anthropological perspectives on the sacred—guide and direct legal and ethical interpretations. The sacred dimension of the Parthenon Sculptures calls attention to misleading advertisements of the purported 'universality' of the 'super-artefacts' on display in universal museums that distort the sacred and the universal in equal measure (e.g., Cuno 2006: 26–27). The inward turn of the frieze upon the gallery space resembles an inward-looking perspective that relies on a problematic and outdated colonial paradigm in legislation premised on protecting the integrity of its collections by any means.

Responsibilities and obligations inhere in sacred cultural material that has survived long and complex histories. The Athenians' and the mummified monk's sacrifices draw out dimensions of responsibility and respect which individuals owe to one another and to their communities. The form of justice which the mummy of Zhanggong Zushi demands is not reliant on rights-frameworks, but on mutual respect and broad interpretations of comity. The missing relic holds the space for a more comprehensive theory of responsibility for the repatriation of sacred cultural material.

Restitution claims give ontological primacy to the tangible. The ontological primacy of things temporarily posits culture as alienable and retrievable, tempting us to treat the tangible as an 'index' for the intangible. When claims relate to physical material, technological reproduction cannot capture the intangible heritage that must accompany full form restitution (Roodt 2022). A common understanding of the sacred grounded in perception, intuition, and theory would enable recognition of specific sacred practices deserve protection as forms of spiritual expression. Recognition of the vulnerability of our own society may unlock generosity which is capable of taxonomic difference. Primary rules may be suspended. The ingrained dichotomisation of procedure and substance might shift when limitation periods have expired. Categorisations may give way to acknowledge that the sacred is far more than a body, a corpse, or data.

Different conceptions of the role of law prevail across legal traditions. Its scope, focus, level of governance, and legal force depends on location and normative interaction. The terrain of restitution and repatriation claims is definedby the intersections of (international and national) cultural heritage law, (public and private) international law, domestic systems of property law, intellectual property law, colonial law, and customary law, to name a few. 'What ought to be done,' 'what the law requires,' or 'what distributive justice requires' invites contestation. Both PublIL and PrIL provide broad interpretive parameters for adjudicators to determine restitution claims. Normative conflicts may see PrIL principles interacting with the bases of restitution claims in PublIL. The confluence of restitutory (PrIL) claims and reparation claims for reparative justice may generate normative leverage to suspend rules, and shift the dividing line between procedure and substance. The 'new problems of responsibility' associated with especially grievous historic wrongs require legal disciplines to overcome artificial distinctions between them, dispense with the 'law versus morality' positions in public and private law, and be more alive to the intersection between public policy and critical provenance research, so that the gaps in the 'common rules of adjudication' may be identified. The PrIL method justifies the application and non-application of legal norms with reference to legal and ethical standards located in other legal disciplines and normative formats. Ideally, PublIL must remain open to the public policy direction of PrIL, supporting the optimisation of PrIL governance to ensure access to justice alongside greater moral and social responsibility.

The vocabulary of any single discipline in law and ethics will be too limited to capture the nuances of the normative interplay between thems. No single discipline can engage fully with provenance questions in the context of normative conflict. Moreover, conceptions of culture, tradition, and religion, are not static, and decisions and policies about the ethics of collecting, restitution, and repatriation are subject to change. This study proposes the adoption of a non-legal factor that is more universally agreeable than legal rules and criteria to stabilise rulings in respect of *locus standi*, choice-of-law, classification, and the application of foreign public law. Any non-legal factor that hopes to give legal decision-making a steer would have to be premised on a common understanding across history, applied philosophy, and primary and secondary legal norms. PrIL's connectivity derives from its capacity for interdisciplinarity within the interlocking network of domestic, provincial, national, regional, international, and transnational norms. PrIL connects to judicial as well as extra-judicial principles and subjects, including applied ethics and history. This facility enriches the discourse about colonial contexts and has the capacity to refine human rights thinking. PrIL's worth and capacity for interdisciplinarity allows it to break new ground for the practice and theory of the restitution and repatriation of sacred cultural property and heritage taken in the colonial era. Given that many dismiss PrIL as 'marginal' because of its self-limiting attachment to the unduly technical only underlines the importance of reflecting on how it is taught and to whom the potential of its ethic and its worth are communicated (Ruiz Abou-Nigm 2019: 384).

Bibliography

Arts Council England, 2022. *Restitution and Repatriation: A Practical Guide for Museums in England*, 5 August 2022 <https://aim-museums.co.uk/guidance-restitution-repatriation-released-arts-council-england>

Banu, Roxana. 2013. 'Assuming Regulatory Authority for Transnational Torts: An Interstate Affair? A Historical Perspective on the Canadian Private International Law Tort Rules' *Windsor Yearbook on Access to Justice* 31(1): 197–211.

Banu, Roxana, 2018. *Nineteenth Century Perspectives on Private International Law* Oxford: OUP.

Banu, Roxana. 2022. 'Teaching by Historicising Private International Law' *International Journal of Law in Context* 18(4): 383–392.

Barad, Karen. 2003. 'Posthumanist Performativity: Towards an Understanding of How Matter Comes to Matter' *Signs: Journal of Women in Culture and Society* 28(3): 801–831.

Bergson, Henri. 1935. *The Two Sources of Morality and Religion* (tr R Ashley Audra and Cloudesley Brereton) London: MacMillan and Co Ltd.

Bonell, Michael J. 2011. 'Limitation Periods' in Arthur S. Hartkamp, Martijn W. Hesselink, Ewoud Hondius, Chantal Mak & C. Edgar Du Perron (eds.) *Towards a European Civil Code* 4th ed., Alphen aan den Rijn: Kluwer Law International 715–732.

Brown, Michael F. 2005. 'Heritage Trouble: Recent Work on the Protection of Intangible Cultural Property' *International Journal of Cultural Property* 12(1): 40–61.

Byrne, James G. 2015. *Factors Determining the Repatriation of Cultural Heritage from Museums; the Place of Cultural Rights in British Museums Practice* Master Thesis, SOAS University of London.

Cacot, Margaret Fleming. 2021. *Cultural Heritage: Property, Personhood, and International Returns* LLM Thesis by Research, University of Glasgow.

Campfens, Evelien. 2021. *Cross-Border Title Claims to Cultural Objects: Property or Heritage?* PhD Thesis, Leiden University (Meijers-reeks Eleven).

Carruthers, Janeen. 2005. *The Transfer of Property in the Conflict of Laws: Choice of Law Rules in Inter Vivos Transfers of Property* Oxford: OUP.

Chechi, Alessandro. 2017/2018. 'When Private International Law Meets Cultural Heritage Law: Problems and Prospects' *Yearbook of Private International Law* 19: 269–293.

Chen, Zhen. 2022. 'Is a Mummy a Person or a Property: The Classification and Choice of Law of Cultural Objects in Private International Law' *The Chinese Journal of Comparative Law* 10(2): 274–296.

Childress III, Donald Earl. 2011. 'Introduction' in Donald E Childress III (ed.) *The Role of Ethics in International Law* Cambridge: CUP 1–8.

Colwell, Chip. 2017. *Plundered Skulls and Stolen Spirits: Inside the Fight to Reclaim Native America's Culture* Chicago: University of Chicago Press.

Cuno, James. 2006. 'View from the Universal Museum' in John Henry Merryman (ed.) *Imperialism, Art, and Restitution* Cambridge: CUP 15–36.

Cuno, James. 2008. *Who Owns Antiquity? Museums and the Battle over Ancient Heritage* Princeton NJ: Princeton University Press.

D'Aspremont, Jean. 2019. 'The Implausibility of Coordinating Transborder Legal Effects of Domestic Statutes and Courts' Decisions by International Law' in Horatia Muir Watt, Lucia Bíziková, Agatha Brandão de Oliveira & Diego P. Fernández Arroyo (eds.) *Global Private International Law: Adjudication without Frontiers* Cheltenham: Edward Elgar Publishing 282–301.

Dawson, Peter. 2016. *The Design and Development of Digital Return Platforms for Northern Indigenous Heritage; Knowledge Synthesis* Final Report for the Social Sciences and Humanities Research Council of Canada.

Díaz-Andreu, Margarita. 2018. 'Archaeology and Imperialism: From Nineteenth-Century New Imperialism to Twentieth-Century Decolonization' in Bonnie Effros and Guolong Lai (eds.) *Unmasking Ideology in Imperial and Colonial Archaeology: Vocabulary, Symbols, and Legacy* Los Angeles, CA: Cotsen Institute of Archaeology Press 3–28.

Douglas, Susan & Melanie K. Hayes. 2017. 'Ethical Databases: Case Studies and Remaining Gaps in Cultural Heritage Information Sharing' in Alessandro Chechi & Marc-Andre Renold (eds.) *Cultural Heritage Law and Ethics: Mapping Recent Developments* Genève: Schulthess 143–170.

Effiboley, Emery Patrick. 2020. 'Reflections on the Issue of Repatriation of Looted and Illegally Acquired African Cultural Objects in Western Museums' *Contemporary Journal of African Studies* 7(1): 67–83.

EU. 2014. Communication from the Commission to the European Parliament, the Council, the European Economic and Social Committee and the Committee of the Regions, *Towards an Integrated Approach to Cultural Heritage for Europe* COM/2014/0477final/.

EU Commission. 2020. *A Union of Equality: EU Anti-racism Action Plan 2020–2025* COM(2020) 565 final 18.9.2020.

Federal Ministry for Arts, Culture, the Civil Service and Sport. 2023. *Recommendations of the Advisory Committee for Guidelines for Collections in Austrian Federal Museums from Colonial Contexts* 20 June 2023, Vienna: BMI Digital Print Center.

Ferrando, Tomaso. 2019. 'Global Supply Chains: Doe v Nestle' in Horatia Muir Watt, Lucia Bíziková, Agatha Brandão de Oliveira & Diego P. Fernández Arroyo (eds.) *Global Private International Law: Adjudication without Frontiers* Cheltenham: Edward Elgar Publishing 236–244.

Francioni, Francesco. 2012. 'Public and Private in the International Protection of Global Cultural Goods' *European Journal of International Law* 23(3): 719–730.

Fresnedo de Aguirre, Cecilia. 2019. 'Public Policy in Private International Law: Guardian or Barrier?' in Verónica Ruiz Abou-Nigm & Maria Blanca Noodt Taquela (eds.) *Diversity and Integration in Private International Law* Edinburgh: Edinburgh University Press 341–361.

Frigo, Manlio. 2023. 'Restitution of Cultural Property and Decolonization of Museums: Issues of Consistency Between Fulfilment of Legal Obligations, Ethical Principles and Identity Links' in Laura Pineschi (ed.) *Cultural Heritage, Sustainable Development and Human Rights: Towards an Integrated Approach* London: Routledge.

Garnett, Richard. 2012. *Substance and Procedure in Private International Law* Oxford: OUP.

German Museums Association (DMB) (Ahrndt Wiebke (Chair), Hans-Jörg Czech, Jonathan Fine, Larissa Förster, Michael Geißdorf, Matthias Glaubrecht, Katarina Horst, Melanie Kölling, Silke Reuther, Anja Schaluschke, Carola Thielecke, Hilke Thode-Arora, Anne Wesche, Jürgen Zimmerer, Veit Didczuneit & Christoph Grunenberg). 2018. *Guidelines on Dealing with Collections from Colonial Contexts*, Berlin, July 2018 <https://www.museumsbund.de/wp-content/uploads/2019/10/dmb-guidelines-colonial-context.pdf>

German Museums Association (DMB). 2019. *Guidelines for German Museums: Care of Collections from Colonial Contexts* (2nd ed 2019) <https://www.museumsbund.de/publikationen/guidelines-on-dealing-with-collections-from-colonial-contexts-2/>

German Museums Association (DMB). 2021. *Guidelines for German Museums: Care of Collections from Colonial Contexts* 3rd ed, April 2021 <https://www.museumsbund.de/wp-content/uploads/2021/03/mb-leitfaden-en-web.pdf>

Girard, René. 1972. *Violence and the Sacred* (tr Patrick Gregory) Baltimore: The Johns Hopkins University Press.

Goldmann, Matthias. 2021. 'Imperial Law's Ambiguity: A Postcolonial Approach to Restitution and Reparation Claims', Keynote Presented at 'Imperial Artefacts: History, Law and the Looting of Cultural Property', Conference organised by the University of Leiden, 27–28 January 2021.

Good, Anthony. 2018. 'Law and Anthropology: Legal Pluralism and 'Lay' Decision-making' in Dawn Watkins & Mandy Burton (eds.) *Research Methods in Law* 2nd ed., London: Routledge 211–238.

Graveson, Ronald. 1974a. *Conflict of Laws: Private International Law* 7th ed., London: Sweet and Maxwell.

Graveson, Ronald. 1974b. 'Problems of Private International Law in Non-Unified Legal Systems' *Collected Courses of the Hague Academy of International Law* 141: 186–254.

Haller, John S. 1971. 'Race and the Concept of Progress in Nineteenth Century American Ethnology' *American Anthropologist* 73(3): 710–724.

Hansard HL Deb. vol 834, cols. 1992–2006, 14 December 2023.

Hartley, Trevor C. 2009. *International Commercial Litigation* Cambridge: CUP.

Hatzimihail, Nikitas E. 2021. *Preclassical Conflict of Laws* CUP online.

Hodgson, Geoffrey M. 2013. 'Editorial Introduction to 'Ownership' by AM Honoré (1961)' *Journal of Institutional Economics* 9(2): 223–255.

Hooper, John & Ted Plafker, 'The Body in the Buddha' *The Economist*, 4 May 2017.

Huber, Ulrik. 1689. *Praelectiones Juris Romani et Hodierni* Vol II Book 1 Tit. iii 'Conflictu Legum Diversarum in Diversis Imperiis' (text, translation and introduction reprinted in D. J. Llewelyn Davies. 1937. 'The Influence of Huber's De Conflictu Legum on English Private International Law' *British Year Book of International Law* 18: 64–78).

Hubert, Jane. 1992. 'Dry Bones or Living Ancestors? Conflicting Perceptions of Life, Death and the Universe' *International Journal of Cultural Property* 1(1): 105–128.

Human Rights Council Report, *Repatriation of Ceremonial Objects and Human Remains under the UN Declaration on the Rights of Indigenous Peoples*, A/HRC/45/35 21 July 2020.

ICPRCP. Twenty-fourth Session, UNESCO Headquarters, 29–31 May 2024, 4:33:01. <https://www.youtube.com/watch?v=hIF_Br8ZeT0&t=17551s>

ILA Committee on the Participation in Global Cultural Heritage Governance. 2022. Resolution 01/2022 <https://www.ila-hq.org/en_GB/documents/resolu-1-1>

Jakubowski, Andrzej. 2009. 'Return of Illicitly Trafficked Cultural Objects Pursuant to Private International Law: Current Developments' in Ana Filipa Vrdoljak & Francesco Francioni (eds.) *The Illicit Traffic of Cultural Objects in the Mediterranean* (EUI Working Paper 2009).

Jayme, Erik. 2005. 'Globalization in Art Law: Clash of Interests and International Tendencies' *Vanderbilt Journal of Transnational Law* 38(4): 927–945.

Kakaounaki, Marianna. 'A Greek Archaeologist's Dig into the Elgin Archive' *Kathimerini* 2 April 2024.

Kalibani, Mèhèza. 2021. 'The Less Considered Part: Contextualizing Immaterial Heritage from German Colonial Contexts in the Restitution Debate' *International Journal of Cultural Property* 28(1): 43–53.

Kennedy, Duncan. 2006. 'Three Globalizations of Law and Legal Thought: 1850–2000' in David M. Trubek & Alvaro Santos (eds.) *The New Law and Economic Development. A Critical Appraisal* CUP Online 19–73.

Kennedy, Duncan. 2010. 'Savigny's Family/Patrimony Distinction and its Place in the Global Genealogy of Classical Legal Thought' *The American Journal of Comparative Law* 58(4): 811–841.

Klabbers, Jan. 2016. 'Reflections on Mimesis and International Law – An Epilogue' in Vincent Négri & Isabelle Schulte-Tenckhoff (eds.) *Mimesis. Towards International Normativity: Between Mimetism and Dissemination* Paris: A. Pedone 249–261.

Kono, Toshiyuki. 2020. 'Impact of Uniform Laws on the Protection of Cultural Property – The 1995 Convention', Keynote delivered at the 1995 UNIDROIT Convention Conference on Cultural Objects at the Crossroads of Rights and Interests, Rome, 8–9 October 2020.

Krupa, Krystiana L. & Kelsey T. Grimm. 2021. 'Digital Repatriation as a Decolonizing Practice in the Archaeological Archive' *Across the Disciplines* 18(1/2): 47–58.

Krygier, Martin. 2024. 'Well-Tempered Power: "A Cultural Achievement of Universal Significance"' Adam Smith Lecture, 10 June 2024, University of Glasgow.

Kynourgiopoulou, Vasiliki. 2011. 'National Identity Interrupted: The Mutilation of the Parthenon Marbles and the Greek Claim for Repatriation' in Helaine Silverman (ed.) *Contested Cultural Heritage: Religion, Nationalism, Erasure and Exclusion in a Global World* 155–170. New York: Springer.

Last, Kathryn V. 2007. 'Cultural Pluralism and the Return of Cultural Heritage' in Stephen Tierney (ed) *Accommodating Cultural Diversity* Burlington: Ashgate 123–143.

Linn-Tynen, Erin. 2020. 'Reclaiming the Past as a Matter of Social Justice: African American Heritage, Representation and Identity in the United States' in Veysel Apaydin (ed.) *Critical Perspectives on Cultural Memory and Heritage: Construction, Transformation and Destruction* London: UCL Press 255–268.

Liu, Zuozhen. 2017. 'Will the God Win?: The Case of the Buddhist Mummy' *International Journal of Cultural Property* 24(2): 221–238.

Loukaki, Argyro. 2008. *Living Ruins, Value Conflicts* London: Routledge.

Lyotard, Jean-Francois. 1988. *The Differend: Phrases in Dispute* (tr George Van Den Abbeele) Minneapolis: University of Minnesota Press.

Machado Haertel, Letícia. 2021. 'The Past, Present: The Parthenon Sculptures Dispute as an Example of the ICPRCP's Role on Claims Barred by the Non-Retrospectivity of the 1970 UNESCO Convention' *International Journal of Cultural Property* 28(4): 479–504.

Magri, Geo. 2017. 'Directive 2014/60/EU and Good Faith Acquisition of Cultural Goods in Italy' in Simona Pinton & Lauso Zagato eds. *Cultural Heritage Scenarios 2015–2017* Edizioni Ca' Foscari Digital Publishing 227–244.

Manacorda, Stefano. 2011. 'Criminal Law Protection of Cultural Heritage: An International Perspective' in Stefano Manacorda & Duncan Chappell (eds.) *Crime in the Art and Antiquities World: Illegal Trafficking in Cultural Property* Springer 17–48.

Michaels, Ralf. 2019. 'Private International Law as an Ethic of Responsivity' in Verónica Ruiz Abou-Nigm & Maria Blanca Noodt Taquela (eds.) *Diversity and Integration in Private International Law* Edinburgh: Edinburgh University Press 11–27.

Mills, Alex. 2019. 'Indigenous Norms and Judicial Anthropology: Song Mao' in Horatia Muir Watt, Lucia Bizikova, Agatha Brandao de Oliuveira & Diego P. Fernandez Arroyo (eds.) *Global Private International Law: Adjudication without Frontiers* Cheltenham: Edward Elgar Publishing 118–130.

Moran, Mayo. 2019. 'The Problem of the Past: How Historic Wrongs Became Legal Problems' *University of Toronto Law Journal* 69(4): 421–472.

Muir Watt, Horatia. 2014. 'Future Directions?' in Horatia Muir Watt & Diego P. Fernández Arroyo (eds.) *Private International Law and Global Governance* Oxford: OUP 343–382.

Muir Watt, Horatia. 2016a. 'Jurisprudence Without Confines: Private International Law as Global Legal Pluralism' *Cambridge Journal of International and Comparative Law* 5(3): 388–403.

Muir Watt, Horatia. 2016b. 'Conflicts of Laws Unbounded: The Case for a Legal-Pluralist Revival' *Transnational Legal Theory* 7(3): 313–353.

Muir Watt, Horatia. 2017. 'Hospitality, Tolerance, and Exclusion in Legal Form: Private International Law and the Politics of Difference' *Current Legal Problems* 70(1): 111–147.

Museum am Rothenbaum Kulturen und Kunst der Welt. n.d. 'Digital Benin: Reconnecting Royal Art Treasures' <digital-benin.org>

Neidhardt, Alberto Horst. 2018. *The Transformation of European Private International Law A Genealogy of the Family Anomaly* PhD Thesis, European University Institute.

North, Peter M. & James J. Fawcett. 2004. *Cheshire and North's Private International Law* 13th ed., Oxford: OUP.

Oruç, Pinar. 2022. 'Rethinking Who Keeps Heritage: 3D Technology, Repatriation and Copyright' *GRUR International* 71(12): 1138–1146.

Paterson, Robert K. 2017. 'Maori Preserved Heads: A Legal History' in Peter Mosimann & Beat Schönenberger (eds.) *Kunst & Recht/Art & Law* Bern: Stampfli Verlag 71–86.

Paul, Joel R. 1988. 'The Isolation of Private International Law' *Wisconsin International Law Journal* 7(1): 149–178.

Pavis, Mathilde & Andrea Wallace. 2019. 'Statement: Response to the 2018 Sarr -Savoy Report' *Journal of Intellectual Property, Information Technology and E-Commerce Law* 10(2): 115–125.

Prott, Lyndel V. 1989. 'Problems of Private International Law for the Protetion of the Cultural Heritage' *Collected Courses of the Hague Academy of International Law* 217: 215–317.

Prott, Lyndel V. 1992. 'Movables and Immovables as Viewed by the Law' *International Journal of Cultural Property* 1(2): 389–392.

'Qingdao Recommendations for the Protection and Return of Cultural Objects Removed from Colonial Contexts or Acquired by Other Unjustifiable Means', adopted at the International Conference on the Protection and Return of Cultural Objects Removed in Colonial Contexts, hosted by the Alliance for Cultural Heritage in Asia in Qingdao, China, on 20 June 2024.

Report from the Select Committee of the House of Commons on the Earl of Elgin's Collection of Sculptured Marbles. 1816. London: W. Bulmer and Co.

Riles, Annelise. 2005. 'Taking on the Technicalities. A New Agenda for the Cultural Study of Law' *Buffalo Law Review* 53(3): 973–1034.

Roodt, Christa. 2007a. 'Reflections of Theory, Doctrine and Method in Choice of Law' *Comparative and International Law Journal of Southern Africa* 40(1): 76–102.

Roodt, Christa. 2007b. 'A Wider Vision in Choice of Prescription Law' *Yearbook of Private International Law* 9: 357-373.

Roodt, Christa. 2015. *Private International Law, Art and Cultural Heritage* Cheltenham: Edward Elgar Publishing.

Roodt, Christa. 2019. 'The Holy Family on an Unholy Odyssey: Legal Ownership of Stolen Trophy Art' in Jane Milosch & Nick Pearce (eds.) *Collecting and Provenance: A Multi-Disciplinary Approach* Lanham, Maryland: Rowman & Littlefield 343–358.

Roodt, Christa. 2022. 'The Role of Digital Technology in the Restitution of Cultural Artifacts' *Georgetown Journal of International Affairs* Online (18 July).

Roodt, Christa. 2024. *Restitution of Cultural Property and the Law: Complex Colonial Histories*. London: Routledge.

Rubin, Alfred P. 1997. *Ethics and Authority in International Law* Cambridge: CUP

Rudenstine, David. 2021. 'Trophies for the Empire: The Epic Dispute Between Greece and England Over the Parthenon Sculptures in the British Museum' *Cardozo Arts & Entertainment Law Journal* 39: 377–505.

Ruiz Abou-Nigm, Verónica. 2019. 'Bridging and Balancing: Diversity and Integration in Private International Law', in Verónica Ruiz Abou-Nigm & Maria Blanca Noodt Taquela (eds.) *Diversity and Integration in Private International Law* Edinburgh: Edinburgh University Press 362–388.

Salmond, Sir John William & Patrick John Fitzgerald. 1966. *Salmond on Jurisprudence* 12th ed., London: Sweet & Maxwell.

Sarr, Felwine & Bénédicte Savoy. 2018. *The Restitution of African Cultural Heritage: Toward a New Relational Ethics* <https://www.about-africa.de/images/sonstiges/2018/sarr_savoy_en.pdf>

Schaepe, David on behalf of the Nooksack Indian Tribe. 2005. *Stone T'ixwelatsa Repatriation Report & Supplement Report I* Stó:lo Research & Resource Management Centre.

Silverman, Raymond A. (ed.) 2015. *Museum as Process: Translating Local and Global Knowledges* London: Routledge.

Spitra, Sebastian M. 2021. 'The Administration of Culture in International Law Since the 19th Century: A New Historical Narrative' *University of Vienna Law Review* 5(1): 121–158.

Stahn, Carsten. 2023. *Confronting Colonial Objects: Histories, Legalities, and Access to Culture* Oxford: OUP.

Stamboulakis, Drossos. 2023. *Comparative Recognition and Enforcement: Foreign Judgments and Awards* Cambridge: CUP.

Struycken, Antoon Victor Marie. 2009. 'Co-Ordination and Co-Operation in Respectful Disagreement: General Course on Private International Law' *Recueil des Cours* 311(2004): 8–551.

UNESCO. 2015. *Operational Guidelines for the Implementation of the Convention on the Means of Prohibiting and Preventing the Illicit Import, Export and Transfer of Ownership of Cultural Property* (20 May 2015), C70/15/3. MSP Operational Guidelines.

Valeonti, Foteini, Antonis Bikakis, Melissa Terras, Chris Speed, Andrew Hudson-Smith & Konstantinos Chalkias. 2021. 'Crypto Collectibles, Museum Funding and OpenGLAM: Challenges, Opportunities and the Potential of Non-Fungible Tokens (NFTs)' *Applied Sciences* 11-9931: 1–19.

Van Vliet, Lars P.W. 2006. 'The Boundaries of Property Rights: Netherlands National Report 2006' in Sjef van Erp & Lars van Vliet (eds.) *Netherlands Reports to the Seventeenth International Congress of Comparative Law: The Principles of the Law of Restitution* OUP: Utrecht.

Von Savigny, Friedrich Carl & William Guthrie. 1869. *A Treatise on the Conflict of Laws, and the Limits of their Operation in Respect of Time and Place, tr. with notes by William Guthrie; with an appendix containing the treatises of Bartolus, Molinaeus, Paul Voet, & Huber* 2nd ed., revised, Edinburgh: T & T Clark.
Wilde, Lawrence. 2013. *Global Solidarity* Edinburgh: Edinburgh University Press.
Woodhead, Charlotte C. 2002. 'A Debate Which Crosses All Borders – The Repatriation of Human Remains: More than Just a Legal Question' *Art Antiquity and Law* 7(4): 317–347.
Yntema, Hessel E. 1953. 'The Historic Bases of Private International Law' *The American Journal of Comparative Law* 2(3): 297–317.
Yuen, Waifong. 2018. *Homeless Cultural Property in the Netherlands: The Case of the 'Liuquan Mummy'* Masters Dissertation in Museum Studies, University of Leiden.
Zeidler, Kamil. 2016. *Restitution of Cultural Property: Hard Case, Theory of Argumentation, Philosophy of Law* Gdańsk: Gdańsk University Press.

4 Towards a coherent theory of responsibility for the ‘sacred’

4.1 Introduction

The modern understanding of restitution law and practice is constrained by museological discourses that maintain that national and international law do not provide suitable pathways for settling ownership issues surrounding acquisitions and takings in colonial contexts. The normative effect of mimesis is nurtured through objectification of others’ sacred cultural heritage. All the case studies in the study—the Parthenon Sculptures dispute, the Zhanggong Zushi mummy cases, the sacred medicine bundles in bundle culture, and the Herero and Nama remains and sacred objects implicated in ongoing litigation against Germany—demonstrate the objectification of material and human remains, the dispersion of fragments of complexes of material, the scattering of the ‘limbs of other civilisations’, and facets of the inexorable drive to digitise and control the digital. Objectification of the villagers’ ancestor, the Zhanggong Zushi mummy, occurred at the hands of the social systems of power and western ideology that are imprinted on the market. If the will to power defines the ultimate horizon of possibility for reasonable responses to the special social question raised by restitution claims of sacred cultural heritage, a ‘near-universal loss of meaning’ would become unavoidable. An unstoppable mimesis will be generated by recourse to power and capitalising on the normative effects achieved by means of power.

This study makes the case for a clearer articulation of the law and ethics of restitution of cultural heritage whose sacred character remains unacknowledged or underacknowledged. An alien ontology envelops sacred objects entangled in contested definitions and disagreements about their status. The restitution of sacred cultural property and heritage relies on criteria for ethical judgments concerning substantive conflicts in trans-border claims. The study demonstrates what is at stake when developing such criteria, and indicates when ethical reasoning can change outcomes. It is constructed around a definition of the ‘sacred’ that cuts across the social sciences and humanities and the colonial proclivities and behaviours of the time. It also makes observations about technological advances in the dissemination of archival and artefactual information in repatriation processes, and argues for balanced decisions in the area.

The scope of the field of the study is broad. There is no single common counter-document to the General Act of the Berlin Conference on West Africa of 26

DOI: 10.4324/9781003583967-4

February 1885 that can confine its parameters (Stahn 2023: 59).t In any event no codification can provide theultimate 'holy grail' of legal certainty for the conflict of laws of sacred cultural property (Szabados 2020: 323ff). The 'holy grail' is a common definition of and approaches to the sacred that lays the ground for restitution law and practice in international civil litigation. Legal uncertainty is unavoidable in matters of public policy. It is the overarching juridical framework of exception that steadies the application of the law on a case-by-case basis. If courts use legal reasoning formalistically to disclaim important contextual aspects, the route to the juridical framework in which the content of the law expresses itself remains blocked. The strongest claim advanced by the village committees—that exchanging the Buddha mummy for other collector items with a collector of unknown identity, just before the legal proceedings got under way, was contrary to the public order—was not contextualised properly. The public policy of promoting the return of stolen and illegally exported heritage to their countries of origin deserves to be applied in courts, no matter where they are in the world. Stolen, looted, and illegally exported sacred cultural material invoke the juridical framework of exception, which renders exchange agreements concluded with a third party while proceedings were pending, contrary to public order. The Dutch court should have been briefed on the sacred quality of the Zhanggong Zushi mummy as well as on the implications of such agreements.

To withstand the unfettered circulation of sacred cultural material, the law must be restored in all its dimensions. Special laws passed by former European colonial powers create exceptions to the general rule of inalienability. Far from adopting uniform primary legal norms, governments move at their own pace. Glimmers of 'best' practice impart a sense of what is possible. Detailed policies for the museum sector go a long way to improve the likelihood of successful returns of sacred and ceremonial items (Zeidler 2016: 203, 213–214; Butt 2009: 5). Their guidelines for the care of their collections from colonial contexts indicate which ethical yardsticks, procedures, and criteria they apply, and help them to communicate their position in a transparent way (DMB *Guidelines on Care of Collections* 2021: 48). Moral codes deserve to remain open, and their moral defensibility open to review, through lenses provided by history, culture, community, law reform, and policy. No attempt should be made to compare and rank values that have no common measure. The relational and material elements do not inhabit 'the same order of existence.'

While the basic requirements of a legal theory are easy to identify, it is more challenging to devise an integrative theory on responsibility in respect of claims to cultural heritage looted and trafficked during the colonial era. Stale and superficial arguments befuddle the claims to have the Parthenon Sculptures returned to Greece. The momentum stirring in restitution discourse and practice offers Private International Law (PrIL) scholars, adjudicators, and policymakers an opening to wield the methods and techniques of PrIL as a lever to achieve more effective activism at the normative and applied levels. The theoretical ground of PrIL is solid and offers a stable place to stand. Its capacity to accommodate other legal systems and local rules that adhere to a different world view and chronosophy is a beacon of light amid the value clashes and legal conflicts that mark restitution cases. Instead of facilitating the effects of liberal capitalism and economic expansion, a connective PrIL can articulate the exceptions that deserve respectful attention and responsiveness in claims for restitution of sacred material removed or trafficked in complex colonial contexts. The potential of PrIL method, techniques, and perspectives to bring order to our thinking on restitution of colonial-era and Indigenous cultural property, rests in common PrIL arguments that can resist the normative effects of mimetics. Public policy and the comity of nations inform the application of the juridical framework of exception. Strengthening PrIL's ethical dimension can replenish the depleted substantive normativity in adjudication relating to removals during the colonial era.

Western priorities in the restitution debate tend to be linked to western conceptions of time which impact the formation of organisational structures and instruments in interpretations that shape how objects are defined, categorised, and treated in law. Conceptions of time will likely also affect the way in which provenance is established and how provenance gaps are filled by working forwards or backwards in provenance research or contextualising their deprivation.

Just title of sacred heritage such as the Parthenon Sculptures, sacred medicine bundles, and artefactual and ancestral human remains, cannot and must not be judged by past standards alone. Where the past behaviours of colonial powers impacted sacred cultural property and heritage, the juridical framework of exception, or the operation of the transitional rules of PrIL can provide solid reasons for rescinding the chronology of historical time. Devising exceptions to the rule of intertemporal law may also clear the pathway to a relational ethic. By bringing normative phenomena, responsibilities, and obligations into sharper focus, institutional accountability for bureaucratic machinations can be promoted, and the weakness of doublespeak that overemphasises the 'universal' at the cost of the particular, exposed.

The coordination potential of secondary legal norms vis-à-vis the application of primary legal norms and conflict rules liberates PrIL from its isolation. Their potential to limit the risks associated with overlapping norms and gaps in normativity is a neglected field of study for colonial contexts. The encased mummy of Zhanggong Zushi, the material removed from the Herero and Nama people during the 1904–1907 genocide, sacred medicine bundles, and the Parthenon Marbles were stripped from their respective contexts along with the knowledge and skills that give them meaning. Their connection to their places of origin was severed without the consent of the people for whom the heritage mattered. The communities who produced this sacred material heritage are actively seeking and campaigning for their return but their claims have ended in frustration.

The claims for the return of the Parthenon Sculptures take on a special significance against the backdrop of the policy gap in ethical guidelines and recommendations in respect of sacred cultural material in public and private collections. As a symbol of a body that demands its limbs back, the Parthenon is like any body that is part of all humanity, but its sacred quality is borne of the place where it originated (interview conducted by Eri Vardaki with Nikos Stampolidis 2021).

Assembling the fragments of the Parthenon inspires the method adopted in this study. Just as each carving of the Temple of the Acropolis was made to fit at a unique angle, a unitary vision must guide the the joining up of the loose parts and the restoration of the law of restitution of colonial-era sacred artefacts. Gathering in the architectural fragments, frieze portions, statues and sculptures, cultural sites, and sacred stones keeps the normative effect of mimetism in check. The Athenians alone had the right to decide to carve up the Parthenon. Their position in the dispute offers a strong commentary on British cultural institutions' use of the law in the debate about 'belonging.' It prompts reflection on the role of the law in the different versions of colonial history.

Like looting and destruction of the sacred, massacres disrupt values that help individuals and communities cope with calamity and tragedy. The Athenians are expected to accept that the British Museum may continue to possess their Parthenon Marbles and display their classical aesthetic and historical value as individual works of art. The Chinese villagers who revere the mummy of Zhanggong Zushi are expected to accept that an anonymous dealer owns it and that its whereabouts are unknown. In both instances, the value these objects hold for the communities helped to fashion them. The cases have a certain in-betweenness that highlights the challenges involved in the classification of complex cultural material and human remains, the value of which is not fully comprehended.

Lack of success in the courtroom does not mean that a case is devoid of merit. Determining whether a different outcome is achievable can contribute to the evolution of the law and an increased understanding of the importance of seized material for the communities of origin. This may be conducive to greater efforts made by societal orders to reconcile contradictions in value systems and resolve conflicts. The failure to secure restitution through adjudication never ends the call to justice, for the 'problem of the past' can generate pressure to respond in ways that legal proceedings cannot contain.

4.2 'Common rules of adjudication' versus PrIL methods and tools in collecting contexts

Should 'common rules of adjudication' take over the function of PrIL methods? Even in an ideal world in which all courts have agreed to apply 'common rules of adjudication,' there would still be a considerable need for PrIL theory and tools to provide a map for disputes arising from public and private collecting contexts.

The formalistic reasoning the Amsterdam District Court used to determine that the Chinese village committees lacked legal standing suppressed the contextual information needed for an evaluation of the merits of the claim. Having pre-selected the juridical framework, the restitution claim could not progress. The harm done with this approach goes beyond the practical outcome for it also cuts short the open dialogue PrIL needs to have with other disciplines (Ruiz Abou-Nigm 2019: 385).

Chechi proposes 'common rules of adjudication' for cultural heritage disputes which are intended to compensate for the shortcomings of PrIL rules and techniques (Chechi 2014: 246). These common rules of adjudication avoid adversarial approaches to restitution that encourage recourse to the law of ownership. Instead of treating restitution claims as title claims, the rules steer in the direction of reciprocal loans, information-sharing about acquisitions, and collaboration in scholarship, conservation, and archaeological investigation (Chechi 2014: 300–302). The intangible knowledge carried by contentious objects in museum collections or documented in museum records is not mentioned in express terms in any of the proposed common rules. Perhaps the implementation of the common rules of adjudication will encourage the formation of more culturally-sensitive rules that could include this aspect. He argues in favour of a 'common rule of adjudication' by which to recontextualise cultural objects that are claimed by Indigenous communities, minorities and former colonies (Chechi 2014: 285–287). Chechi's proposal pursues simplicity as the main tool for integration in law, which raises the question of whether theoretical depth and the techniques, methods, and approaches that grapple with diverse views and approaches to the problem of cultural conflict in PrIL offers a better way by which to achieve integration (Riles 2008: 277). A 'common rule of adjudication' could potentially raise awareness regarding the crucial role fulfilled by 'recognition' in transnational litigation.

In the colonisers' eyes, the colonised and what they produce are objects (Fanon 1986: 77). The objectification of so-called 'non-western' human cultures culminated in a geographical classification of all material culture in public museums, designed along an evolutionary aesthetic, which was expected to reveal the complete history of man. A category error reduced ethnographic objects to subjects of analysis (Hicks 2021: 5–6). The epistemologies implicit in the order and use of the collections in former colonisers' museums made it possible to usurp the cultural identity and history of the Other, while the research tradition and methods were hailed as 'neutral' and 'objective.' The same flawed thinking concerning the Other seeped into different fields of knowledge and scholarship and affected also perspectives from religions. Recognition of what the sacred means to the Other is a crucial ethic. PrIL technique facilitates it, and policy guidelines that bridge legal diversity and facilitate our understanding of what it means to ourselves, can stregthen the application of these techniques. In PrIL, 'recognition' provides room for preserving the integrity of the cultural heritage of each nation and adopting a respectful stance and a holistic view of the cultural heritage of Indigenous communities. The forum may decide to recognise the classification conferred on cultural material by any potentially applicable foreign law and may also decide to recognise and enforce the laws of the country of origin to support a claim. Recognition forms part of the ethic of PrIL. There are instances where PrIL techniques got in the way of ensuring 'respect for alterity' or promoting active reflection on the 'reception of the foreign' but the Chinese litigation proved its potential to reconcile clashing world views, cultural interests, and categorisations that pervaded the materiality and sacrality of the mummified monk.

Constructing a more complete, stable legal concept of *res extra commercium* beyond what cultural property and heritage conventions currently accomplish, will promote the practice of due diligence in respect of sacred cultural material. Given that harmonised or uniform law is inadequate as a potential common legal basis for restitution claims in respect of cultural material removed unethically during the colonial era, PrIL's connective capabilities must be liberated to accommodate conceptions of cultural property and heritage in customary law and traditional protocols in transnational litigation. A connective PrIL can articulate the exceptions that deserve respectful attention and responsiveness, so that it becomes possible to resist power plays. PrIL rulings have concrete and symbolic implications which should encourage adjudicators to identify when laws and practices have promoted power imbalances in the trade in art and cultural objects and when force, forced sale, or duress taint the provenance of cultural material. These disputes present complex economic, political, moral, and legal questions in an international context. A conflation of law and ethics will hinder a full understanding of the role of international law which was entrenched in legal colonialism, but acknowledgement of the underlying moral theory and the relationship between law and ethics can support restitution claims.

4.3 Novel contributions of this study

This study demonstrates the effects of setting the stolen sacred as a priority. Its main method turns on law and ethics approaches that restore the capacity of cultural material to challenge or decenter the discourse about retention of sacred material in cultural institutions in the West. Broadly speaking, two different approaches were used. First, a theory of the sacred was used to indicate what difference the sacred status of cultural material can make to restitution claims as opposed to a general 'heritage art' status of cultural objects. The sacred was the subject of an in-depth study in *Restitution of Cultural Property and the Law: Complex Colonial Histories* (Roodt 2024). As a non-legal factor that guides legal decisionmaking based on primary and secondary legal norms, the sacred inspires novel questions about the legal basis of restitution claims. It highlights structural weaknesses in the legal frameworks and jurisprudential schemes, and provides a steer on priorities: Which legal obstacles should be tackled first to expedite a settlement or return and strengthen the decision-making and dispute settlement processes? What sustains the essence of life—its fullness and sacrality—stands as the theoretical grounding and the foundation for litigated claims. The second approach was to expand the usual perspective. Both approaches were permeated by the parallels between the Parthenon Marbles dispute and the restitution claim for the artefactual encased human remains in Buddhist statuary to show that a common understanding of the sacred casts light on the ground for restitution claims, illuminating the legal pathways available to restore sacred cultural property and heritage to deprived communities, institutions, states, and individuals. The paradigmatic Parthenon Sculptures disputes has valuable lessons to teach about navigating the political reality of a deadlock in lawmaking. Unlocking this dispute remains the critical turning point the world needs to see. Both examples offer countless opportunities to evaluate whether policy and norm creation is reasonable and sound.

This study identified the gaps and fragmentation evident in the treatment of cultural material and their associated knowledge systems. Undesirable and unintended consequences arise from decoupling the 'private' and the 'public' and from driving a wedge between moral, ethical, and regulatory frameworks. PrIL can ill afford to operate in isolation from Public International Law (PublIL), but it is also inappropriate to blindly perpetuate the uncritical engagement with the state-centered premises of PublIL in disputes concerning material removed during the colonial eras. PrIL's response to non-legal factors such as the sacred and the role of provenance research in relation to the sacred (including also the implications the sacred has for facts that cannot be proven), was considered, and insights were offer in respect of both internal and external normative conflicts in complex colonial contexts. Considering the restrictions which capitalisation and colonialism have imposed on the full operation of secondary legal norms in dispute settlement for the belonging of complex contested material, the study demonstrated the importance of integrating internal conflicts of law and heritage debates that focus on the ethical and ownership dilemmas of imperial artefacts *and* developing the law for external conflict of laws that determine the legal position and status of such artefacts. One of the most important tools for this integration is the public policy exception.one of the focal points of the study was the context for investigating when and how the limits of tolerance may be extended. *When* ethical reasoning invokes the juridical framework of exception is linked to *why* substance ought to prevail over form. Just as the public policy exception of PrIL remains rooted in the basic requirements of the domestic public order, *jus cogens* norms remain immutably rooted in the basic requirements of the international public order where temporal and spatial dimensions in the law that tend to hinder restitution may be tackled. Together, PublL and PrIL provide a firm grounding from which to resist and surmount fragmentation, truncate mummified assumptions about normativity and normative conflicts, and dismantle the time factor as a hurdle to claims. This potential is amplified by progressive case studies that model alternative approaches based on soft law besides the 2017 case involving the *Quimbaya Treasure.* A bilateral agreement was signed between Mexico and Sweden in June 2022 in respect of the Maaso Kova, a sacred ceremonial deer head removed from the Yaqui peoples of Mexico by Danish anthropologists in 1934. The basis for this return is to be found in Article 12(2) of the 2007 UNDRIP. The retroactive application of this instrument enabled the repatriation. There is also a growing number of instances where courts apply ethical standards underpinned by broad consensus in the international community and manifest in conventions even when the parties are not from signatory states. When bilateral agreements cannot be achieved and treaties provide no recourse, a coherent theory of responsibility and justice in the restitution and repatriation of unethically removed sacred material is needed as a basic point of orientation for adjudicators and policymakers.

This study also highlighted the ethic of responsiveness of PrIL. The contribution which PrIL's ethic can make in respect of claims for restitution of colonial-era and Indigenous cultural property lies in encouraging decisionmakers and policymakers to consider the role of comity in rulings on standing to sue and recognition and enforcement, and in their decisions on expired time limits. Rethinking the application of expired time limitations in transnational claims for sacred remains and belongings is of fundamental importance in this field. Lived time (durée) rather than linear time is what matters to the sacred. Apart from taking on board the 'common rule of adjudication' on the time factor, this study also provides much-needed perspectives on human timescales that erode dispute settlement potential. Timescales that promote more constructive combinations of chronological and non-chronological time, which speak to a widening sense of humanity, were advocated for.

An important contribution of this study is the reflection it invites, both in legal evaluation and in provenance research, on the normative leverage which restitution claims require to see adjudicators suspend ordinary primary commercial rules, reconsider the dichotomisation of procedure and substance, shift the ingrained dividing lines between PrIL categories, and engage with crucial justifications for the non-application of prescription rules, statutes of limitation, and the objectives of procedural protections. A certain normative leverage is discernible in the confluence of restitutionary and reparative justice claims in cases marked by violent looting and theft during the colonial era.

Having argued that a considerable need exists for PrIL theory and tools to provide a map for disputes arising from the public and private contexts of collecting, it remains for the broad outlines of a coherent theory and unifying model to be set out.

4.4 Towards a coherent theory and unifying model for restitution claims of 'sacred' cultural material

Responsibility for cultural takings and returns tends to be based on past wrongdoing, a broad structural relationship to the wrong, and human rights that transform relations between humans and objects (Stahn 2023: 459–467). Recipients of legal norms are more numerous than recipients of moral norms. They include any person or institution whose behaviour the law seeks to modify, including any person, institution, or community. Scholarly disagreement prevails over whether the circumstances of acquisition can constitute an international wrongful act. It has been argued that, even if conditions of removal were to be measured against the normative shifts that statutory and treaty law have undergone since, a claim based on the circumstances of acquisition as potentially constituting an international illegal act cannot succeed (Lubina 2009: 140–141). Such a view limits the potential to characterise disputes over the ownership and belonging of sacred cultural heritage as violations of international law. Many commentators believe that a human rights framework offers a unifying model that would bolster systematic analysis of restitution claims relating to the colonial era in the social and human sciences. A human rights framework places responsibilities on the international community of states; States Parties to the United Nations Educational, Scientific and Cultural Organization (UNESCO) and UNIDROIT Conventions; Indigenous peoples; the World Intellectual Property Organisation (mandated to address issues related to traditional knowledge, traditional cultural expressions, and genetic resources); the Expert Mechanism of the Human Rights Council; the Permanent

Forum on Indigenous Issues; as well as the Special Rapporteur on the rights of Indigenous peoples whose customs and traditions are bound to embody obligations (UN General Assembly *Report of the Expert Mechanism on the Rights of Indigenous Peoples, Repatriation of Ceremonial Objects, Human Remains and the Intangible Cultural Heritage under the United Nations Declaration on the Rights of Indigenous Peoples* 21 July 2020: para 14). Disappointingly, a human rights framework is not free from disempowering side effects. Human rights discourse has undeniable imperial features that enabled the colonial powers to justify expeditions and interventions in the name of their 'civilising mission' as 'humanitarian' missions. The abolition of slavery or the suppression of human sacrifice provided scope for the justification of Britain's colonial subjugation in West Africa, for instance (Stahn 2023: 42). In relation to the role of norms in civil claims involving architectural and artistic cultural works that have survived for millennia, indeterminate human rights language fails to establish a clear connection with the cultural rights at stake. This study submits that further refinement of pertinent human rights is needed to make them justiciable and actionable.

Claims for return of cultural material deriving from untold histories of racial injustice or resistance to societal distributions of power, require more active acknowledgement of the non-material values in cultural property and heritage than restitution or repatriation claims do for other material. When culturally-sensitive ethnographic material and potent objects are 'imprisoned' in vitrines, their historical record of legal ownership is 'frozen' in time and not easily rectified, especially if labels assigning objects to supposed 'ethnic' or geographical categories are all that remain. Sacred objects and collections become trapped in places that insist on their 'protection.' Many are in a liminal zone of (colonial) time and place. In 1867, Richard Rivington Holmes (1835–1911), an assistant in the manuscripts department of the British Museum since 1854, was appointed archaeologist to the Abyssinian Expedition to Maqdala in Ethiopia. Emperor Tewodros II took British diplomats and European missionaries hostage in 1864 and held them at Maqdala. Ransom demands prompted a military intervention under the command of General Robert Napier (1810–1890). All the European hostages were released unharmed before the attack on Maqdala could be commenced, yet Napier proceeded to bombard, siege, and sack Maqdala (Kostal 2005: 427–428). During the expedition Holmes purchased a collection of material on behalf of the British Museum, but instead of handing over 'Christ with Crown of Thorns' (Kwer'ata Re'esu), he kept it for himself. The painting is by an unknown artist's hand and is dated to around 1520 (Bailey 2024). Proof of Holmes' involvement in the work's provenance is the inscription he made on the back of the painting during the battle. However, precisely how the painting ended up in the possession of the Ethiopian emperor is unclear. The painting was sold via Christie's auction house after Holmes died. In 1998, it was discovered in a bank safe in Portugal that was registered to an heiress of Portuguese art historian Luiz Reis Santos. It remains unknown how the painting ended up in her possession (P55.ART 2023). Now considered part of Portuguese cultural heritage, Portuguese export controls prevent this loot from being returned to Ethiopia. 'Provenance' runs a distinct risk of creating meanings that may suppress and override the intended sacred meanings and functions they have in the communities and families they were made for. Only a critical provenance that takes account of the normative gradients of 'hard' and 'soft' law can provide direction in such cases.

A claimant may decide to characterise the dispute over ownership and belonging of sacred cultural material as a property dispute or a moral claim, but a unifying model must consider the cultural material that is subject to a restitutory claim as well as the obligations this material carries. All rights are exercised against persons, but restitution policies also apply to the 'empire of things' which comprises, inter alia, inalienable objects, gifts, and objectified objects that are scattered and 'unsettled' in the sense that where they are is not where they belong (Myers 1996: 3ff). This study argued that the normative conflicts that characterise complex colonial contexts require a theory of the sacred that recognises the responsibilities and duties that inhere in sacred cultural material, and that this theory must acknowledge the intangible cultural heritage that honours and promotes the human capability of those who produced the heritage as the basis of any restitutory claim. Girard's theory of the sacred imparts clues on the responsibilities and obligations that inhere in the sacred. Read together with Mauss's 'The Gift,' it provides a theory of obligations. The sacred engenders obligations that could potentially invalidate collectors' schemes and exchange agreements. It re-defines the relationship between rights, duties, and obligations in respect of private, common, and cultural property heritage removed from fragile cultures. These same obligations question artificial classifications and absurd distinctions drawn for purposes of adjudication. Obligations that precede rights expand on the usual understanding of the moral considerations that justify derogation from the law. The party who returns an object is indirectly extending recognition to the recipient. The legitimacy this confers on the recipient may strengthen any claim the group may have to self-government (Last 2007: 128).

Critical studies in jurisprudence that interrogate duty-oriented conceptions of communal responsibility probe the 'phenomenology' of both legal obligation and moral obligation. They have shown that the correlation of a right and a duty is not inescapable. gift economies allow exchanges based on altruism, reciprocity, mutual obligation, or the desire for a higher social status. They carry no expectation of monetary reward and may be characterised by offering services and goods to other members of the community. Western legal philosophers nonetheless pondered whether the gifts exchanged in gift economies, like those in Potlatch ceremonies, were given freely without the expectation of reciprocity or were obligational reciprocal performances in which rights have a part to play. If the ethical divide takes precedence over the ontological, existence confers an infinite obligation that precedes and exceeds all past and all future 'correct' settlements. Being 'prior,' obligation infers an 'asymmetrical gift' (Van der Walt 2018: 35–37, 60–61, 64). An enquiry into the origin of obligations ultimate reveals the 'metaphysics of generosity' to be the most fundamental experience of reality. This enquiry into the theory and practice of repatriation of sacred and ceremonial objects, human remains, and intangible cultural heritage confirms that obligations may exist without rights. An obligation to transfer a collection piece to a claimant may take precedence over a contractual loan agreement, and acknowledging the obligation created by a sacred thing could clarify the reason for this position to contractants. However, cultural property such as sacred medicine bundles also bear duties that are different from legal norms that have specific addressees. Conaty observes that the true owners of medicine bundles are the gods who have the right to repossess their gifts:

> [b]ut because these gifts were given by the gods to men, they can no longer be given by men to other men, except in special circumstances or for extraordinary reasons. On the other hand, what men may (and even must) give are the benefits, the positive effects emanating from the powers contained in these objects from the beginning. (Conaty 2015: 60)

While the power of the bundles infuses the social structure and lives of many Indigenous communities across the Americas, the sharing of their benefits engenders obligations for the recipient communities.

Restrictions in visibility and access to sacred cultural heritage reinforce their sacrality (Berlo et al. 1995: 8). Best practice proposals concerning the intellectual property dimension of restitution suggest that 'culturally sensitive' sacred and religious objects deserve to be shielded against digitisation practices in the same way human remains do. Some communities reject photographs and descriptions of the material. Returning images, photographs, drawings, impressions, film and sound recordings, and anthropometric data or other documents, restores control over the management of archives and anthropological photo collections (Dobbin 2013: 128–143). The collective ownership structures of blockchain may accommodate the various interests associated with objects over time, support fair settlements, and make fair(er) trade possible (Whittaker et al. 2021: 324). Blockchain mirrors the structure of the chain of title theory, but has an added advantage that the information it stores is more complete and better accessible to multiple owners, possessors, and agents than traditional title records. However, the issues of consent and the ownership of the digital representations deserve to be at the forefront in conversations about restitution and new policies in the field.

Full form restitution or repatriation would encompass the physical return of sacred corporeal cultural heritage along with control over associated archives and its intangible dimensions and databases that offer access to information about the material. In this sense, a more complete restitution becomes possible through digitisation (Boast & Enote 2013: 103–113). Because repatriation encompasses tangible as well as the intangible heritage embodied in the relationships and knowledge that the material evokes, returned collection items should be accompanied by relevant documentation and archive material as a matter of principle. The repatriation of archaeological and historical archival materials contribute to the decolonising of archives. The important principle is that digital technology must not be made to act as a replacement for repatriation, and digitisation and digital resources must never become a tactical manoeuvre that substitutes for the restitution of physical material. To expect communities to engage with 3D models of ethnographic collections, or to rely on digital archives and digital reunification alone, could lead to concerns over intellectual property risks and the hijacking of information. More importantly, they do not satisfy the need for processes of embodiment in the present, which rituals can provide. A virtual reunification of the Parthenon Marbles cannot achieve what Greece is seeking. Each carving was made to fit into the Parthenon at a unique angle and specific place, with seemingly similar proportions hiding innumerable differences. The Athenians' sacrifice is a unique intangible dimension of the Sculptures. More than the stock of knowledge the Athenians possessed, the sacred reconciles the ontological with the ethical in their restitution claim.

It is submitted that PrIL's capacity to refine human rights thinking and connect to extra-judicial principles and tools can be better communicated. Improved communication would emphasise that nationalist or community bias on the part of the adjudicator will make it impossible for them to maintain a strong commitment to the entire international community. What is at stake in restitutory international civil proceedings is more than just the interest of a state's own citizens. Cicero observed that '[t]his, then, ought to be the chief end of all men, to make the interest of each individual and of the whole body politic identical' (Cicero 44BC: 6 sub 'the conflict between the right and the expedient').

To ignore the interests of foreigners is to destroy human society (Struycken 2009: 195–196). This value underpins an important guiding principle for PrIL. The potential that the secondary legal norms of PrIL have for ethical reasoning comes alive through concepts that reflect the interests of foreigners or human society at large, such as efficiency, non-discrimination against foreign citizens, and 'meta-justice' (Brilmayer 2011: 102). When foreigners receive different treatment before judicial and administrative authorities only because they are foreigners, or when foreign law is treated as inferior, there is no meaningful engagement with the Other (Ruiz Abou-Nigm 2019: 387).

The analysis of the histories, behaviours, and overlapping norms and gaps in normativity in relation to material removed in the colonial past must match the analysis of the nature and complexity of the material in question. The restitution question throws into sharper relief the legal perspective in its complex relationship to ethics, and therefore those guidelines and norms classed as soft law that offer direction, can be used constructively. PrIL must prime domestic courts to diffuse the tensions that arise in cases where complex colonial histories are at play and to take account of the welfare needs of a broader spectrum of people than those within their territory. Taking the long view of time and space does not always require that we re-invent the field in a radical sense but it certainly reorients our thinking about the field (Michaels 2019: 27). It can change the decisions and policies we consider appropriate. Reorienting one's thinking is radical and demanding work. To simplify and clarify its methods and approaches PrIL's pro-active engagement with other disciplines is required (Ruiz Abou-Nigm 2019: 365). A coherent theory and unifying model will also be predicated on the value choices required by provenance research and with the rules of evidence.

Every legal system has rules by which to assess the legal position in circumstances that do not allow for clarification of the facts. Rules of evidence enable courts to come to a decision even when the facts remain unclear. Differences in the culture of courts and their legal areas introduce differences in the rules of evidence including who bears the burden of proving specific facts, and to whose detriment it would be when the facts cannot be proven. Factual evidence in claims concerning ownership of sacred cultural material requires a refined approach since the historical accuracy of the narratives should be verified but there is likely to be facts that cannot be proved. It follows that a workable unifying model will need to pay attention to this facet.

Any taxonomical difference wrought by the sacred relates to the cultural material in international civil litigation in the first instance. Legal counsel has a responsibility to ensure that the judiciary is correctly informed about the sacred quality of the object in question, and claimants' legal representatives should bring the implications of the juridical framework of exception for aspects like standing and recognition to the court's attention.

4.5 Conclusion

Studies on the restoration of the law of restitution of sacred cultural property and heritage removed during the colonial era are few and far between. The preceding study, *Restitution of Cultural Property and the Law: Complex Colonial Histories* (Roodt 2024), sheds light on the nature of the sacred. It is the common ground from which categories and outcomes achieved elsewhere may be recognised and respected. As such, it can change the outcome of restitution claims involving sacred cultural property and heritage of individuals, groups, or states.

This study has formulated novel responses to the new momentum stirring in restitution discourse and practice. It challenged the fragmentation and gaps that plague adjudication and policymaking. It identified openings at the material level and at the level of conceptions of associated systems of knowledge. It made 'present' those PrIL elements that support re-unification of sacred cultural material to replace the old system that excludes this dimension of international law.

Formal legal mechanisms and adjudicatory techniques that are deployed tactically, to keep responsibility for the past at bay, will always prompt uncomfortable questions. If ethical reasoning is locked out of the adjudicatory frame in ownership disputes about complex sacred material, mimesis and injustice will fortify the structures of law and power that already exist within jurisprudence. Formalist tradition can resurge at the least provocation to undercut PrIL's ethic, leaving the commercial thrust of art markets to thrive. Ethical reasoning prompts PrIL adjudicators to look the deprived in the face. It changes the question and makes its appeal to PrIL's disciplinary depth. The perspective can shift and expand because PrIL's theories and methods are techniques of ethics. A more egalitarian, less hierarchical approach comes into view, and it becomes possible to liberalise PrIL jurisprudence for the sacred.

PrIL's theoretical ground is a solid place to stand to dismantle the artificial distinctions that impede the return of sacred heritage looted or trafficked during the colonial era. Instead of facilitating the effects of liberal capitalism and economic expansion in relation to the ethnographic, a connective PrIL articulates the exceptions that deserve respectful attention and responsiveness. An attempt was made to not impose unnecessary bifurcation or artificial distinctions, but rather to simplify the approach, identifying distinctions and artificial procedures that prevent the restoration of the restitution frameworks in existence today.

The theoretical depth and method of PrIL equip it to identify and take account of factors external to law that would improve dispute settlement. Rights-based forms of justice 'project onto its object an image' of the hierarchies and discursive models 'which themselves are complicit in the injustices one aims to address' (Thomas 2020). They are inappropriate for sacred material carrying the cultural knowledge of regrettable losses through violence, theft, and displacement. Attentive forms of justice are needed for the sacred, which is so consistently discounted and misapprehended in current critical analyses of the legal, ethical, curatorial, political, and economic discourses. PrIL's technical aptitude must step into the service of the 'object of humanistic inquiry' (Riles 2008: 1033). Models of responsibility and responsivity that are available in adjudicatory contexts and settlement processes resonate globally, for they relate to the very core of human life and its flourishing. It is up to PrIL scholars, adjudicators, and policymakers to wield the methods and techniques of PrIL to achieve more effective activism at the level of the normative and applied theory.

Bibliography

Bailey, Martin. 2024. 'Investigation by Portuguese Newspaper Reveals Grappling Between Politicians and Museums Over Future of Kwer'ata Re'esu' *The Art Newspaper*, 5 February.

Berlo, Janet C., Ruth B. Philips, Carol Duncan, Donald Preziosi, Danielle Rice & Anne Rorimer. 1995. 'The Problematics of Collecting and Display, Part I' *The Art Bulletin* 77(1): 6–23.

Boast, Robin & Jim Enote. 2013. 'Virtual Repatriation: It Is Neither Virtual nor Repatriation' in: Peter F. Biehl & Christopher Prescott (eds.) *Heritage in the Context of Globalization: Europe and the Americas* New York: Springer 103–113.

Brilmayer, Lea. 2011. 'The Problem of Provenance: The Proper Place of Ethical Reasoning in the Selection of Applicable Law' in Donald Earl Childress III (ed.) *The Role of Ethics in International Law* Cambridge: CUP 101–124.

Butt, Daniel. 2009. *Rectifying International Injustice: Principles of Compensation and Restitution Between Nations* Oxford: OUP.

Chechi, Alessandro. 2014. *The Settlement of International Heritage Disputes* Oxford: OUP.

Cicero, M. Tullius. 44 BC. *De Officiis III*. Tr Walter Miller 1913, Cambridge, MA: Harvard University Press.

Conaty, Gerald T. 2015. 'The Development of Museums and Their Effects on First Nations' in Gerald T. Conaty (ed.), *We Are Coming Home!: Repatriation and the Restoration of Blackfoot Cultural Confidence* Athabasca, Edmonton: AU Press 37–69.

Dobbin, Kristen. 2013. '"Exposing Yourself a Second Time": Visual Repatriation in Scandinavian Sápmi' *Visual Communication Quarterly* 20(3): 128–143.

Fanon, Frantz. 1986. *Black Skin, White Masks* (tr by Charles Lam Markmann 1952) London: Pluto Press.

Federal Ministry for Arts, Culture, the Civil Service and Sport, Recommendations of the Advisory Committee for Guidelines for Collections in Austrian Federal Museums from Colonial Contexts (20 June 2023), Vienna: BMI Digitalprintcenter.

German Museums Association (DMB). 2021. *Guidelines for German Museums: Care of Collections from Colonial Contexts* 3rd ed, April 2021. <https://www.museumsbund.de/wp-content/uploads/2021/03/mb-leitfaden-en-web.pdf>

Hicks, Dan. 2021. *Necrography: Death-Writing in the Colonial Museum*, British Art Studies 26 February Issue 19: 3–6.

Human Rights Council Report. 2020. *Repatriation of Ceremonial Objects and Human Remains under the UN Declaration on the Rights of Indigenous Peoples*, A/HRC/45/35 21 July.

Kostal, Rande W. 2005. *A Jurisprudence of Power: Victorian Empire and the Rule of Law* Oxford: OUP.

Last, Kathryn V. 2007. 'Cultural Pluralism and the Return of Cultural Heritage' in Stephen Tierney (ed) *Accommodating Cultural Diversity* Burlington: Ashgate 123–143.

Lubina, Katja. 2009. *Contested Cultural Property: The Return of Nazi Spoliated Art and Human Remains from Public Collections* PhD Thesis, Maastricht: University of Maastricht.

Mauss, Marcel. 2016. *The Gift: Expanded Edition Selected, Annotated, and Translated by Jane I. Guyer* Chicago, Illinois: Hau Books.

Michaels, Ralf. 2019. 'Private International Law as an Ethic of Responsivity' in Verónica Ruiz Abou-Nigm & Maria Blanca Noodt Taquela (eds.) *Diversity and Integration in Private International Law* Edinburgh: Edinburgh University Press 11–27.

Myers, Fred R. 1996. 'Introduction' in Fred R. Myers (ed.) *The Empire of Things: Regimes of Value and Material Culture* Santa Fe, New Mexico: School of American Research Press 3–61.

P55.ART. 2023. '"Kwer'ata Re'esu": Ethiopian Icon that Remains in Portugal', 12 December <https://www.p55.art/en/blogs/p55-magazine/kwer-ata-re-esu-icone-da-etiopia-que-permanece-em-portugal>

Riles, Annelise. 2008. 'Cultural Conflicts' *Law and Contemporary Problems* 71: 273–308.

Roodt, Christa. 2024. *Restitution of Cultural Property and the Law: Complex Colonial Histories* London: Routledge.

Ruiz Abou-Nigm, Verónica. 2019. 'Bridging and Balancing: Diversity and Integration in Private International Law', in Verónica Ruiz Abou-Nigm & Maria Blanca Noodt Taquela (eds.) *Diversity and Integration in Private International Law* Edinburgh: Edinburgh University Press 362–388.

Stahn, Carsten. 2023. *Confronting Colonial Objects: Histories, Legalities, and Access to Culture* Oxford: OUP.

Struycken, Antoon Victor Marie. 2009. 'Co-ordination and Co-operation in Respectful Disagreement: General Course on Private International Law' *Recueil des Cours* 311(2004): 8–551.

Szabados, Tamás. 2020. 'In Search of the Holy Grail of the Conflict of Laws of Cultural Property: Recent Trends in European Private International Law Codifications' *International Journal of Cultural Property* 27(3): 323–347.

Thomas, Christopher. 2020. '"Silence is Violence": Simone Weil on the Impossible Demands of Justice' <https://thephilosophicalsalon.com/silence-is-violence-simone-weil-on-the-impossible-demands-of-justice/> 31 August.

UN General Assembly. 2020. *Report of the Expert Mechanism on the Rights of Indigenous Peoples, Repatriation of Ceremonial Objects, Human Remains and the Intangible Cultural Heritage under the United Nations Declaration on the Rights of Indigenous Peoples* UN Doc. A/HRC/45/35, 21 July.

Van der Walt, Johan. 2018. 'The Origins of Legal Obligations: Towards a Fundamental Phenomenology of Moral and Legal Obligation' in Daniel Matthews & Scott Veitch (eds.) *Law, Obligation, Community* London: Routledge 35–70.

Vardaki, Eri. 2021. Interview with Nikos Stampolidis 'Ο Παρθενώνας Είναι το Σώμα-Σύμβολο που Ζητά τα Μέλη του Πίσω' BHMAgazino 19.09.2021 <https://www.tovima

.gr/2021/09/19/vimagazino/nikos-stampolidis-o-parthenonas-einai-to-soma-symvolo-pou-zita-ta-meli-tou-piso/>

Whittaker, Amy, Anne Bracegirdle, Susan de Menil, Michelle Ann Gitlitz & Lena Saltos. 2021. 'Art, Antiquities and Blockchain: New Approaches to the Restitution of Cultural Heritage' *International Journal of Cultural Policy* 27(3): 312–329.

Zeidler, Kamil. 2016. *Restitution of Cultural Property: Hard Case, Theory of Argumentation, Philosophy of Law* Gdańsk: Gdańsk University Press.

Index

For Product Safety Concerns and Information please contact our EU
representative GPSR@taylorandfrancis.com
Taylor & Francis Verlag GmbH, Kaufingerstraße 24, 80331 München, Germany

www.ingramcontent.com/pod-product-compliance
Lightning Source LLC
LaVergne TN
LVHW021127300926
849160LV00010B/897

* 9 7 8 1 0 3 2 9 5 2 6 0 4 *